THE WORKS OF SHAKESPEARE

EDITED FOR THE SYNDICS OF THE
CAMBRIDGE UNIVERSITY PRESS

BY

JOHN DOVER WILSON

MACBETH

MACBETH

CAMBRIDGE

AT THE UNIVERSITY PRESS

1968

PUBLISHED BY
THE SYNDICS OF THE CAMBRIDGE UNIVERSITY PRESS

Bentley House, 200 Euston Road, London, N.W. 1
American Branch: 32 East 57th Street, New York, N.Y. 10022

First edition 1947
*Reprinted 1951
1960
First paperback edition 1968

* Places where slight editorial changes or additions
introduce variants from the first edition are, when
possible, marked by a date 1950 in square brackets.

First printed in Great Britain at the University Press, Cambridge
Reprinted in Great Britain by Hazell Watson & Viney Ltd,
Aylesbury, Bucks

CONTENTS

To

former colleagues and fellow-students of

THE UNIVERSITY OF EDINBURGH

'GODBAIRN' OF THE KING FOR WHOM
MACBETH WAS WRITTEN

*this recension is gratefully dedicated
by the editor*

INTRODUCTION

This is a difficult play to edit. Few of Shakespeare's have been more discussed; yet, though the greatest critics have given their mind to it, they have not always done so wisely or with cogency. In few again is the textual basis so obscure or the necessity for a definition of it so compelling. With many plays one can pass direct to the dramatic problems without troubling about the history of the text,[1] but not with *Macbeth*; while the wildest and most divergent textual theories are current, are indeed endorsed by eminent writers. Readers of this Introduction are, therefore, asked to accept its long second section as a necessary evil, if they do not decide to skip it as they well may. On the other hand, I find my path eased by excellent and scholarly modern editions, among which special acknowledgements are due to that of Sir Edmund Chambers (1893), that of Sir Herbert Grierson and Dr J. C. Smith (1914), and that of Professor Kittredge (1939).[2] Further, the problem of contemporary staging, so important in *Macbeth*, which relies upon supernatural machinery more than any other play of Shakespeare's, and the kindred problem of contemporary demonology, have recently been much illuminated by *The Globe Playhouse* of Professor J. C. Adams (1943) and *Shakespeare's Philosophical Patterns* of Professor W. C. Curry (1937); books that reached me from across the ocean in a happy hour.

[1] Cf. *Hamlet* ('New Shakespeare'), pp. xi–xii.
[2] Unfortunately the interesting edition by Professor J. Q. Adams (1931), which anticipates some of my findings, did not come to my hands until November 1946, when this edition was already in the press.

I. *The Macbeth myth, and what Shakespeare owes to it*

Little is known for certain about the historical Macbeth, who reigned in Scotland 1040–57; but what is, seems to point to a vigorous, successful, and, for his age, even religious, ruler. That he killed his predecessor, Duncan I, and was in turn killed by his successor, Duncan's son Malcolm III, is simply in the nature of things monarchical in tenth- and eleventh-century Scotland. Out of the nine kings who reigned between 943 and 1040 all but two were killed, either in feud or directly by their successors. And this state of affairs was the result, not so much of the general barbarism of the age, as of the ancient law or custom of alternate or collateral succession, which preceded the law of primogeniture in Scotland, Ireland and some other parts of Europe during the Dark Ages, and meant that, on the decease of a king, his crown passed, not to the direct descendant, but to the brother or cousin or even remoter collateral who seemed the strongest person within a certain family group. It was a system of obvious utility in a period when strength at the helm was a condition of survival for any institution; but it encouraged assassination, because the strong man would generally wish to 'mak sikker' by ending the ruling king's reign at a convenient moment for himself in advance of its natural term. Sometimes, however, it worked the other way. Malcolm II, for example, broke custom by killing off the members of the alternate branch in order to secure the throne for his grandson Duncan I. But by oversight or negligence he left one alive, a woman, Gruoch; and she later had a son by her first husband, and later still took as her second husband a formidable person called Macbeth, son of Findlaech, mormaer (earl) of Moray. Findlaech was not of Scottish blood royal. But Macbeth's mother is said by some to have been Malcolm II's sister; and, though this is doubtful, Macbeth could claim the crown on behalf of his wife and her son. Thus from the eleventh-century standpoint Duncan was the usurper, and Macbeth the vindicator of the true line of succession.

But views change with changes in social custom, and if we ask how Macbeth came to figure in the chronicles and in Shakespeare as the crowned monster of Scottish history, the answer is first that the triumph of primogeniture during the twelfth and thirteenth centuries taught men to regard the events of the preceding age in a new light; and second that Macbeth belonged to the House of Moray, which, unrelated to the royal stock and controlling a district still largely outside the authority of the Scottish kings, played a conspicuous, and being unsuccessful a discreditable, part in the later dynastic struggles that led to the aforesaid triumph of primogeniture. Thus, as one of a brood of traitors and would-be usurpers, and himself the slayer of Duncan I, who was now considered the rightful heir of Malcolm II, Macbeth was shaping well for the role of arch-usurper and tyrant by the end of the thirteenth century. It was however an event at the end of the following century which blackened his character finally and irredeemably. This was the occupation of the throne by a new dynasty, that of the Stewarts, a family which, reaching Scotland from Brittany, via Shropshire, where it had received lands from Henry I, stood in special need of an indigenous Scottish ancestry. A mythical genealogy was accordingly invented, with a mythical founder named Banquo, who was added to the ranks of royal martyrs credited to the House of Moray by means of a mythical murder at the hands of the already mythically infamous Macbeth, followed by the flight of a mythical son Fleance to Wales, from the borders of which the historical Stewarts are known to have come. And Fleance, it may be noted in passing, was important for another reason, since he was said to have married a Welsh princess. Thus the house of Stewart could claim to be descended from Arthur himself; a claim of considerable value to its possessors in the fifteenth, sixteenth and seventeenth centuries.[1] Furthermore, the legend of Macbeth had by this date developed features which made it a peculiarly appropriate starting-point for the chronicle of a great line of kings, as may be seen by comparing the account of his reign in *The Orygnale Cronykil of Scotland* by Wyntoun (*c.* 1424), a more than usually fabulous metrical history of the universal type, which knows nothing of Banquo, with that in the *Scotorum Historiae* (1527) by Hector Boece, who perhaps invented him, though he builds upon Wyntoun, the *Chronica Gentis Scotorum* of Fordun (ob. 1385) and other chronicles.

The Macbeth of Wyntoun is a most sinister person. To begin with, his mother, though described as Duncan's sister, is clearly some kind of witch, if one may judge from her suspicious delight in 'hailsume aire' and the woods, and from the fact that one day she meets there 'ane fayre man', alias the Devil, who becomes Macbeth's father and gives her a promise that the boy will prove a great warrior, invulnerable to all of woman born. Tenderly nurtured by his uncle Duncan, the infant no sooner grows to manhood than he attests his diabolical origin by murdering his kinsman and benefactor, marrying his widow (whom Wyntoun[2] identifies with Gruoch), and seizing his crown. But the most interesting part of the story is the vision which prompts Macbeth to perpetrate this crime. He dreams that he is hunting with Duncan when they encounter 'thre werd systrys' who hail him in turn Thane of Cromarty,

[1] See R. F. Brinkley, *Arthurian Legend in the Seventeenth Century*, 1932, p. 16.

[2] See Bk. vi, l. 1877 (ed. Scottish Text Soc. iv, 275).

Thane of Moray, and King of Scotland. Here was a golden opportunity for the chroniclers of the House of Stewart, inasmuch as all sound genealogical tales from the Book of Samuel downwards have opened with prophecy. It only needed to take dream for reality, substitute Banquo for Duncan as Macbeth's hunting companion, and continue the prophecy of the Weird Sisters in such terms as would make the promise equivocal to Macbeth and both sure and of eternal import to Banquo. Who first took this step we do not know, but we find the two legends combined in Boece, from whom, with the aid of a translation by Bellenden,[1] Holinshed adopted the whole story and passed it on to Shakespeare. As an illustration of legendary accretion in other directions, it may be noted that whereas Wyntoun says nothing about Macdowald's[2] rebellion or the Norwegian invasions, which derive from Boece, he relates nearly all the facts we find in Shakespeare about Macduff, who is probably another mythical personage. With Wyntoun, however, the man not of woman born who slays Macbeth is an unnamed knight; with Boece it is Macduff himself.[3]

Though it must never be forgotten, and will be made clear in the Notes, that the witch-scenes probably owe much to Reginald Scot's *Discoverie of Witchcraft*, 1584, to *Newes from Scotland*, 1591, which describes a famous witch-trial in which King James was involved, and to the *Dæmonologie*, 1597, written by the king himself, Shakespeare's main historical source for *Macbeth* was the second edition (1587) of Holinshed's

[1] Boece is fuller than Bellenden, and Holinshed often reverts to the original.   [2] See note 1.2.9.

[3] The foregoing paragraphs are indebted to conversations with Dr W. Croft Dickinson, Fraser Professor of Scottish History at Edinburgh, who, however, must not be held answerable for the views expressed.

Chronicles of England, Scotland, and Ireland, which he had already used for his English histories.[1] And he made the most of it. Holinshed's account of Duncan and Macbeth furnished him, of course, with the majority of his 'facts'; but he borrowed the circumstances of Duncan's murder from the murder of King Duff by Donwald, while the voice that Macbeth hears crying 'Sleep no more', together with his insomnia and the terrors he suffers, were clearly suggested to him by the account of King Kenneth.[2] Moreover, as Sir Herbert Grierson has pointed out, he found in Holinshed not only the details of the story,

...but the tone and atmosphere of the Celtic and primitive legends of violent deeds and haunting remorse. He recognised in these turbulent Scottish kings and thanes a type of criminal quite distinct both from the hard, unscrupulous, remorseless, and ambitious Norman nobles...of the early 'histories', and from the subtle and soulless Italian artist in crime such as he had portrayed in Iago. Story after story told him of men driven by an irresistible impulse into deeds of treachery and bloodshed but haunted when the deed was done by the spectres of conscience and superstition.[3]

We catch a glimpse here of something already noted in our introductions to the 'histories': Shakespeare's debt to Holinshed on the side of incident has been stressed enough, and more than enough; on the side of character it has still to be appreciated to the full.

Apart from the incorporation of such elements from other parts of the *Scottish Chronicle,* Shakespeare made free as usual with Holinshed's account of Macbeth's

[1] See W. G. Boswell-Stone, *Shakespeare's Holinshed,* p. x. Cf. note 1. 3. S.D. below.

[2] Cf. note 2. 2. 35.

[3] *Macbeth,* ed. by Sir Herbert Grierson and Dr J. C. Smith, 1914, pp. xviii–xix.

reign. First, he compressed its seventeen years into about ten weeks; much as he had done with the reign of Henry IV and for much the same motives of dramatic art.[1] In retailing, for example, the valiant deeds of Macbeth before the meeting with the Witches, he fused into one three separate campaigns referred to by Holinshed: (i) the revolt and defeat of Macdowald in Lochaber;[2] (ii) the invasion of Fife by Sueno, King of Norway;[3] (iii) the second invasion of Fife by King Canute, in revenge for his brother's defeat;[4] though it remains doubtful how much of this condensation belongs to his original draft and how much to the later processes of compression or abridgement. He transmuted, again, references to Duncan's 'feeble and slothful administration'[5] and to his 'too much of clemencie'[6] into a winning and gracious benevolence, which seems to overflow with generous impulses, while I suspect that the second phrase came to be associated in his mind with Macbeth himself. On the other hand, he suppressed every hint of a Macbeth who 'set his whole intention to maintayne justice', 'to punishe all enormities and abuses', and to furnish the realm with 'commendable lawes',[7] traces of the vigorous and firm ruler which had survived the tides of denigration above described, while he was careful to exclude also suggestions, likewise still discernible in Holinshed, that Macbeth possessed some claim to the throne.[8] Shakespeare's Macbeth is a mere usurper (5. 8. 55), an 'untitled tyrant' (4. 3. 104), who after the murder of Duncan respects neither justice nor mercy. Here again there are good dramatic reasons for the change; but

---

[1] See Introduction to *1 Henry IV*, p. xxi.
[2] Holinshed's *Scottish Chronicle* (ed. 1805), pp. 335–6.
[3] *Ibid.* pp. 336–7. [4] *Ibid.* p. 339.
[5] *Ibid.* pp. 341, 343. [6] *Ibid.* p. 335.
[7] *Ibid.* p. 341. [8] *Ibid.* p. 340.

there are other reasons too. The process of defamation begun in the thirteenth century culminates in this play by a 'servant' of King James and a writer for the King's company of players. That the same writer also succeeds in endowing the 'tyrant bloody-sceptred' with enough nobility and 'human kindness' to claim our pity, is simply to say that he is Shakespeare.

But it was in his representation of the character of Banquo that he departs most strikingly from his source. And here also the desire to please his royal master and the demands of his art seem inextricably blended. Oddly enough Boece makes Banquo an accomplice in the murder of Duncan. 'At length', writes Holinshed of Macbeth, expanding Boece a little, 'communicating his purposed intent with his trustie friends, amongst whom Banquho was the chiefest, upon confidence of their promised aid, he slue the king at Envernesse.'[1] Traces of this complicity remain in the veiled approaches which Shakespeare's Macbeth appears to make towards Banquo at 1. 3. 153–5 and 2. 1. 20–9, while on the second occasion Banquo is thought by many, in my view mistakenly, to be aware that treachery is afoot.[2] But Shakespeare could never have exhibited the ancestor of King James before his very eyes as a murderer's confederate. On the contrary, he makes him the soul of honour and loyalty, and (as I think) entirely unsuspicious of Macbeth's intentions beforehand, while to him is given the lofty protestation afterwards:

> In the great hand of God I stand, and thence
> Against the undivulged pretence I fight
> Of treasonous malice.

Yet these brave words are followed by no action. And Bradley deduces from this and from his speech at

[1] Holinshed, *op. cit.* p. 340.   [2] See note 2. 1. 25.

3. 1. 1—10 that, though no accomplice, Banquo becomes an accessory after the act. Commenting upon the
speech, he writes:

> When next we see him, on the last day of his life, we find
> that he has yielded to evil. The Witches and his own
> ambition have conquered him. He alone of the lords knew
> of the prophecies, but he has said nothing of them. He has
> acquiesced in Macbeth's accession, and in the official theory
> that Duncan's sons had suborned the chamberlains to
> murder him.[1]

The passage shows Bradley at his weakest, treating
Shakespeare as if he were a historian, answering questions that should not be asked of Elizabethan drama,
and drawing deductions which assuredly the dramatist
never in the least intended. For King James's ancestor
could no more be a cowardly time-server than he could
be privy to the assassination of his liege lord. And as if
to prevent anyone supposing it for a moment, Shakespeare makes Macbeth pay a special tribute to 'his
royalty of nature', the 'dauntless temper of his mind',
and 'a wisdom that doth guide his valour'.[2] Bradley
quotes this to illustrate Macbeth's fear that Banquo is
plotting against him, but fails to observe that it reflects
upon the character of Banquo himself. Yet why is it
that, despite Macbeth's fears, Banquo never gives a hint
of meditating any action, violent or otherwise? And
why, a point Bradley overlooks, is his reply to the
invitation to supper couched in respectful, almost
obsequious, terms, although uttered immediately after
his soliloquy referring to Macbeth's guilt? Is it not at
least true to say, in the words of Sir Herbert Grierson,
who does not subscribe to Bradley's explanation, that
'Banquo's position at Macbeth's court is a very

[1] *Shakespearean Tragedy*, pp. 384–5.
[2] 3. 1. 49–53.

ambiguous one'?¹ Some ambiguity there certainly is;
and I think it may be accounted for, like other ambigui-
ties in the text, by assuming that Banquo was given
scope to make his position clear in the full-length play,²
either by soliloquy³ or in conversation with other thanes.
Yet, even as the text stands, King James, we may be
sure, perceived nothing but what was plain and right
and proper; for his ancestor would be simply following
the precepts of his most distinguished successor.
Usurper, tyrant, murderer as he was, Macbeth had been
crowned at Scone; and according to James's ideas of
kingship, as expounded in his *Trew Law of Free
Monarchies*,⁴ once a king has been anointed, be he 'an
idolatrous persecuter' like Nebuchadnezzar or 'a bloody
tyrant' and 'monster to the world' like Nero, his subjects' duty as laid down in Holy Writ, is perfect
obedience and even prayers for his prosperity.⁵ But the
'right of kings' was hereditary as well as divine.⁶ There
was one person, therefore, who might raise the standard
against the usurper, and in whose cause Macbeth's
subjects might take up arms against him, viz. the lineal
heir of Dunçan, Malcolm Prince of Cumberland.
Macduff knows this and acts upon it; and it may well be
that Banquo, with a 'wisdom that doth guide his
valour' was made privy to his purposes in the unrevised
play; certainly, the plot would gain from a scene

¹ Grierson and J. C. Smith, *op. cit.* p. 119.
² See § 11, below.
³ For example, by extension of the speech at the opening
of 3. 1.
⁴ Published in 1598, and reprinted in 1603, in both cases
without James's name, though his authorship was an open
secret.
⁵ *The Political Works of James I*, ed. by C. H. McIlwain,
1918, pp. 60–1.
⁶ *Ibid.* p. xxxiii.

between the two immediately after 2. 3. in the existing text. Until Malcolm appears on Scottish soil, however, Banquo must behave to the reigning monarch like a loyal and respectful subject, as we find him doing.

It has long been supposed that Lady Macbeth is almost wholly a child of Shakespeare's invention; a supposition which rests on the assumption that Holinshed was Shakespeare's only historical source. Holinshed tells us that Macbeth had a wife 'verie ambitious, burning in unquenchable desire to beare the name of a queene', who 'lay sore upon him to attempt the thing', and that Donwald also had a wife who 'counselled him (sith the King oftentimes used to lodge in his house without any garde about him, other than the garyson of the castell which was wholly at his commaundement) to make him away and shewed him the meanes whereby he might soonest accomplishe it'; which he did, 'though he abhorred the act greatlie in heart'.[1] And that is all. Shakespeare, however, as Mrs Stopes pointed out in 1916,[2] though no one appears to have noticed it, was probably acquainted with another source of Scottish history, since several of his points seem to be taken from it, points mostly connected with Lady Macbeth. This source was a manuscript of William Stewart's *Buik of the Croniclis of Scotland*, a metrical and expanded translation of Boece, said to have been made for King James V at the command of Queen Margaret, widow of James IV, and finished in 1535, though not printed until 1858. Stewart, who often gives us the actual words of his characters, relates that Macbeth's wife rated him and called him a coward, who 'durst nocht

---

[1] Holinshed, *op. cit.* pp. 295, 340.
[2] C. C. Stopes, *Shakespeare's Industry*, 1916, pp. 93, 102–3.

tak on hand' the task of removing King Duncan;[1] that Donwald's wife bade him

> Blyn of your baill, 'se ye be blyth and glaid.[2]

which may be translated:

> Give o'er this gloom; see you look blithe and gay,

look, that is, as Macbeth's wife bids him look, at 1. 5. 62 ff.; that when the murder was discovered Donwald pretended to faint—

> Dissimulat syne for to fall in swoun,
> As he wer deid thair to the erth fell doun[3]—

as Lady Macbeth does; and that he afterwards ran up and down

> With mony schout ay squeilland like a kid,[4]

as she promises to do at 1. 7. 78–9. Moreover, the prophecy to Banquo, which in Holinshed runs 'of thee those shall be borne whiche shall gouerne the Scottishe kingdome by long order of continuall discent',[5] becomes

> Bot of thi seed sall lineallie discend,
> Sall bruke the crown onto the worldis end,[6]

which brings it close to Shakespeare's

> What, will th' line stretch out to th' crack of doom?

---

[1] Cf. note 1. 7. 43. Here Stewart keeps close to Boece who writes: 'acerrimis dictis incitat, ignavum ac timidum appellans, qui cantibus superis satisque portendentibus aggredi rem non audeat tam egregiam tamque praeclaram.'

[2] William Stewart, *Buik of the Croniclis of Scotland*, ii, l. 35,983 (Rolls Series, 1858).

[3] *Ibid.* ll. 36,161–2.

[4] *Ibid.* l. 36,172.

[5] Holinshed, *op. cit.* p. 340.

[6] Stewart, *op. cit.* ii, ll. 39,729–30.

Now James knew the native chronicles of Scotland well. A Latin Boece and "the Scottis Chronicle, wrettin with hand" were among his books.[1] The latter may have been Stewart, and anyhow Stewart which contained this version of the prophecy is likely to have been particularly interesting to him. Lastly, the lines in which Stewart describes the character of Macbeth himself may be quoted:

> This Makcobey, quhilk wes bayth wyss and wycht,
> Strang in ane stour, and trew as ony steill,
> Defendar als with of the commoun weill...
> Syne throw his wyfe consentit to sic thing,
> For till distroy his cousing and his king:
> So foull ane blek for to put in his gloir,
> Quhilk haldin wes of sic honour befoir.[2]

Boece and Holinshed have nothing corresponding to this, and yet how well it sums up the pity of Macbeth's fall as Shakespeare represents it![3]

The nature of the three Weird Sisters has been much discussed by critics;[4] yet it seems to have occurred to none of them that it was in all probability much discussed also by Shakespeare's public. The operation of spirits and devils was a favourite subject of speculation, not only among experts on demonology like King James, but with all students of 'philosophy', which we should now call science. And readers, busy with Scottish history at the beginning of James's reign, in order to become *au courant* with the new dynasty, could not possibly remain ignorant of the story, as told by Holinshed, of Banquo being promised that the House

---

[1] G. F. Warner, *The Library of James VI* (*Misc. Scot. Hist. Soc.* 1893, p. xxxiv).　　[2] *Ibid.* ll. 39,822–30.

[3] For another parallel with Stewart v. note 1. 6. 14–18.

[4] See, for example, Spalding, *Elizabethan Demonology*, 1880, pp. 87–124; Kittredge, *Macbeth*, 1939, pp. xvi–xx; Curry, *Shakespeare's Philosophical Patterns*, 1937, ch. III.

of Stewart should occupy the throne, and of the Norn-like 'goddesses of destiny' who as 'women in strange and wild apparell, resembling creatures of an elder world'[1] uttered the great prophecy in question. So familiar was it indeed that students of St John's College. dressed as 'tres quasi Sibyllae' had met James on his visit to Oxford in 1605 and recited Latin verses to him,[2] while, when the astrologer Simon Forman made notes of a performance of *Macbeth* seen at the Globe in 1611, his impressions were clearly influenced by memories of Holinshed's account.[3] Yet, as such readers listened to the opening scenes of Shakespeare's play, they may well have asked themselves whether the august and auspicious figures which Holinshed describes and which appear as great ladies in his illustrations,[4] could possibly be the same as the foul hags rising from hell to claps of thunder, grinning and capering in obscene dances, gloating over parts of dismembered bodies, whom Shakespeare presents, 'Weird Sisters' though he might call them. On the other hand, he seems careful never to call them witches;[5] and though they behave as such at the beginning of 1. 3 and 4. 1, they have, as all critics have noted, something at once sublime and abysmally evil about them which marks them sharply off from the ordinary mortal witches such as his England and especially his Scottish king were thoroughly acquainted with. We can ourselves realise this distinction by comparing them with the witches in contemporary drama: with the merely nauseous hags of Jonson's *Masque of Queens*, for example,

[1] Holinshed, *op. cit.* p. 339.

[2] Cf. article by H. N. Paul in *J. Q. Adams: Memorial Studies* (1948), pp. 253ff. for links between this Oxford 'show' and *Macbeth* as we have it. [1950.]

[3] See *The Review of English Studies*, July 1947.

[4] See Frontispiece.

[5] The term is only applied to them by the 'rump-fed ronyon' who is well punished for it.

with the pitiful old village crone in *The Witch of Edmonton*, with the well-to-do wife and mother who practises witchcraft in Heywood's *Lancashire Witches*, or with the meretricious sylphs whose trivial amours bore us in Middleton's *Witch*. Too witch-like to be Norns, too Norn-like to be witches, what then are they? The answer is that, borrowing from both conceptions, Shakespeare made something new of his own, as truly his own, Coleridge observes, 'as his Ariel and Caliban'. They had to be sufficiently like witches at first view for his audience to accept them as creatures within their ken; they had to seem increasingly mysterious and forbidding on further acquaintance to be recognised as creatures more terrible than witches. The Weird Sisters in *Macbeth* are the incarnation of evil in the universe, all the more effective dramatically that their nature is never defined. 'They are', writes Lamb, 'foul anomalies, of whom we know not whence they are sprung, nor whether they have beginning or ending. As they are without human passions, so they seem to be without human relations. They come with thunder and lightning, and vanish to airy music. This is all we know of them.'[1] And that, we can fancy Shakespeare echoing, is all ye need to know.

But one thing can be said of them: though 'Parcae' is the word in Boece which Bellenden translates 'weird sisters', they are not Fates or anything corresponding with that conception in Shakespeare; for Macbeth exercises complete freedom of will from first to last. They set the play moving because they bring with them 'the filthy air' of ineffable evil which is its atmosphere, but they are no more the agents of what follows than 'the infernal Serpent' is the author 'of all our woe' in Milton's epic. Just as *The Book of Job* and

[1] *Works of Charles Lamb*, ed. E. V. Lucas, 'Miscellaneous Prose', p. 55.

Goethe's *Faust* begin in Heaven, so by introducing the Weird Sisters into his introductory scenes Shakespeare begins *Macbeth* where Milton begins *Paradise Lost*, in Hell. For the theme of both is Temptation and Fall, the assault by Hell upon two great human souls.

II. *The three* Macbeths

But before we turn and consider *Macbeth* as a dramatic masterpiece, we have first to make up our minds what the *Macbeth* we are to consider precisely is. Does the only text which has survived, namely that in the First Folio, represent the play as Shakespeare left it, or does it, as W. J. Lawrence declares and many others believe, resemble the ruin of some 'vast and venerable Gothic cathedral, tastelessly tinkered by an unimaginative restorer'?[1] To few questions about Shakespeare have the answers been more various and more disparate. Pass these answers in review, however, and two points emerge: first, that, if we ignore modern throw-backs like the 'Arden' edition of 1912, which rejects as 'spurious' some 167 lines, opinion among scholars has grown steadily more optimistic since 1872, when the old Cambridge editors actually queried 300 lines in their Clarendon Press edition; and second, that the literary critics who are most sweeping in their condemnation of the text are often loudest in their praise of the play. Mr Masefield, for example, in a recent little book on *Macbeth*, estimates that at least thirty pages were torn from Shakespeare's manuscript 'by men who preferred a jig or a tale of bawdry, or were certainly asleep',[2] and yet at the same time displays boundless enthusiasm for

[1] W. J. Lawrence, 'The Mystery of *Macbeth*', *Shakespeare's Workshop*, 1928, pp. 24–5.

[2] John Masefield, *A 'Macbeth' Production*, 1945, p. 8.

the dramatic wreck such botchers would undoubtedly have left behind them. Again, while all agree that *Macbeth*, which, with its 2,084 lines, is the shortest play but two in the canon,[1] must at one time have been longer, few will quarrel with another recent critic who notes that 'no significant scene seems to be missing' and pronounces it 'incomparably brilliant as it stands, and within its limits perfect'.[2] From such a dilemma only one escape appears possible: if our incomparable *Macbeth* is an abridged text, Shakespeare himself must be the chief abridger.

Nor does this solution rest on common sense alone; for it is possible to argue that during the first dozen years of the seventeenth century three distinct *Macbeths* were produced: (i) an original play by Shakespeare of unknown length and unknown date; (ii) an abridgement of this, also by Shakespeare, intended as the brevity of the Folio text suggests[3] for a performance limited to about two hours; and (iii) a rehandling of this abridgement in turn by the 'unimaginative restorer' mentioned above, whom it will be convenient to rid our hands of first.

The 'restorer' is now generally identified with Thomas Middleton, whose *Witch*, as Steevens first noted, contains the full text of the two songs referred to by title only in the Folio stage-directions of *Macbeth* at 3.5.33 and 4.1.43, while the influence of the same play is evident also in the context of these stage-directions. The most extravagant theories of Middleton's interference with other scenes have been advanced from time to time, but the majority of serious students will to-day

[1] *The Tempest* runs to 2015 lines and *The Comedy of Errors* to 1753 according to Mr Hart's count; v. *The Review of English Studies*, viii, 21.

[2] Mark van Doren, *Shakespeare*, 1939, p. 252.

[3] See E. K. Chambers, *William Shakespeare*, i, 471.

subscribe to Sir Edmund Chambers's verdict that his interpolations are in the main

confined to three passages (3. 5; 4. 1. 39–43; 4. 1. 125–32) in the witch-scenes, which can be distinguished from the genuine text by the introduction of Hecate, by the use of an iambic instead of a trochaic metre, and by prettiness of lyrical fancy alien to the main conception of the witches.[1]

I confess to finding with others a non-Shakespearian flavour in Macbeth's comment upon the third Apparition in 4. 1, while I am tempted, again with others, to assign the more vapid of the numerous couplets to Middleton whose attested plays show him to have a fondness for that form of verse.[2] But I am satisfied that, apart from the passages specified by Chambers, the Folio *Macbeth* is substantially of Shakespeare's composition.

On the other hand, I am equally sure that it does not contain all Shakespeare left in his manuscript when he last handled it; for the sorry state of the second scene, the only blot, but a real blot, upon the play's perfection, is demonstrably the work of an alien hand. The scene has undoubtedly been drastically and crudely cut, and may even be a cento of two or more original scenes not too carefully stitched together; and if one asks why so many nineteenth-century students have believed *Macbeth* to be mutilated throughout by an unintelligent adapter, the answer is that they jumped to the con-

---

[1] E. K. Chambers, *op. cit.* I, 472.

[2] See notes below, 2. 1. 60–1; 2. 4. 40–1; 4. 1. 153–4; 4. 3. 239–40; 5. 2. 29–30; 5. 4. 19–20 and D. L. Chambers, *The Metre of 'Macbeth'*, 1903, who shows (p. 18) that, whereas *Macbeth* has 108 lines of rhymed pentameters, *Hamlet* (almost twice as long) has only two-thirds of this, and *Antony and Cleopatra* (a little shorter than *Hamlet*) one-third.

clusion after perusing this scene. The verse, except for a word or two here and there, is certainly Shakespeare's;[1] but the broken lines, the irregular metre and lineation, and the abrupt transitions, together with a number of little obscurities or difficulties in construction and meaning,[2] tell a tale which can have but one interpretation. One of these difficulties, a favourite theme of editors since Dr Johnson, concerns the treacherous Thane of Cawdor, whose title is conferred upon Macbeth, and who is spoken of at 1. 2. 52–4 in terms implying that he is an ally of the King of Norway and fighting by his side against Macbeth; an implication not only inconsistent with Macbeth's astonishment, twice expressed, when he hears of Cawdor's treachery in the next scene, but dramatically exceedingly inept, inasmuch as the prophecy of the second witch loses more than half its virtue if Macbeth knows already that Cawdor is a notorious and defeated traitor. The real explanation is, as Angus hints at 1. 3. 111–16 in reply to Macbeth's second expression of astonishment, that Cawdor had been *secretly* in league with both Norway and the rebel Macdonwald;[3] and we need not doubt that this was

---

[1] Few question this to-day; those who do may be referred to J. M. Nosworthy's note on the scene in *The Review of English Studies*, April 1946.

[2] Most of these are brought out in the notes on 1. 2 below.

[3] I owe this point to Kittredge, who, however, claims that Angus's words prove the difficulty about Cawdor to be 'quite imaginary'. He forgets that a dramatic explanation must be absolutely clear to be effective, whereas this one is so obscure that nobody seems to have tumbled to it before himself. He forgets too that an explanation of Macbeth's ignorance, furnished after the Witch's prophecy, is furnished too late. See *Macbeth*, ed. G. L. Kittredge, 1939, pp. vii–viii and notes therein on 1. 2. 52; 1. 3. 72–3.

made perfectly plain in 1. 2 before the adapter got to
work upon that scene and cut out the relevant passage.
But why did he not make it plain then also, as he might
have done in three words? Here is the reference to
Cawdor as it stands in the Folio context:

> And fanne our people cold.
> *Norway* himselfe, with terrible numbers,
> Assisted by that most disloyall Traytor,
> The *Thane* of Cawdor, began a dismall Conflict.

He had only to rearrange the lineation and add a
phrase like 'in secret wise' after 'numbers' and all would
have been well. That he failed to do so can, I think, be
explained in one way alone: he knew enough of the
play to realise the importance of preparing for the prophecy in 1. 3 by a mention of the treachery of Cawdor
in 1. 2; he did not notice that it was equally important
to retain some reference to its secrecy. In a word, he
was not the author.

I suggest that this botcher is Middleton, who, having
interpolated some fifty lines of his own in the witch-
scenes, is here seen robbing Shakespeare of lines in ex-
change in order not unduly to increase the length of
the play in performance. There are, of course, pretty
obvious traces of cutting elsewhere. Chambers, for
example, notes that the short lines at 2. 3. 103; 3. 2. 32,
51; 3. 4. 4; 4. 3. 28, 44 are abrupt and give rise to
obscurities,[1] while Bradley finds it 'difficult not to
suspect some omission or curtailment' at 1. 4. 33–43,
where the naming of Malcolm as Prince of Cumberland
is 'extremely sudden', and 'the abruptness and brevity
of the sentence in which Duncan invites himself to
Macbeth's castle are still more striking'.[2] But none of

---

[1] E. K. Chambers, *op. cit.* i, 471.

[2] Bradley, *op. cit.* p. 468. Cf. also notes 3. 1. 129, 137
below.

these are as crude as those in 1. 2, and though some
of them may be Middleton's all may equally well be
Shakespeare's. The important point is that Shakespeare
can be completely acquitted of the murder of his second
scene; how important we shall see when we come to
consider the problem of Macbeth's character.

At what date was Middleton concerned with *Macbeth*? The answer depends upon the date of his *Witch*,
which, not printed before 1778, has come down to us
in a late transcript conjecturally assigned to 1620–7.[1]
But we now know that the scribe was Ralph Crane, one
of the scriveners of the King's men;[2] and we can therefore accept with some confidence his statement in the
title of the MS. that the play was 'long since acted by
His Majesty's servants at the Blackfriars', and deduce
therefrom that it was acted in or after the autumn of
1609 when the King's men probably first occupied that
theatre.[3] Further, I find it difficult to set aside Lawrence's
argument that *The Witch* can hardly be much later than
Ben Jonson's *Masque of Queens*, produced at Whitehall
on 2 February 1609, seeing that it clearly owes much to
the Antimasque of Witches with which that masque
opens, while its Hecate scenes may even have been
played by the same performers, dancing the same dances
in the same costumes.[4] In a word, late 1609 or early
1610 seems a highly probable date for *The Witch*. And
I accordingly assign a date somewhere in 1610 or 1611
to Middleton's production of *Macbeth*, since, being
chiefly concerned with the addition of witch-songs and
witch-dances to the text,[5] he would naturally be using

[1] Greg, *Elizabethan Dramatic Documents*, pp. 358–9.
[2] See the article on Crane by Prof. F. P. Wilson in
The Library, 1926, vii, 194–215.
[3] E. K. Chambers, *Elizabethan Stage*, ii, 510.
[4] W. J. Lawrence, *op. cit.* pp. 28–33.
[5] See notes on 4. 1 below.

the same performers and costumes once again. As his cuts in 1. 2 seem to display anxiety not to exceed a two hours' performance, I am inclined to think this production was intended once again for the court. But if so, it was first tried out in the popular theatre or was shortly after transferred thither, since the old astrologer Simon Forman witnessed a performance at the Globe on 20 April 1611.[1]

Forman records the earliest performance of *Macbeth* for which we have external evidence. We have, however, internal evidence of a positive kind that it was being acted in 1606, and we can be almost certain that it was one of the plays given at Court on the occasion of King Christian of Denmark's visit to his sister Anne and his brother-in-law James. Date and occasion were first suggested by Malone[2] who pointed out that the drunken Porter's welcome to Hell of 'an equivocator that could swear in both the scales against either scale, who committed treason enough for God's sake, yet could not equivocate to heaven' was obviously intended to refer to Henry Garnet, Provincial of the Jesuit Society in England, who was tried on 28 March 1606, for his complicity in the Gunpowder Plot (on which day King James himself attended the trial incognito),[3] confessed to the use of equivocation and was hanged on 3 May. Further, the words 'yet could not equivocate to heaven',

---

[1] For Forman's account, and the date of his visit, which he writes '1610' in error, see the reprint of his MS. *Bocke of Plaies* in E. K. Chambers, *William Shakespeare*, ii, 337–41, and cf. pp. lxix–lxx, below. The *Bocke* has recently been declared a Collier forgery by Dr Tannenbaum (*Shakesperian Scraps*, 1933, pp. 1–35) following a suggestion by Prof. J. Q. Adams (*Macbeth*, 1931, p. viii). But for evidence in favour of its authenticity see *The Review of English Studies*, July 1947. [2] See Boswell's *Malone*, ii, 407 ff.

[3] G. B. Harrison, *Jacobean Journal*, 28 March 1606.

and the assumption that the equivocator had already
found his way to Hell, surely imply that Garnet was a
dead traitor when the speech was first uttered. And this
is supported by another passage which, as Bradley noted,
actually links equivocation with the hanging of traitors.
'What is a traitor?' asks little Macduff of his mother,
and the dialogue continues:

> *Lady Macduff.* Why, one that swears and lies.
> *Son.* And be all traitors that do so?
> *Lady Macduff.* Every one that does so is a traitor, and
> must be hanged.[1]

'It is to be feared', comments Bradley, 'that the audience
applauded this passage',[2] and I think it safe to assume
that both it and the Porter's speech were written after
the great Jesuit had paid the last penalty. As against this
we have to reckon with the echoes of *Macbeth* noted
below[3] in Marston's *Sophonisba*, entered in the
Stationers' Register on 17 March, i.e. before Garnet's
trial and certainly acted some weeks earlier; echoes
which led Sir Edmund Chambers 'tentatively' to 'put
Macbeth early in 1606'.[4] But it was customary for the

---

[1] 4. 2. 46–50.

[2] Bradley, *op. cit.* p. 397, n. 1.

[3] The following are the chief parallels to *Macbeth* noted
in plays acted or printed in 1606–7: 'In stead of a Iester,
weele ha the ghost ith white sheete sit at vpper end a' th'
Table' (*The Puritan*, 4. 3. 89; perhaps by Middleton: probably acted 1606); another obvious reference to Banquo's
ghost at 5. 1. 20–30 of *The Knight of the Burning Pestle*
(*c.* 1607) which is quoted on p. lxix below; and several
slight, but convincing, echoes in Marston's *Sophonisba*
pointed out by Bradley (p. 471), e.g.

'Upon whose tops the Roman eagles streachd
Their large spread winges, which fan'd the evening ayre
To us cold breath.' (1. 2; cf. *Macbeth*, 1. 2. 50–1.)

[4] *William Shakespeare*, i, 475.

players to 'exercise themselves' before acting at court by first trying the play out on the popular stage, and the other echoes of *Macbeth* traceable in the drama of 1606 and 1607 make it certain that Shakespeare's tragedy was being publicly performed at this time. The foregoing apparent conflict of evidence may accordingly be resolved if we suppose the allusions to Garnet were added to the text after these public performances, while that they *are* additions will presently be shown. A further complication must, however, be noticed in passing, viz. that the Jesuit doctrine of equivocation had been a subject for stage jesting at least since the time of *Hamlet*.[1] It is not necessary to suppose therefore that a general expression like 'th' equivocation of the fiend' (5. 5. 43) was intended as a reference to Garnet.

Christian IV's visit lasted from 17 July to 11 August, and the passages on the hanging and damnation of equivocators, written, I assume, after 3 May, bring the play close to that period. Its production at court cannot be proved but is strongly suggested by its brevity,[2] and by the fact that the passages in question together with others seem to have been added, for the entertainment of the royal audience, to an already existing text. Examine in its context, for instance, the dialogue just quoted from 4. 2. Although the boy's first question is

---

[1] See *Hamlet*, 5. 1. 134, and my note thereon.

[2] See A. W. Pollard on short plays in *Aspects of Shakespeare*, pp. 13–14 and a Note by R. C. Bald in *The Review of English Studies*, iv, 429–31. It seems unlikely that all plays given at Court were short, though plays for particular occasions, i.e. for weddings or as *part* of an evening's entertainment might well be, especially when the chief guest was a foreigner with but slight understanding of English, as was probably the case with King Christian in 1606 and the German bridegroom of Princess Elizabeth before whom *The Tempest*, another short play, was given in 1612.

preceded by another, 'Was my father a traitor, mother?' which harks back to l. 4, 'traitors' is there used in a very different sense, while 'hanging' has no relevance to Macduff whatever. And when it is further observed that the dialogue stands at the beginning of a prose passage (ll. 44–63) which occurs in the middle of a scene otherwise in verse, the likelihood of an insertion is increased.

And a quite certain example of rewriting may, I think, be seen at 4. 3. 97–100, which is the culmination of Malcolm's self-detraction, that innocent deception practised on Macduff in order to test his loyalty and followed by a recantation. The episode, as every commentator has noted, is little more than a paraphrase of Holinshed. What has not been noted is that whereas Malcolm 'unspeaks' the three vices, lechery, avarice, and falsehood, which Holinshed names, and repudiates the third with particular emphasis, he does not actually accuse himself of this third vice at all; for after following his source faithfully with the first two, Shakespeare suddenly deserts it and makes Malcolm confess to a crime not even hinted at therein, that of contentiousness. A strange vice and expressed in strangely modern terms!

> Nay, had I power, I should
> Pour the sweet milk of concord into hell,
> Uproar the universal peace, confound
> All unity on earth.

That we have here an instance of rewriting after the composition of the original dialogue cannot, I think, be denied. Nor is it difficult to see for what purpose the change was made. Shakespeare had come to know more of his royal master's mind in the interval and to realise, as a modern apologist puts it, that 'he was haunted by thoughts of the unity of the Christian world under one faith',[1] or, to use the words of a less favourable historian, that he was 'the most thorough-going pacifist who ever bore rule in Britain'.[2] It seems that the crowning horror in Malcolm's self-indictment is violent opposition to King James's cherished foreign policy! Yet the words have a special point as well, appropriate to the summer of 1606 and to no other time. For Rome followed up the outrage of the Gunpowder Plot in England by laying the ancient republic of Venice under an interdict, and it was confidently predicted in this country that the act would precipitate a general European War with England, France, and Venice on one side, and Spain and the Pope on the other. At an interview on 14 June 1606, James unburdened himself of a 'long discourse' on the subject to the Venetian ambassador, his conclusion being that the Jesuits were 'authors and instruments of all the great disturbances' in the world.[3] Clearly Shakespeare's Malcolm poses as a kind of Jesuit. Need we hesitate to assume that this *bonne bouche* was concocted for the dish which His Majesty was to share with a foreign monarch?[4]

Similarly, I suspect with others that the episode of the King's Evil (4. 3. 140–59), which has but slight

[1] See Prof. Sisson's essay on James I in *Seventeenth Century Studies presented to Sir Herbert Grierson*, p. 60.

[2] G. M. Trevelyan, *History of England*, p. 385. Cf. *Calendar of State Papers (Scotland)*, 1936, vol. x, p. xvi.

[3] *Calendar of State Papers (Venice)*, 1603–7, vol. x, pp. 359–61. Cf. F. A. Yates in vol. vii of *The Journal of the Warburg and Courtauld Institutes*.

[4] H. N. Paul, *The First Performance of 'Macbeth'* (Shakespeare Assoc. Bulletin, Oct. 1947) shows that 4. 3. 97–100 reflects a seditious 'uproar' in the streets when a Latin speech, celebrating Concord, Heavenly Peace, and Briton's Unity, was delivered on 31 July 1606 to welcome King Christian, and infers therefrom that *Macbeth* was the play given at Hampton Court on 7 August. [1950.]

dramatic relevance and is so self-contained that it may be omitted without damage to the context either in metre or meaning, was also added in 1606. It is another *bonne bouche*, since though based on Holinshed, it flattered James by emphasising his descent from St Edward the Confessor, by hinting, in the reference to the latter's 'heavenly gift of prophecy', that James was also inspired as his bishops were fond of saying,[1] and by paying tribute to the miraculous healing power of his sacred touch, which he affected to smile at while he delighted in showing it off.[2] Moreover, his dear brother Christian of Denmark could lay claim to none of these 'king-becoming graces'.

We have, then, proof that passages of *Macbeth* were written in the summer of 1606 and pretty clear evidence that other passages were added to an already standing text to please Shakespeare's royal master. Is there anything to show that some, if not all, of these additions were part of a general revision, that the 1606 text was in fact an abridgement of a longer play, as its brevity suggests and as many critics have supposed? If Shakespeare undertook such an abridgement, one thing is certain: he went to work in a very different fashion from Middleton in the second scene. It may well be that some of the short lines and abrupt transitions outside that scene were left by his cuts, but the splendour of the play as a whole indicates that the abridgement, if abridgement there was, must have been a masterly operation, involving no doubt the sacrifice of speeches, episodes, scenes for which room could not be found within the narrower frame, but proceeding in the main by compression, readjustment, recasting and rewriting.

[1] See Harington, *Nugae Antiquae* (1804), i, 181–2 and note 4. 3. 157 below.
[2] Cf. note 4. 3. 146.

In a word it was a process not of botching but of gestation.

It follows that it will be far less easy to detect than it was to catch Middleton out in 1. 2. Yet if we look closely, it is possible, I think, to find a birthmark or two in the re-born *Macbeth*, pointing to its previous existence as a longer text. An obvious example, obvious because it has given rise to much comment, but actually so inconspicuous that it passed unnoticed until one Hans Koester drew attention to it in 1865,[1] is Lady Macbeth's taunting reference at 1. 7. 47 ff. to an occasion on which her husband first broached the 'enterprise' of Duncan's murder. No trace of any such occasion is to be discovered in the text as it stands, and efforts have been made to explain it away, both (i) on psychological grounds as a bold lie[2] or as an exaggeration,[3] based on his letter to her, and (ii) on technical grounds, as an 'episodic intensification' like the allusion to Lady Macbeth's children,[4] or as a piece of dramatic legerdemain resorted to in order to stress at this juncture the less admirable side of Macbeth's character.[5] The trouble with this last explanation, in some ways the most plausible of the four, is that as no spectator or reader apparently observed the point until 1865, it can hardly

---

[1] *Shakespeare Jahrbuch*, I, 146.

[2] *Macbeth*, ed. par James Darmesteter, Paris, 1887, p. 35, and ed. by Sir Herbert Grierson, 1914, p. 107.

[3] Bradley, *op. cit.* p. 483. See also his whole Note CC, 'When was the murder of Duncan first plotted?'

[4] See note 4. 3. 216, and Schücking, *Character Problems in Shakespeare*, pp. 113–6. The best discussion of this matter is the earliest, i.e. by Goethe, in *Conversations with Eckermann*, April 18, 1827, quoted below in note 1. 7. 54.

[5] R. Bridges, 'The Influence of the Audience on Shakespeare's Drama' (*Shakespeare: Stratford Edition*), 1907, vol. 10, and *Collected Essays, etc.* 1927, i, 13–19.

have been intended to stress anything. And if it had been, why should Shakespeare write the first six scenes in such a manner that practically all readers since then have imagined quite another state of affairs and *continued to imagine it* after reading the passage which is troubling us?[1]

Moments of dramatic tension are not the time a practised playwright chooses for the communication of new and important facts; and the truth is the highly emotional situation leaves us no wits to notice that Lady Macbeth is speaking of something which transforms our idea of Macbeth's character, still less of something which has never taken place at all. And yet, *once our attention is directed to her words*, we see that they are far too positive and too pointed to be susceptible of any of the foregoing explanations. Consider, for instance, the following:

> Nor time nor place
> Did then adhere, and yet you would make both:
> They have made themselves, and that their fitness now
> Does unmake you.

She is recalling him to a situation fresh in the minds of both (and surely, we now feel, also in the minds of the audience), to a time before Duncan arrived at Inverness or was expected to arrive there, to a discussion between them of how nevertheless the assassination might be contrived; and she is comparing his behaviour then with his behaviour now. This earlier conversation had taken place; of that there can be no reasonable doubt, as we read the passage by itself. Yet, if so, when? On the

---

[1] My question is a free paraphrase of a sentence in Bradley. It need hardly be added that there is nothing in common between Lady Macbeth's allusion and those improbabilities in the antecedents, ἔξω τῆς τραγῳδίας, common in Greek drama, such as the ignorance of Oedipus in the *Oedipus Tyrannus* of Sophocles.

one hand, the previous scēnes are so closely knit together
as to allow no moment anywhere when it could have
taken place, while on the other, critics who imagine
Macbeth and Lady Macbeth discussing the murder
before the play opens, or in some scene that has dropped
out or been 'cut' out, only do so by ignoring the plain
sense of the scenes before them. They must overlook,
for example, 1. 3. 130–42, which depicts the terror of
Macbeth's soul when the idea of murder *first* comes to
him;[1] and 1. 5. 14–24, in which Lady Macbeth makes
it clear that so far he has refused to entertain any but
honourable thoughts; while the dialogue at the end of
1. 5 may be read as either implying an earlier conversation or as the earliest occasion upon which the
murder has ever been talked of between them.

We seem to be turning round and round; and critics
will continue so to do while they think of the play as
without a history, or as a text shortened merely by the
omission of scenes and episodes. But believe that Shakespeare revised his own play, that the earlier *Macbeth* was
not rough-hewn but re-born as the *Macbeth* of 1606,
and all is plain. The mysterious conversation to which
Lady Macbeth so positively alludes is then seen to belong to the longer play, and to have been squeezed out
in the tightening-up process. That in such circumstances
Shakespeare by inadvertence or indifference should
have left a reference to it standing at 1. 7. 47 is likely
enough and has many parallels in the texts of his other
plays. He knew an audience would not notice the
implications and it added another lash to the Lady's
chastising tongue. Nor is there any difficulty in supposing that another and larger dramatic frame contained
a scene in which the Thane of Cawdor designate called at
Inverness on his way to Forres, told his wife of the Weird
Sisters, and—no doubt prompted by her—confessed

[1] See p. lv below.

that 'thoughts of murder had crossed his mind'; a scene, in fact, that probably supplied much of the material for the first thirty lines of the surviving 1. 5.

Yet if 1. 5 be a reconstructed scene it must contain material from the original scene in which Lady Macbeth receives news of Duncan's approach under her battlements; for it will be granted, I hope, that such a scene was to be found in the earlier play. And part of this material was, I think, an invocation to the spirits 'that tend on mortal thoughts' very similar to, if not identical with, the speech we now have; since, unless I am much mistaken, the speech in question reveals a second indication of something lost or squeezed out. The whole point of Lady Macbeth's invocation is that she intends to murder Duncan herself. She speaks of '*my* knife' and of '*my* fell purpose'. And the same resolve is implied in everything she says to Macbeth after his entry. She bids him put

> This night's great business into *my* dispatch;

she tells him he need do nothing but look the innocent and kindly host; she dismisses him with the words 'Leave all the rest to me'. All this seems obvious directly it is pointed out, though once again no one appears to have noticed it before,[1] simply because in the end the murder is of course performed by Macbeth himself; and must be, however the drama is shaped. But that implies a change of plan and such an important change ought by all dramatic rights to be explained to the audience. This was originally done, I suggest, by means of a further dialogue between husband and wife, preceded perhaps by a scene in which, going to the bedroom knife in hand, she cannot bring herself to the action; and I further suggest that when he reached this point in 1606 Shakespeare found he had no room for such

[1] See, however, J. Q. Adams, *Macbeth*, 1931, pp. 150–3, 164–5.

developments and had to extricate himself as best he could. And how triumphantly he does it! First he writes a soliloquy ('If it were done, when 'tis done') for the beginning of scene 1.7, which conveys the impression that Macbeth was intending all along to do the deed himself; he then later in the same scene makes the guilty pair talk as if they were proposing to do it *together*; and finally, though he sends Macbeth to the bedroom alone, he brings Lady Macbeth on to inform us that she has already been there, and—crowning touch—that

> Had he not resembled
> My father as he slept, I had done't.

The broken thread, as I believe it to be, is so dexterously woven back into the new stuff that no one, not even lynx-eyed Bradley himself, has noticed the join. Yet the words just quoted tell the whole story, since they provide us, not only with the dramatic reason for the change of plan as it was explained, I believe, in the original dialogue, but also with a technical reason for the introduction by Shakespeare of a change of plan at all. One thing can be said with certainty about the longer *Macbeth*, that it shed greater light, light we would willingly recapture, upon the character of Lady Macbeth. How much more effective would be this unexpected revelation of *her* 'human kindness', had the audience been first led to believe that she, and not Macbeth, was to do the murder! Yet when she prays

> That no compunctious visitings of nature
> Shake my fell purpose,

she at once acknowledges her weakness and gives spectators their warning. These words and those cited above form, I suggest, the two ends of the original thread.

Nor is the extrusion of material like this the end of the matter. Apart from the short and abrupt lines noted above, the puzzles of Banquo's behaviour after Macbeth's coronation[1], the appearance of a third murderer in 3.3[2], and Macduff's desertion of his wife are also best explained by compression, while once this factor be admitted it becomes obvious that many original scenes and episodes may have been sacrificed without leaving a trace, unless it be in 'the multiplicity of very brief scenes' to which Greg draws attention.[3]

But if the 1606 *Macbeth* be an abridged text, what can one say about the length, character and date of the earlier play? Nothing, I fear, but guesses; one or two of which may perhaps be hazarded, if only to provoke better guesses by others.

First, then, my impression is that while the process of compression affected the play throughout, it was most drastic in the first half. Many spectators and readers are, I think, conscious of something a little wrong, or unusual, about the balance of the plot: the murder of Duncan, which forms as it were its peak, belongs by rights to Act 3 and not the beginning of Act 2. And this hypothesis would help to account for another phenomenon, the fact that irregularity of verse-division, which is so marked a feature of the Folio text, is almost entirely confined to the earlier scenes. My second guess—a confident one—is that the earlier and longer *Macbeth* was intended for King James just as much as the shortened version of 1606. Indeed, I cannot believe that this chronicle-play of the house of Stewart, with its witch-scenes full of points likely to be of interest to the author of *Dæmonologie*, was written for any eyes but his.[4] And if readers be ready to grant this royal interest

[1] See above, pp. xvi–xvii.
[2] See notes 3. 1. 129, 137; 3. 3 (head).
[3] Greg, *The Editorial Problem in Shakespeare*, p. 147, and *Alcazar and Orlando*, p. 94, n. 3.
[4] See below, pp. xliv–xlv.

in the play, they will allow at least the possibility that
the abridgement of 1606 was undertaken by express
command of His Majesty who wished his brother of
Denmark to witness what he probably looked on as his
own special piece.

My next guess, though at first sight irreconcilable
with the foregoing, and founded upon the contentious
ground of style, can at least show powerful support for
part of its claim. It was the considered opinion of a
supreme taster of poetic vintage, George Saintsbury,
an opinion twice expressed, that those who believe
Shakespeare wrote the whole of *Macbeth* in 1605–6
'must have curious standards of criticism', inasmuch as
portions of it, and in particular 'the second scene, are
in verse and phrase whole stages older than the bulk of
the play'.[1] And this verdict, Sir Herbert Grierson,
Saintsbury's successor at Edinburgh, has endorsed with
certain modifications.[2] Encouraged by a hint from
Coleridge,[3] I would dare to offer a modification in my
turn, question the words 'whole stages older', and setting
the second scene of *Macbeth* beside the Pyrrhus speech in
Hamlet, suggest that they belong to approximately the
same date. It is unnecessary here to note the many
striking similarities in imagery and phrasing, since that
task has recently been performed by Mr Nosworthy.[4]
What I would point to are the echoes in the two scenes
of contiguous lines from Marlowe's description of the
slaughter of Priam in *The Tragedy of Dido*. Here are
the three passages:

[1] *Cambridge History of English Literature*, v, 203.
Cf. Saintsbury's *History of English Prosody*, ii, 41–2.
[2] *Macbeth*, ed. Grierson and Smith, p. xii.
[3] Raysor, *Coleridge's Shakespearean Criticism*, i, 67
(opening paragraph on *Macbeth*).
[4] *The Review of English Studies*, April 1946, pp. 126 ff.

But with the whiff and wind of his fell sword
Th' unnerved father falls.   *Hamlet* 2. 2. 477–8.

Till he unseamed him from the nave to th' chops.
                              Macbeth 1. 2. 22.

Which he disdaining whiskt his sword about,
And with the wind thereof the king fell down:
Then from the navell to the throat at once
He ript old Priam.   *Dido* 2. 1. 283–6.

It seems likely that what put Shakespeare in mind of
Marlowe's lines was his desire to contrast his Prince
of Denmark with Pyrrhus, the classical type of ruthlessness, and, if this is so, the line in *Macbeth* must be,
not 'whole stages', but only some four or five years
older than the rest of the play. Again, it has often been
observed that Hamlet and Macbeth are complementary
characters; the one never being able to begin, the other
never being able to leave off; [1] while I find further
similarities in rhythm and phrase, thought and action,
when I compare the scene in which Macbeth provokes
the murderers to kill Banquo (3. 1. 73 ff.) with that in
which Claudius eggs Laertes on to a like purpose (4. 7).
In a word, my guess is a very daring one, viz. that
the earlier *Macbeth* was the next play undertaken after
Hamlet, i.e. that it was written in the second half of
1601 or early in 1602.

That means pushing back into Elizabeth's reign a
play just claimed as intended from first to last for King
James. 'How shall we find the concord of this discord?'
At this point I tremble, and then, remembering I am on
good Scottish soil, take the boldest step of all.[2] Shakespeare's fellows are recorded as acting before the Queen

[1] See Saintsbury, *loc. cit.* Cf. note 4. 3. 44–132, below.
[2] The bolder that it follows the now discredited
F. G. Fleay; v. his *Life and Work of Shakespeare*, 1886,
p. 43.

in the winter of 1602;[1] but nothing is known of *his* doings during her last years after the fall of Essex. We do know, however, that 'English comedians' were in Scotland from 1599 onwards, to the scandal of the Edinburgh Kirk Sessions[2], and that they were led by one Laurence Fletcher, whose name later appears with Shakespeare's as one of the principal members of the King's company constituted by royal patent on 19 May 1603. We know too that players can do nothing without plays; and, though no title or tittle of what they acted has survived, it is at least conceivable that Shakespeare's longer *Macbeth* was first produced by Fletcher's company in the capital city of Scotland. Indeed, if I may continue to live dangerously, it is even possible that Shakespeare visited Scotland himself. Somehow or other he learned that the Setons were the royal armour-bearers[3] and seems to have become acquainted with William Stewart's *Croniclis of Scotland*.[4] The only surviving copy of this found its way from Scotland to Cambridge via Bishop Moore's library,[5] but there are not likely to have been many copies in England at any time, and Holinshed does not use it. Did Shakespeare read it in Edinburgh? But enough of guessing.

III. *'The Tragedy of Macbeth'*

One of the most difficult of Shakespeare's tragedies to classify, or seemingly to fit into our modern conception of tragedy at all, *Macbeth* has meant different things to different generations. In Shakespeare's own day,

[1] E. K. Chambers, *Elizabethan Stage*, ii, 205–6.
[2] *Ibid*. pp. 266, 270; and A. J. Mill, *Medieval Plays in Scotland*, 1927, p. 299.
[3] See note 5. 3. 29 S.D.
[4] See also notes 4. 3. 107; 5. 8. 33.
[5] See Preface to Stewart's *Croniclis*, *op. cit*. pp. vi–vii.

Seneca being the ideal for tragedy, the end of poetry being 'to teach and to delight', and the components of true tragedy being therefore Seneca and instruction, the Senecan *Macbeth*, with its exhibition of a tyrant in action, its revelation of his innermost soul, and its demonstration of the just retribution that inevitably awaits him, probably seemed to critics a more satisfactory tragedy than any other of his plays.[1] Indeed, it almost looks as if in the writing of it Shakespeare had consciously in mind Sidney's famous description of

...high and excellent tragedy that openeth the greatest wounds, and sheweth forth the ulcers that are covered with tissue;[2] that maketh kings fear to be tyrants, and tyrants manifest their tyrannical humours; that, with stirring the affects of admiration and commiseration, teacheth the uncertainty of this world and upon how weak foundations gilden roofs are builded; that maketh us know

> Qui sceptra saevus duro imperio regit,
> Timet timentes, metus in auctorem redit.[3]

Every point tallies, including the quotation from

[1] That Shakespeare knew Seneca's *Hercules Furens* at least, if not other dramas of his, will appear from the notes on 1. 7. 8–12; 2. 2. 37–40, 59–63; 5. 3. 22, 40. As Grierson and Smith point out, '*Macbeth* has three pairs of neighbouring passages paralleling three pairs of neighbouring passages in *Hercules Furens*', while the parallel at 2. 2. 59–63 makes it pretty certain Shakespeare read it in the Latin (see my note). Cf. too J. W. Cunliffe, *Influence of Seneca on Elizabethan Tragedy*, 1893.

[2] Cf. *Hamlet* 3. 4. 147–9:
> 'It will but skin and film the ulcerous place,
> Whiles rank corruption mining all within
> Infects unseen.'

[3] Sidney, *Apology for Poetry* (Gregory Smith, *Elizabethan Critical Essays*, i, 177). The verse comes from *Oedipus*, ll. 705–6.

Seneca's *Oedipus*, which might have stood as a motto on Shakespeare's title-page had he elected to publish this play. When we remember too that Macbeth was *the* tyrant of Scottish history, and that the play was written for the delight of a Scottish[1] king, who was in his own conceit the inspired exponent of the rights and duties of Christian monarchy,[2] its didactic implications for Shakespeare's original audience become still more obvious. Lastly, think of *Macbeth* as a tragic 'mirror for magistrates',[3] and you have an entirely satisfactory explanation of the dialogue between Malcolm and Macduff in 4. 3, on bad kings and good, which seems to us a tiresome digression chiefly because we have ceased to interest ourselves in a topic that much engaged the minds of the British Solomon and his court. It had engaged his indeed from boyhood; for had not that stern tutor, George Buchanan, dedicated to him, while still a lad of ten, a Senecan tragedy on Herod and John the Baptist, 'quod tyrannorum cruciatus, et, cum florere maxime videntur, miserias dilucide exponat'?[4]

But James was interested in it for another reason also. As Shakespeare's most direct and elaborate treatment

[1] Cf. an interesting article by J. W. Draper, '*Macbeth* as a compliment to James I', *Englische Studien*, 1937–8, pp. 207 ff.

[2] See *The Political Works of James I*, ed. by C. H. McIlwain, 1918, *passim* and p. xvi, above.

[3] Cf. E. M. W. Tillyard, *Shakespeare's History Plays*, pp. 315–16. Dr Tillyard does not refer to the dialogue in question, and I do not subscribe either to his interpretation of *Macbeth* or to the notion, which runs through his book, that Shakespeare drew much inspiration from *The Mirror for Magistrates* itself, a volume I doubt whether he ever looked into, unless to read Sackville's contributions.

[4] Dedication to *Baptistes* by George Buchanan, 1576.

of the mysterious yet very actual realm of evil, which pressed close upon men's minds in that age, and was believed to be thronged with malignant spirits able at once to direct the operations of nature and to influence the human soul, *Macbeth* undoubtedly appealed even more powerfully to the author of *Dæmonologie*, 1597, than did its anatomy of tyranny to the author of the *Trew Law of Free Monarchies*, 1598, and *Basilikon Doron*, 1599. Indeed, just as a knowledge of ghost-lore is necessary to the full understanding of *Hamlet*, so the present-day spectator of *Macbeth*, who lives in a scientific age from which witchcraft has been long since banished, and in which the terrors of hell have given place to the terrors of the atomic bomb, must miss not only more than half the feeling of awe and dread which the play originally inspired, but also a very great deal of the point and relevancy of the text. This is a matter to which I must return later. At the moment it is enough to note that *Macbeth* still retained this appeal in some measure throughout the eighteenth century, and that the following account, written in 1774, of the emotions aroused in the breast of one enthusiastic and intelligent spectator probably gives us a fair idea of the attitude of an audience in Shakespeare's day. After citing *Macbeth* as an example of Shakespeare's power of exhibiting the process of change in human character, Maurice Morgann continues:

The Weird Sisters rise, and order is extinguished. The laws of nature give way, and leave nothing in our minds but wildness and horror. No pause is allowed us for reflection: Horrid sentiment, furious guilt and compunction, air-drawn daggers, murders, ghosts, and inchantment, shake and *possess us wholly*. In the mean time the *process* is completed. Macbeth changes under our eye, *the milk of human kindness is converted to gall; he has supped full of horrors*, and his *May of life is fallen into the sear, the yellow leaf*; whilst we, the fools of amazement, are insensible to the shifting of place and the lapse of time, and till the curtain drops, never once wake to the truth of things, or recognise the laws of existence.[1]

Is this how Mr Gielgud's or Mr Wolfit's audiences experience *Macbeth*? I think not. Nor do I think them capable of entering with much understanding into the 'process' of the hero's 'change' as Shakespeare first conceived it, which was no other than the history of a human soul on its way to Hell, a soul at first noble, humane, innocent; then tempted through ambition to commit an appalling crime; and last, passing through the inevitable stages of torment and spiritual corruption that precede damnation. And what of the play's 'inchantment', the atmosphere supplied by witchcraft and apparitions, thunder and lightning, 'fog and filthy air'? Does it not seem more than a little childish to spectators *blasé* with synthetic mickey-mouse magic? Yet it was just this, we can be sure, that most arrested groundlings and judicious alike in Shakespeare's day. *Macbeth* was, indeed, a triumph of the latest stage-technique—the witches rising up and down from the 'cellarage' or 'hell' through traps, or vanishing into artificially created mists, the stage likewise artificially darkened in the scene after Duncan's murder, the 'blood-boltered' Ghost of Banquo suddenly appearing upon Macbeth's stool, the three apparitions springing out of the blazing cauldron in the cave, the wonderful 'show of eight kings' passing one by one across the back of the stage. Nothing of its kind so bold or so elaborate had been seen before, and it was the desire to exploit these purely theatrical attractions still further which led to the degradation of the text at the hands first of Middleton

[1] Maurice Morgann, *Essay on the Dramatic Character of Falstaff*, 1777, p. 69. The italics are his. For 'May of life' see note 5. 3. 22 below.

and later of D'Avenant. No: Shakespeare's *Macbeth* possessed a fascination and a meaning for King James and his Jacobeans which have now to a large extent passed away and even passed out of mind.

Yet, their date was not out for another hundred and fifty years. Though, debased in D'Avenant's recension and padded out with songs and dances, the *Macbeth* which Pepys and Restoration London admired for its 'divertisement' became a kind of tragic opera,[1] its moral and spiritual appeal remained unchanged. Pepys speaks of it as 'a deep tragedy', by which he meant no doubt that it was profoundly edifying, while the neo-classic principles upon which this conception was based were still inspiring Johnson in 1765 when he added a postscript to the play which concluded with these words, words that might have been written by Sidney himself:

> The passions are directed to their true end. Lady Macbeth is merely detested; and though the courage of Macbeth preserves some esteem, yet every reader rejoices at his fall.[2]

If Lady Macbeth is no longer 'merely detested', and we now admire in Macbeth something more than courage, that is due to what may be called the Shakespearian character-writers, who were already getting to work in Johnson's day, just as the play's original appeal was beginning to fade. The first serious study of the hero, which was written in 1770, by Thomas Whately, uncle of the famous archbishop, drew special attention to the 'apprehensions' which are so marked a feature of his character and distinguish it in particular from Shakespeare's earlier Senecan figure of Richard III. Hazlitt praised this essay and borrowed from it, while it seems

---

[1] See Stage-History, pp. lxx, lxxii, and Pepys's *Diary* (Globe edition), p. 453.

[2] Cf. his *Preface to Shakespeare*, 'the end of writing is to instruct; the end of poetry is to instruct by pleasing'.

likely that Coleridge had read it too, since his notes on the play are largely taken up with just those 'recoilings' and 'terrors' which are Whately's theme. But while Coleridge followed his predecessors in associating these with a troubled conscience, he originated the idea, which most have since held, that Macbeth seems himself to be largely unaware of the conscience that troubles him. It was he too that first stressed the essential womanliness of Lady Macbeth, who was only a 'monster' to Steevens and other eighteenth-century critics, and 'a splendid fiend' even to her great impersonator, Mrs Siddons. Yet, as we shall see, Coleridge to some extent darkened counsel, while it is strange that the author of *Biographia Literaria* should never have attributed an 'imagination' to Shakespeare's greatest man of imagination, or that the creator of *The Ancient Mariner*, which owes so much to this play, should not even have spoken of him as a poet. It was left to Andrew Bradley to discover these things, and they were great discoveries indeed. But when Bradley insists that the imagination is limited, that Macbeth 'shows no sign', for example, 'of any unusual sensitiveness to the glory or beauty in the world or in the soul', and when he gives this as in part the 'reason that we have no inclination to love him and that we regard him with more of awe than of pity', one is amazed. For are not

> And pity like a naked new-born babe,

and

> Scarf up the tender eye of pitiful day,

a distillation, as it were, of all that Blake wrote of innocence and experience? Does not

> Ere the bat hath flown
> His cloistered flight, ere to black Hecate's summons
> The shard-borne beetle with his drowsy hums
> Hath rung night's yawning peal, there shall be done
> A deed of dreadful note

read like a passage from some lost masterpiece by
Collins; and

> Can such things be
> And overcome us like a summer cloud
> Without our special wonder,

match Wordsworth at his most inspired? Or does not

> This my hand will rather
> The multitudinous seas incarnadine,
> Making the green one red,

offer an angel-view of the whole ocean-girdled globe,
which out-soars even Milton 'towering in his pride of
place'; while

> But here upon this bank and shoal of time

extends that horizon across the vasty deep of eternity?
In truth, as John Bailey has said, 'there is no one in
all Shakespeare who so continually, almost invariably,
speaks the very greatest poetry as Macbeth'.[1] But it is
in his reluctance to pity Macbeth that Bradley seems
to come most short; and is at the same time most surprising, since pity is of the very essence of tragedy.
Yet he could hardly help himself; since, though he
sets it down as an effect of Macbeth's poetic limitations,
his hesitation really sprang from quite other causes,
causes connected with the textual situation discussed
in our second section.

For critical opinion about Macbeth had taken another
turn in the second half of last century. With the exception
of Johnson, the majority of eighteenth-century critics
who speak of him as he was before he met the Witches
discover a very noble soldier, full of that 'milk of human
kindness' which his wife herself attributes to him. And

[1] John Bailey, *Shakespeare*, 1929, p. 182.

even Johnson was so moved by the proud magnanimity of

> I dare do all that may become a man;
> Who dares do more is none,

that he declared the lines 'ought to bestow immortality on the author, though all his other productions had been lost'.[1] Schlegel perhaps best expressed the general view when he declared that, though he might have portrayed 'a hardened villain', Shakespeare preferred

> to exhibit a more sublime picture: an ambitious but noble hero, yielding to a deep-laid hellish temptation; and in whom all the crimes to which, in order to secure the fruits of his first crime, he is impelled by necessity, cannot altogether eradicate the stamp of native heroism.

And, in taking leave of the play, he adds:

> However much we may abhor his actions, we cannot altogether refuse to compassionate the state of his mind; we lament the ruin of so many noble qualities.[2]

Goethe implied the same when he ranged Macbeth with Hamlet and Brutus, and found him driven like them into a toil from which he was unable to extricate himself.[3] Coleridge too spoke of his 'heroic character'.[4] Yet his references elsewhere to an early 'birth-date of guilt'[5] and to a 'mind rendered temptable by previous dalliance of the fancy with ambitious thoughts'[6] raised doubts of this nobility for the first time; and the doubts seemed amply confirmed by Koester's article[7] in

[1] Raleigh, *Johnson on Shakespeare*, p. 171.
[2] Schlegel, *Dramatic Literature* (Bohn's Library), pp. 408–9.
[3] Goethe, *Shakespeare und kein Ende* (1813–16).
[4] Raysor, *Coleridge's Shakespearean Criticism*, i, 82.
[5] *Ibid.* p. 70.   [6] *Ibid.* p. 68.
[7] See above, pp. xxxiv ff.

1865, which came to be accepted by most as proof that Macbeth had schemed the murder before the opening of the play.[1] And though Bradley, we have seen, did not accept it as such, it clearly shook him, and led him to scrutinise the text narrowly for evidence of the earlier and more favourable conception of the hero's character, with the result that while admitting 'a keen sense both of honour and of the worth of a good name', and again that 'he was far from devoid of humanity and pity', he found it impossible to subscribe either to his nobility or to his 'human kindness'.[2] Meanwhile Koester's discovery ruled out in the eyes of most subsequent critics even the good that Bradley allowed for; and so Macbeth became the 'hardened villain' which earlier critics believed Shakespeare had rejected in favour of 'a more sublime picture'. Let that honest and sensitive writer John Bailey, who found it impossible to brush Koester aside, speak for all. Campbell, he first reminds us, called *Macbeth* 'the greatest treasure of our dramatic literature', and then he continues:

> I do not know whether anyone would to-day repeat that judgment, which I confess I do not understand. In nearly all the qualities which make up the greatness of a great tragedy it seems to me to come distinctly behind its three great rivals. It neither interests the mind, nor moves the heart, nor fills the imagination, as do *Hamlet* and *Othello* and *Lear*.[3]

He does not explain how, if it satisfies neither mind nor heart nor imagination, it can rightly be called a tragedy at all. Maybe, remembering Aristotle's

---

[1] This deduction was first drawn, not by Koester himself, but by the American, George Fletcher, in *Studies of Shakespeare*, 1845, as Mr Sprague kindly informs me [1950]. For its influence on Irving see below, p. lxxix.

[2] *Op. cit.* p. 351.   [3] Bailey, *op. cit.* p. 180.

exclusion from the category of tragedy all drama which exhibits 'an extremely bad man falling from happiness into misery',[1] he thought it wiser not to try.

It is not easy in any case to regard Macbeth as a tragic hero in Aristotle's sense.[2] But having disposed of Koester we can at least return to the old notion, which Shakespeare found explicit in Stewart's *Croniclis*, of a character that begins by being admirable and falls from grace under the stress of great temptation. Such a hero will be capable of moving us to compassion; of making us feel that, given his stature and the strength of the temptation which assails him, we might have endured a like fate; of compelling us to cry out 'God, God forgive us all', as we contemplate the spectacle of his tremendous catastrophe. By setting that cry on the Doctor's lips Shakespeare associated pity with the ruin of his 'fiend-like queen'. Is it not likely that he, of all dramatists, would invite pity also for the other and more human protagonist?[3] And if so, how could he contrive it except by representing Macbeth as a hero in the full sense of that word at the outset of the play, as one who possessed the instincts of a Henry V if without his stability, and above all as a great Elizabethan gentleman, tender, magnanimous and honourable as well as brave? Holinshed offered him, in the three campaigns against Macdonwald, Sweno and Canute, excellent material for the display of such qualities. But we shall never know whether or how far he made use of the opportunity, because some other hand has cut to pieces the scene or

---

[1] *Aristotle on the Art of Poetry*, trans. I. Bywater, § 13.

[2] See the remarks of S. H. Butcher, *Aristotle's Theory of Poetry*, p. 322.

[3] See the eloquent paragraph on *Macbeth* in *A Critical History of English Poetry*, by Sir Herbert Grierson and Dr J. C. Smith, 1944, p. 116.

scenes dealing with these campaigns. All that remains
is the picture of 'Bellona's bridegroom', a skilful general
and a soldier of superhuman strength and bravery.

Yet more may be legitimately inferred. Speaking of
the treacherous Cawdor, Duncan announces in the last
line of the same scene:

> What he hath lost, noble Macbeth hath won.

That word 'noble', thus placed and winged with
rhyme, was surely intended to introduce us in the next
scene to something more than a great soldier.[1]
Mr Masefield, again, noting the politeness with which
he takes leave of Ross and Angus at the end of this same
next scene, remarks on 'the delicate good manners,
which make him so winning a man', and bids actors
who play him 'ever remember that Shakespeare gave
Macbeth an exquisite sensibility, a charm hard to resist,
an eloquence like the tongue of an angel'.[2] When I read
this, it carried instant conviction; for I recollected not
only that Shakespeare bestowed his finest poetry upon
him, but that he wrote it for the golden voice of Richard
Burbage. Nor do I doubt that Lady Macbeth (perhaps
played in 1606 by the young eyas who was presently to
'boy' Cleopatra's greatness) was meant to be equally capti-
vating. They make, in fact, the perfect host and hostess;
and the lovely sunlit scene in which she welcomes
Duncan under her battlements is, for all the irony that
mocks it, none the less a thing of sheer delight in its
display of beautiful courtesy on both sides. Further,
having endowed his hero with supreme poetic genius,
could Shakespeare deny him what in his own experience
was inseparable therefrom, a human heart? He found
in Holinshed a Macbeth 'somewhat cruell of nature';

[1] Bradley, *op. cit.* refers to this passage in a footnote to
p. 351, but dismisses it as irrelevant to Macbeth's character.
[2] Masefield, *op. cit.* p. 38.

and his Macbeth after he has 'supped full with horrors'
becomes cruel enough, though never I believe 'of
nature'. But before the first murder he is, Lady
Macbeth tells us, 'too full o'th' milk of human kindness'.
She speaks no doubt in impatience and with some contempt. But impatient contempt makes the testimony
more and not less striking.[1] And, as Kittredge points
out, it is confirmed by Macbeth's unconscious self-
revelation in the great tribute to Pity in the soliloquy
of scene 7.[2] For my own part, I suspect that Shakespeare, reading in Holinshed that Duncan 'had too
much of clemency', translated the phrase into his own
words and transferred the quality to the yet untempted,
unstained Macbeth.

Assuming then, that Macbeth was no criminal to
start with but an honourable soldier, cast in titanic
mould, and that the initial step in his tragedy was

> So foull ane blek for to put in his gloir,
> Quhilk haldin wes of sic honour befoir,

I propose to round off this section by tracing in brief
outline his spiritual development, utilising for the

---

[1] Bradley (*op. cit.* p. 351) tries to make light of it by saying
she 'did not fully understand him'. But this is not *dramatic*
criticism. Shakespeare gives her the words to illuminate
Macbeth as well as herself; that she does not 'fully understand' his poetic imagination is another matter. Sir
Edmund Chambers makes light of it in another fashion, by
paraphrasing 'the milk of human kindness' as 'the commonplace ordinary qualities and tendencies of human kind'.
A sentence or two earlier he writes: 'Away from the battlefield his greatness is gone, he sinks to the level of quite
common men' (*Shakespeare: a Survey*, p. 235). To this had
Macbeth come in 1904–08 when these words were first
written.

[2] Kittredge, *op. cit.* p. 112.

purpose at once the findings of modern Shakespearian critics and our limited knowledge of what the original audience thought and felt about the forces of evil in the universe, which form the background of the tragedy as is made clear by the prologue-like appearance of the Weird Sisters in the first and third scenes.

Temptation first comes to Macbeth with the fulfilment of the second prophecy of the Sisters immediately upon their disappearance. The 'start' he gives when hailed 'King hereafter' shows indeed that his mind had been 'rendered temptable by previous dalliance of the fancy with ambitious thoughts'.[1] But *murderous* thoughts are not born until Ross and Angus bring tidings that he is Thane of Cawdor and he realises that 'the devil can speak true'. The thoughts come suddenly, and obviously quite unexpectedly. They fill him with horror; his hair stands on end; his heart knocks against his ribs; he is lost in trance. It is an astonishing glimpse this, of a stricken soul at the very moment of temptation; and it is given us that we may be under no misunderstanding. For if the thought that now 'shakes so his single state of man' had long been his, if he were not an innocent spirit reeling under an utterly unforeseen attack, the symptoms we are shown would be meaningless. The internal struggle is also quite obviously a conscious one, while the assault of the Tempter seems at first repelled; for Macbeth flings free with

If chance will have me King, why, chance may crown me
Without my stir.

Yet his next aside,

      Come what come may,
Time and the hour runs through the roughest day,

---

[1] Coleridge, *op. cit.* i, 68.

is less positive, and there are other signs that ambition,
like
>   rank corruption mining all within,
> Infects unseen.

Thus when the next direct attack comes with Duncan's
public nomination of Malcolm as his heir, which
destroys all possibility of ambition being satisfied except
by unholy means, Macbeth's powers of resistance have
clearly weakened. For, though the thought is no less
detestable and the deed is as terrible as ever, still too
terrible to be named, he has moved appreciably nearer
to it.

>   Stars, hide your fires!
> Let not light see my black and deep desires:
> The eye wink at the hand; yet let that be
> Which the eye fears, when it is done, to see.

'Yet let that be!'—there speaks an already lost soul.
And he has still to encounter Satan's sworn ally at his
own hearth in the person of his wife and 'dearest love'.

To get the full measure of Lady Macbeth's inter-
vention, it is necessary to realise the appalling character
of the prayer she offers to the spirits of murder and
destruction, when on her first appearance she hears of
Duncan's impending visit. To take this as a mere
rhetorical expression of her determination is to miss
more than half the horror of it. When Jacobean
spectators heard

>   Come, you spirits
> That tend on mortal thoughts, unsex me here,
> And fill me, from the crown to the toe, top-full
> Of direst cruelty....Come to my woman's breasts,
> And take my milk for gall, you murd'ring ministers,
> Wherever in your sightless substances
> You wait on nature's mischief,

they interpreted the words literally: she was in fact
invoking the Powers of Hell to take possession of her

body, to suck her breasts as demons sucked those of witches, to expel from her not only all signs of grace but the least 'compunctious visitings of nature'. Many of Shakespeare's audience must have imagined her as indeed 'possessed' from this time onwards. Yet Shakespeare himself leaves it open. The demons she summons do not rid her of all 'visitings of nature', since when it comes to the point Duncan's resemblance to her father as he slept *does* shake her fell purpose, while the sleep-walking scene shows that her creator still felt and claimed pity for her. Yet here was a temptress more inescapable than the Witches themselves, one whom Goethe, not without reason, names the Super-witch.

That she knows her man is shown in her comments upon his letter, and when they meet she rides him at first on the snaffle: she hints at the deed, no more; and once assured by his downcast eyes that he is hers, instead of pressing her advantage by forcing him to speak of it openly, she leads him unconsciously forward by removing from his path the terror that immediately confronts him. 'No,' she says in effect, 'there is no need for you to think about the night's business at all. Your task is to look like the innocent flower....Leave all the rest to me.' There follows, we have seen, a dramatic lacuna of some kind;[1] and when we are next allowed to look into Macbeth's mind, the great soliloquy which opens 1. 7 reveals a fresh stage of his disease. The assassination, never named before, is now debated, at first quite coolly, and not on moral grounds at all but purely from the point of view of self-interest. What alone checks his hand, he tells himself, is the thought of the evil consequences that may ensue for the assassin, in this world. Assassination is catching, and others may try it on him; as kinsman, subject and host he will seem a

[1] See above, pp. xxxvii–xxxviii.

triple traitor in men's eyes; Duncan is so virtuous and
excellent a king that his death will excite the pity of the
whole world and draw down a universal curse upon the
murderer: such is the drift. Coleridge seems to suggest
that until after the murder Macbeth succeeds in hiding
from his conscience,[1] and Stoll that that conscience is
conceived by Shakespeare as something external to the
criminal.[2] There is no evidence for such views before
this soliloquy. On the contrary, the struggle between
good and bad has clearly, I said, been internal and perfectly conscious up to this point, and the chief purpose of
the soliloquy is to show that the struggle is ceasing, that
evil is very nearly triumphant. Yet the voice of the good
angel can still be heard by us, though not by Macbeth,
speaking through the poetry which reveals his sub-
conscious mind.[3] 'We'ld jump the life to come' shows
him far gone indeed on the road to perdition; yet in the
same breath he uses a metaphor, 'this bank and shoal of
time', which shows that thoughts of eternal issues are near
at hand. And the angel-voice grows yet more audible in
the Blake-like imagery which comes to him as he contemplates the martyrdom of his King; calls up awe-
inspiring visions of Doomsday, and Pity, and God's
all-seeing cherubim; and works up to a tremendous
climax which leaves the speaker exhausted.

Coleridge sums up the soliloquy: 'Macbeth enume-
rates the different worldly impediments to his scheme
of murder: could he put them by, he would "jump the
life to come".'[4] He does not notice that the impediments enumerated all proceed on the assumption that
the deed is to be performed openly: could Macbeth

[1] Coleridge, *op. cit.* i, 75, 80; ii, 270.
[2] Stoll, *Shakespeare Studies*, pp. 349–51.
[3] A point suggested to me by Dr Duthie.
[4] Coleridge, *op. cit.* ii, 270.

procure Duncan's death without being known as the
murderer, the assassination would trammel up every
consequence he can think of. It is, moreover, still the
problem of the consequences to himself that engages his
conscious thought for the rest of the scene, which can
only be rightly understood if we grasp that fact. For he
is no longer held back by any but 'prudential fears', and
it is these which inspire the objections he now urges
upon his wife, viz. the risk of putting his newly-won
glory in jeopardy, and the risk of failure. What he needs
is the ring of Gyges, the receipt of fern-seed that he may
walk invisible. Lady Macbeth taunts him with
cowardice; tells him his love for her is worthless; shows
herself, a mere woman, far more resolute than he: he
remains sullen, unresponsive through it all. And then,
by teaching him that all suspicion of the murder may
be shifted to the grooms, she suddenly hands him
the talisman his soul craves.[1] He is at once afire, lost
in admiration for her single-minded determination,
and eagerly filling in the details of her scheme! Bailey
calls the latter 'absurd';[2] and Bradley maintains that
she invents it 'on the spur of the moment, and simply
in order to satisfy' him.[3] Perhaps so; but at any rate
he *is* satisfied. 'I am settled', he declares; and never
after swerves from his purpose. She has given him his
orders; the tactical plan lies clear before him. How
soldier-like it all is! As for conscience, it is now utterly
insensible, and only reawakens for a time when he finds
himself confronted, there on Duncan's bed, with

The deep damnation of his taking-off.

And between these two points comes the soliloquy of
'the air-drawn dagger', which is *his* sleep-walking scene.

[1] The point was first made, I believe, by Professor W. C.
Curry; v. *Shakespeare's Philosophical Patterns*, p. 119.
[2] Bailey, *op. cit.* p. 185.   [3] Bradley, *op. cit.* p. 367.

The whole is spoken in trance; in, I believe, a horrible smiling trance. He is 'settled'; has at length yielded himself a passive agent; and, when the dagger points him towards the fatal chamber, begins moving softly and involuntarily thither 'with Tarquin's ravishing strides', as if led by some invisible hand.

This tremendous picture of a human being, first tempted, then little by little possessed by the idea of murder, and last so completely under its sway that he becomes oblivious of everything else, has no parallel that I know of in literature except Dostoieffsky's description of the stages through which Raskolnikoff passes on his way to the flat of the old miser; and Shakespeare has something Dostoieffsky lacks, the poet's tongue.

Thereafter, however, the two heroes proceed in opposite directions: Raskolnikoff climbing painfully towards redemption, Macbeth plunging furiously downwards along the road to Hell. I have space for only one or two comments upon this phase of Shakespeare's tragedy. First, it may be asked, of what nature are the 'terrible dreams that shake him nightly', or the 'restless ecstasy' that makes his bed a 'torture of the mind'? And there are other references to night as a time of terror. 'You lack the season of all natures, sleep', his wife says, as if to explain his conduct in the banquet scene; 'Duncan is in his grave', he himself says enviously;

> After life's fitful fever he sleeps well;

while he gives as his reason for Macduff's death

> That I may tell pale-hearted fear it lies,
> And sleep in spite of thunder.

Two things may, I think, be said with certainty about this. On the one hand, as all have noticed, Macbeth himself associates these 'rancours in the vessel of his peace' with a sense of danger and insecurity, so that their effect is to drive him on from crime to crime. Hence his 'fears in Banquo stick deep' and he dreams apparently that he is being murdered by him;[1] fears and dreams that can only be stilled by his death; hence, no sooner is Banquo removed, than Macduff takes his place as the imagined menace; hence at a later stage the unpremeditated and senseless murder of Lady Macduff and her children; hence finally an indiscriminate slaughter, so that Scotland hears

> Each new morn
> New widows howl, new orphans cry, new sorrows
> Strike heaven on the face.

On the other hand, all this is somehow connected with the dreadful voice, which he hears immediately after the assassination of Duncan, crying 'Sleep no more! Macbeth does murder sleep...Macbeth shall sleep no more!' The cry in fact introduces a leading theme of the dramatic poem as a whole, which, enveloped as it is in 'thick night' from first to last, may be described as in one aspect a study in sleeplessness. Furthermore, as scene succeeds scene, Macbeth's nerves get more and more out of hand, intense irritability alternating with lassitude.[2]

Bradley, following Coleridge, puts all this down to a troubled conscience disguising itself as fear; and there is nothing in the text which forbids us to agree with them. Yet there is equally nothing to show that Macbeth's conscience is alive at all during the last three acts, while quite a different explanation no doubt suggested itself to a Jacobean audience, and in particular to the royal author of *Dæmonologie*, viz. that Macbeth, once he had delivered himself up to the Devil by murdering Duncan,

---

[1] See note 3. 2. 18.
[2] See notes 3. 4. 133; 5. 2. 15, 23; 5. 3. 19, 50.

became 'possessed'. Learned doctors disputed whether
demoniacal possession meant that devils actually entered
the minds or bodies of their victims, but all admitted
that God allowed them dominion and power over men
'guilty of grievous offences', whom they strove to ruin
body and soul by 'afflicting, tormenting and vexing
their person', by driving them forward ever deeper
into sin and by procuring their early and violent death.[1]
Furthermore, the theory of Macbeth's possession finds
support in a feature of his character which does not
appear to have attracted much attention among critics:
I mean the defiant impiety that is his after Act 2, and
takes the form of a craving for destruction which involves far more than the death of individual human
beings.

At the thought of Banquo's heirs succeeding him he
cries

> Rather than so, come fate into the list,
> And champion me to th' utterance![2]—

which might be the mere hyperbole of passion, were it
not that a similar determination to proceed to all lengths
is heard shortly afterwards, on a more strident note and
in more precise terms, when he declares that to escape
the terrors that afflict him he is ready to 'let the frame
of things disjoint, both the worlds suffer'.[3] Kittredge
calls this an outburst of 'magnificent egoism'; and he is
right. But it carries with it most shockingly blasphemous
implications, hardly possible to any but those in a state
of damnation. And a willingness to contemplate, if not
to rejoice in, that universal dissolution which the Powers

---

[1] See King James, *Dæmonologie*, 1597, 'Bodley Head
Quartos', ed. by G. B. Harrison, pp. 62–4, and Deacon and
Walker, *Dialogicall Discourses of Spirits and Divels*, 1601,
p. 340.
[2] 3. 1. 70–1.   [3] 3. 2. 16.

of Hell constantly strove to bring about may be seen
again in his conjuration to the Witches:

> Though you untie the winds and let them fight
> Against the churches; though the yesty waves
> Confound and swallow navigation up;
> Though bladed corn be lodged and trees blown down;
> Though castles topple on their warders' heads;
> Though palaces and pyramids do slope
> Their heads to their foundations; though the treasure
> Of Nature's germens tumble all together,
> Even till destruction sicken; answer me
> To what I ask you.[1]

The culminating image here, and one upon which the
speaker obviously dwells in delight, seems to envisage
a stage even beyond the triumph of Hell and the destruction of 'both the worlds', namely the discovery, through
that catastrophe, of the hidden seeds of life whether in
heaven or earth; seeds which, originating in the mind
of God, could not themselves be destroyed but might be
rendered for ever barren, or productive of mere
monstrosity, if tumbled all together in devilish confusion.[2]
In other words, Macbeth speaks of a time when the
Devil will not only have made an end of God's world,
but have rendered its re-creation for ever impossible.
After the contemplation of so dreadful a contingency,
the words

> I 'gin to be aweary of the sun,
> And wish the estate o' th' world were now undone

sound almost tame, and are, I think, intended to mark
the sinking of the volcanic fires before the end.

[1] 4. 1. 52–61.
[2] For 'Nature's germens' v. note 4. 1. 58–60, and
Curry *op. cit.* (ch. II), who does not, however, explain the
point of 'tumble all together'.

To sum up, Macbeth's whole mind is set on destruction. With Milton's Satan he might say

> For only in destroying I find ease
> To my relentless thoughts.[1]

Shakespeare had to avoid blasphemous words; and there is nothing in these passages for the censor to take hold of. But he certainly wished his audience to imagine a Macbeth thinking blasphemous thoughts and, like Satan and Marlowe's Faustus, an enemy of God as of man.[2] Yet when we ask whether he also intended them to imagine him a man 'possessed', all we can say is that, as with Lady Macbeth, he leaves it open for them to do so, and that, contemporary opinion being what it was, many of them probably did, while he left it equally open for those who preferred the theory of a tortured conscience to adopt that explanation instead. Further, we must not forget that regicide, the crime for which he was tormented, was one of a peculiarly appalling nature, especially in the eyes of King James. In short, a study of Elizabethan and Jacobean demonology, as the recent work of Professor Curry has shown, is of first-class importance for *Macbeth*, though not quite for the reasons Professor Curry supposes. What it tells us is not what Shakespeare intended his audience to think of mysterious personages and events like the Weird Sisters, the Ghost of Banquo,[3] the air-drawn dagger, the voice that cried 'Sleep no more', the prodigies that follow the murder of Duncan, the apparitions in the cave; but what he knew they were capable of thinking. Take the voice, for

----

[1] *Paradise Lost*, ix, 129–30. Cf. Bradley, *op. cit.* p. 362 n.

[2] Cf. the important article by Dr Greg on 'The Damnation of Faustus' in *The Modern Language Review*, April 1946.

[3] Cf. note 3. 4. 37 S.D.

example. Was it a devil, a good angel, or conscience speaking, or was it, as Macbeth himself explains the dagger, a mere hallucination,

> a false creation,
> Proceeding from the heat-oppressed brain?

Here are four explanations easily possible for a seventeenth-century spectator, and the other phenomena just mentioned were capable of a similar variety of interpretation. Thus the right attitude towards 'the demonic metaphysics of *Macbeth*' is to think of it and use it in the way Shakespeare himself thought of it and used it, namely as a source of suggestion and atmosphere, not of information. *Macbeth* was not intended to supply the age with a spiritual or psychological exposition of the criminal mind, still less with 'a dialogical discourse of spirits and devils', but to enthral London with a new play in which the author took for his high light, as a change from the themes of *Hamlet*, *Othello* and *Lear*, the mind of a great man turned criminal, and availed himself of the demonological notions of his audience to intensify the chiaroscuro.

Furthermore, Macbeth's heaven-defying fury, which first led me to the foregoing observations, has a purpose more relevant to dramatic art than any revelation of his psychological processes could be: it shows him as a rebel against fate, against the whole 'estate o' the world', against 'both the worlds', natural and supernatural; a rebel refusing to recognise defeat and fighting his last and hopeless battle with growing despair but undiminished resolution. For Macbeth is a Shakespearian hero; and, though

> his face
> Deep scars of thunder had intrenched, and care
> Sat on his faded cheek,

he still looks out at us 'under brows of dauntless courage', still rears a mighty form which

> had not yet lost
> All her original brightness, nor appeared
> Less than Archangel ruined.

I apply to Macbeth words used of Lucifer in Hell because I think either hero helps us to understand the other. That the two figures are closely akin both Shakespeare and Milton acknowledge; Shakespeare by the line

> Angels are bright still though the brightest fell,

which flashes out like a jewel in the midst of a rather ordinary piece of dialogue, and shows what he had in mind; Milton by the fact that he himself contemplated at one time the writing of a play on Macbeth and by the many indications in *Paradise Lost* of his study of Shakespeare's play. In short, *Macbeth* is not a moral treatise, as King James and his successors down to the time of Dr Johnson may have supposed, or a profound psychological analysis of two criminal types as Coleridge and his disciples have tended to assume, or even an essay in Jacobean demonology as modern sociological critics might imagine, but a great tragedy.

Its theme is that of all Shakespeare's mature tragedies, man and the universe, and its purpose is to present us with a 'dazzling vision of the pitiful state of humanity'. The words are Walter Raleigh's, and I know of no account of Shakespearian tragedy in general and of *Macbeth* in particular at once more illuminating and more satisfying than the paragraph that follows them. Written forty years ago, it might have been directly inspired by 'the pitiful state of humanity' of which we to-day are all too conscious. It may serve to remind us also how greatly opinion about *Macbeth*, which stands

from age to age 'an ever-fixéd mark', has changed and
deepened since it was first presented to the view of King
James. Observing that Shakespeare's tragic vision is 'so
solemn and terrible and convincing in its reality' that
we try to escape from it by expounding his tragedies as
moral fables, Raleigh continues:

> But here we have to do with an earthquake, and good
> conduct is of no avail. Morality is not denied; it is over-
> whelmed and tossed aside by the inrush of the sea. There is
> no moral lesson to be read, except accidentally, in any of
> Shakespeare's tragedies. They deal with greater things than
> man; with powers and passions, elemental forces, and dark
> abysses of suffering; with the central fire, which breaks
> through the thin crust of civilisation, and makes a splendour
> in the sky above the blackness of ruined homes. Because
> he is a poet, and has a true imagination, Shakespeare knows
> how precarious is man's tenure of the soil, how deceitful are
> his quiet orderly habits and his prosaic speech. At any
> moment by the operation of chance, or fate, these things
> may be broken up, and the world given over once more to
> the forces that struggled in chaos.[1]

To this I will dare to add but one point: the sense of
exultation and atonement which the spectacle of such
tragedy leaves behind. We rise from the all-engrossing
experience, which Morgann so vividly describes and
Raleigh illuminates, not appalled but awed, not de-
pressed but enlarged. For, though life has been revealed
in the wizard's glass as a thing of overwhelming horror
and pity, we have discovered there too a grandeur and
significance far beyond our own limited unaided vision.
'This dead butcher and his fiend-like queen' is the
world's epitaph upon Macbeth and the woman who
treads the path to Hell with him. But we know better.
For we have caught our breath at the utterances of her
invincible spirit and subjected our imaginations to the

[1] Walter Raleigh, *Shakespeare*, 1907, pp. 196–7.

'most commanding and perhaps the most awe-inspiring
figure that Shakespeare drew';[1] while as for the
husband, of mettle at first less undaunted but always of
finer temper than hers, not all the blood he spills can
extinguish his native humanity or blot out his splendour.
Rather, as the play moves to the inevitable catastrophe
and we sit watching his soul in process of dissolution,
while we never for a moment condone or excuse his
crimes, the personality of the man seems to become at
once more portentous and more appealing. And if we
ask how this can be, the answer is that, by one of those
paradoxes of which Shakespeare possessed the secret,
in this volcanic character which through his 'multiplying villainies', growing callousness and ever-louder
maledictions, holds us tighter and tighter in the grip of
terror, we also see a gigantic reflexion of our sinful
selves thrown upon the immeasurable screen of the
universe, and giving eternal expression, 'with an
eloquence like the tongue of an angel', to the cyni-
cism, disillusion, and despair, which are the wages of
sin, whatever be the creed of the sinner, whatever the
origin of

> that perilous stuff
> Which weighs upon the heart.

J. D. W.

EDINBURGH, *August* 1946.

---

[1] Bradley, *op. cit.* p. 366.

THE STAGE-HISTORY OF
MACBETH

Macbeth has been so constantly acted that only a severely selective record is here possible. As noted above,[1] contemporary allusions point to performances as early as 1606. Perhaps the most obvious of these is that in 5. 1. 26–32 of *The Knight of the Burning Pestle* (*c.* 1607) which runs:

> When thou art at thy table with thy friends,
> Merry in heart, and filled with swelling wine,
> I'll come in midst of all thy pride and mirth,
> Invisible to all men but thy self,
> And whisper such a sad tale in thine ear
> Shall make thee let the cup fall from thy hand,
> And stand as mute and pale as death itself.

These lines, spoken by Jasper 'with his face mealed', were clearly intended to recall the apparition of Banquo on the stage, and suggest that the stage business of dropping the cup, mentioned by Garrick, and used by Charles Kemble and many others,[2] goes back to the original staging at the Globe. The earliest explicit notice of performance, however, as has also been mentioned above,[3] is that by the astrologer, Simon Forman, in his *Bocke of Plaies* (1611), which describes the play as he saw it at the Globe on Saturday, 20 April 1611. His account shows him most of all impressed by the meeting with the Witches, the blood on the hands of the guilty pair, which 'could not be washed of by Any meanes', the

[1] P. xxix, and n. 3.
[2] See A. C. Sprague, *Shakespeare and the Actors*, pp. 261–2.   [3] P. xxviii and note.

ghost of Banquo, which 'came and sate down in his cheier behind' Macbeth as he stood up to 'drincke a Carouse to him', and Lady Macbeth's sleep-walking, in which she 'talked and confessed all'. The detail, if Forman was an accurate observer, shows a different original staging of Banquo's ghost from the traditional plan, represented by Rowe's S.D. (1709) at 4. 3. 92 ('rises just before him'). After Forman's notes, we hear no more of the play in its early years. The Folio's S.D.s for songs borrowed from Middleton's *Witch* at 3. 5. 33 and 4. 1. 43, as well as the fairly certain interpolation of Hecate in these two scenes, prove a re-handling of the play after Shakespeare had finished with it, but this probably took effect before Forman's visit.[1]

After the Restoration, notices of our play come thick as hail. In November 1663, Sir Henry Herbert records in his Accounts a charge of £1 for 'a Revived Play, Mackbethe'; and presumably a performance followed the license; it did so in the case of *Henry VIII*, bracketed with *Macbeth* in this entry, for Pepys saw this at Lincoln's Inn Fields on 10 and 22 December 1663. Pepys tells of seeing our play, 'admirably acted', on 5 November 1664, and eight times more up to 15 January 1669. In December 1666, he found it 'a most excellent play *for variety*', and on 7 January 1667, 'a most excellent play in all respects, *especially in divertisement*, though it be a deep tragedy'.[2] Pepys's admiration must reflect the general verdict, as few plays figure so frequently in the records. It appears in Downes's list of the plays given by the Duke's Company after the opening, in November 1671, of their new Dorset Garden Theatre; and on 16 February 1682 it was acted there before His Excellency 'the Embassador of Morocco', and 'to the satisfaction of H.E.' (*Loyal*

---

[1] See above, pp. xxvii–xxviii. [2] Cf. above, p. xlvii.

Protestant, 18 February).[1] During the union of the
Duke's and the King's Companies (1685–95) it was
acted at Drury Lane, and after the new separation into
two Companies in 1695, each of them continued to
stage it, Drury Lane bravely putting it on each year,
though bereft of their star performers, Betterton and
Mrs Barry. These were scoring triumphs with it at the
Haymarket, where, on 7 December 1707, it was shown
'with the addition of several new scenes proper to the
play'; and in January 1708 it was the last play given
(for Wilks's benefit) before the Companies reunited in
Drury Lane. There it continued to be acted several
times every season. In fact, though Professor Odell
thinks it ranked below *Hamlet*, *Othello* and *Julius
Caesar* in popularity, it would seem, from Professor
Allardyce Nicoll's figures for sample years from 1703
to 1749 (*XVIIIth Century Drama*, 1700–50, pp. 55–9),
to have been more frequently shown than any other
tragedy, averaging four to five performances a year.

Throughout the first part of this period Betterton
was a Macbeth without a serious rival. He was
splendidly supported by his wife, whose Lady Macbeth
'was perhaps her greatest role' (Hazelton Spencer);
even the great Mrs Barry, who succeeded her in the
part, could not, in Cibber's view, command 'the strokes
of terror...at once delightful and tremendous' of her
predecessor. The cast for the revivals from 1672 is
printed in the D'Avenant *Macbeth* of 1674. This shows
the Bettertons aided by Smith as Banquo, Nat Lee as
Duncan (his playing of the part 'ruined him for an
actor', says Downes), Harris and Mrs Long as the two
Macduffs, and Sandford as Banquo's ghost. But
Sandford was usually cast for villain's parts because of

---

[1] Cited by Sybil Rosenfeld, *Modern Language Review*,
October 1935.

'his low and crooked figure'; and the incredible assign-
ment of Banquo's ghost to a different actor, and one so
totally unlike the living Banquo, is best explained as a
printer's error in the 1674 text. Indeed, he almost
certainly played Hecate during these years.[1] It is of
interest to note that, following the pre-Restoration
practice, the Witches were still usually played by men
at this time and for long after, as in the revivals of
Macklin (1746–7), Kemble (1794), Kean (1814),
Macready (1837) and Phelps (1844). After Betterton,
the chief Macbeths were Powell, Mills, and Quin, with
Delane between Quin's early years and Garrick.
Davies in his *Dramatic Miscellanies* criticises Wilks for
partiality in preferring Mills for the leading part to
Powell or Booth, whom he relegated to the lesser roles
of Lennox and Banquo. Quin, who alone could com-
pete with these three, played Macbeth frequently—in
Drury Lane as early as 1717 and as late as 1739, in
Lincoln's Inn Fields between 1718 and 1732, and in
Covent Garden in 1742–4 and 1749–50. No very
notable Lady Macbeth took the place of Mrs Barry
between her time and that of Garrick.

The *Macbeth* which thus held the London stage for
eighty years was, however, a sorry perversion of Shakespeare; the real play was turned into semi-opera. What
the 'divertisements' were which Pepys praised in 1667
we learn from John Downes's notice of the revival after
the Dorset Garden Theatre opened in 1671—'The
Tragedy of *Macbeth*, alter'd by *Sir William Davenant*;
being drest in all it's Finery, as...new Scenes, Machines,
as flyings for the Witches, with all the Singing, and
Dancing in it:...being in the nature of an Opera.'
Pepys's 'most excellent play for variety' suggests that the
singing, dancing, and flyings of the witches were already

---

[1] See Montague Summers, *Playhouse of Pepys*, p. 159.

in full swing in 1666; they were, after all, only an extension of a process which the songs from *The Witch* in the S.D.s of F1 show to have begun in Jacobean revivals. The tampering with the text was much more serious. The 1674 version, ascribed by Downes to D'Avenant, shows wholesale rewriting of the original. The aim was to tone down the more violent effects, to refine and simplify the language, and to procure balance and consistency. But the result was to jettison the finest poetry. Tasteless paraphrases like:

> Nay, they would sooner add a tincture to
> The Sea, and turn the green into a Red;

or

> Behold a sight
> Enough to turn spectators into a stone;

or

> lighted fools
> To their eternal home....

ruin some of the most memorable lines. The panic-stricken fury of

> The devil damn thee black, thou cream-faced loon!
> Where got'st thou that goose look?

becomes the bland inquiry,

> Now Friend, what means thy change of countenance?

while Macbeth decorously expires on the stage with a moral on his lips:

Farewell, vain world, and what's most vain in it, ambition.

Some changes seem purely wanton: 'out, out, that candle'; 'He, after life's short feavor, now sleeps; Well.' Symmetry and decorum dictated abridgement and much cutting (the Porter, of course, goes, and so does the murder of young Macduff), balanced by large additions, extending to a whole set of scenes exhibiting

Macduff and his wife as foils to the two criminals. It is some satisfaction to know that such a travesty of Shakespeare evoked travesties of itself, the best known being the epilogue to Duffett's skit on Settle's *Empress of Morocco* in 1674, announced as 'a new Fancy after the old and surprising way of MACBETH, performed with new and costly MACHINES'.

Yet this was the only *Macbeth* Londoners were allowed to see till Garrick on 7 January 1744 produced the play at Drury Lane 'as written by Shakespeare'. Even that, while removing the scenes between Macduff and his wife, still omitted the Porter and the murder scene (4. 1); and though it discarded most of D'Avenant's 'improvements' of the text, it gave to the dying Macbeth a speech of six lines, which seems to fuse together D'Avenant's edifying moral with some feeble echoes of Dr Faustus's despair. And by Garrick and for long after, even by Irving in 1875, Banquo and Macbeth were still escorted to the blasted heath by an army, an interpolated order to which—'Command they make a halt upon the heath'—were Macbeth's first words. Garrick also kept the 'divertisements' of the witches, which indeed proved hard to get rid of; they still embellished Kemble's and Macready's productions, and, after Phelps had dropped them in 1847, were brought back by Charles Kean in 1853, and in part at least by Irving in 1888.

Garrick's spirited and realistic acting was, after the stilted declamation of Quin, like a new creation; 'heavens!' exclaims Cumberland, 'what a transition!... old things done away...a new order'. But his Drury Lane productions from 1748–68 owed even more to the genius of Mrs Pritchard, who succeeded Mrs Giffard as Lady Macbeth during these years. The greatest in the part till Mrs Siddons, she outshone her rivals in Covent Garden, Mrs Spranger Barry, Peg

Woffington and Mrs Yates even more completely than
Garrick did the corresponding Macbeths of Spranger
Barry, William Powell and Sheridan. The effectiveness
of Garrick's acting was heavily offset by the absurdity
of his costume, the eighteenth-century tie-wig and
officer's red coat. It was left to Macklin to introduce
realism in dress, when, on 23 October 1773, at Covent
Garden, he came on the stage as Macbeth with other
characters in Scottish attire. But his Queen was still
arrayed in the robes of contemporary fashion; and
beyond the partial improvement in dress, there was not
much to be said for his performance—he neither looked
the part, nor, except at moments, rose to tragic heights.
But the play, however presented, never failed of
popularity; from 1742 to 1776 it was shown every
season but four in Drury Lane, and only missed ten of
the years in Covent Garden.

With J. P. Kemble, the play fell into the hands of
the first great producer. His aim was 'by the aids of
scenery and dress to perfect dramatic illusion' (Boaden).
Even so, his tendency to elaboration made him in 1788
retain superfluous spirits, black, white, blue and grey,
while 'the lovely Crouch' as a witch was fashionably
fitted out with 'fancy hat, powdered hair, rouge, and
point lace'. In March 1794, on the other hand, when
Macbeth was played at the opening of the enlarged
Drury Lane, Kemble tried, by new devices, to present
the witches as eerie, sinister beings; and the absence of
a visible ghost at the banquet showed Macbeth to be
the victim of hallucination. Under stress of criticism,
however, he restored a visible Banquo to this scene in
September 1809, at the opening of the new Covent
Garden Theatre. This performance was one of the
most disastrous ever given, for the play was acted
inaudibly from start to finish amid a din of catcalls and
other noises in protest against the enhanced prices. In

the dialogue, Kemble mostly reverted to D'Avenant's spurious text, and, to make matters worse, he included Garrick's pitiful final speech. In staging his tendency was towards the antiquarian realism which reached its zenith with Charles Kean.

Compared with the vivacity and naturalness of Garrick, Kemble's acting was formal and stiff, without, as Hazlitt put it, 'the unexpected bursts of genius and nature', but with 'all the regularity of art'. His sister, Mrs Siddons, far surpassed him in power of genius as Lady Macbeth; this was probably her greatest part, and she was the finest of the many fine actresses in the role. She claimed to have first acted it 'when only 20 years old', that is, in 1775. In 1777, we find her in the part in Liverpool, and in 1779 and 1780 in Bath and Bristol. London first saw her in it at Drury Lane in February 1785, with Smith as Macbeth; the next month her brother joined her in his first London acting of the part, though he had played it earlier for Daly's Company in Dublin, 1781–3. Thereafter their partnership in the play covers nearly a third of a century, the last appearance of both in it being in Covent Garden on 5 June 1817, when Hazlitt regretted Mrs Siddons's return, her 'always slow utterance' being now 'too slow'. Of his first impressions of her he had written: 'Mrs Siddons's Lady Macbeth is little less appalling in its effects than the apparition of a preternatural being.' Her incredible self-possession on the stage was demonstrated when, at Brighton in 1809, Charles Kemble as Macbeth threw the cup violently away from him in the banquet scene so that it passed near her face; she sat, Genest was told, 'as if she had been made of marble'. Mr C. B. Hogan's researches, which he has kindly made available for use in this account, show that in all she acted the part 139 times in London, and in every year but four of the period, while she acted it at least 43 times in other towns, including Dublin and Belfast. In 1785, 1794, and 1809, London saw her in it 15 times each year. Her brother's appearances were less frequent, and but seldom outside London. Sometimes he gave place to others in the title role, to Palmer in 1797 in Drury Lane, to C. M. Young, now first acting it, in Covent Garden in 1809, and to his brother Charles, for the latter's benefit, in 1813, and again in 1816. In January and May 1814, Mrs Faucit and Mrs Renaud in turn took Mrs Siddons's place when Kemble played Macbeth.

Meanwhile, Edmund Kean was challenging Kemble's supremacy in the part. He acted it at Drury Lane with Mrs Bartley on 9 March 1814, and 23 other times before the end of the year. Hazlitt, though later to declare that Kean's acting in general 'has destroyed the Kemble religion', was critical of his Macbeth, preferring his Richard III, though he felt his acting of the scene after the murder 'beggared description'; 'it was a scene', he says, 'which no one who saw it can ever efface from his recollection'. In the fifth act, however, he found him 'lost too poorly in himself', and his delivery of 'My way of life / Is fallen into the sere, the yellow leaf' a failure compared with Kemble's. Kean returned to the part a dozen years later. But some preferred C. M. Young, who continued the Kemble tradition of more formal acting. Macbeth was one of his best parts, his chief performance being in October 1828. During these years (1819–26) Elliston in Drury Lane was bringing back more of the true text, he himself acting Macduff; but his earlier production at the Olympic Theatre had once more turned the play into 'a kind of operatic pantomime'. The culmination of that process was seen at the Royal Coburg Theatre, which, on an unstated date, advertised a 'Grand Historical Caledonian Drama, interspersed with

National Marches, Choruses, Combats, Processions, entitled "Fatal Prophecy, or Scottish Regicide"'.

To Macready belongs the credit of finally reinstating the authentic text in his later revivals. His earlier ones were still tainted with the time-honoured perversions; even in 1837, when he staged the play in his first season as Manager of Covent Garden, he kept at least the music and acrobatics. He first acted Macbeth at this theatre with Mrs Bunn in 1820; Drury Lane saw him in it in 1831 and 1835, and in 1843 it was the last play put on by him as Manager here; the Princess's saw him in it in 1846 and 1848. *John Bull* hailed his revival of 1837 as conveying for the first time 'the poetry of the drama', and praised the new scenic aids, especially the realism of the moving wood of Birnam. Macready was fortunate in his partners, chief among them Mrs Warner (Miss Huddart) both in Drury Lane and Covent Garden, and after her Helen Faucit, Charlotte Cushman and, finally, in 1848, Fanny Kemble. The last had been seen in the part as early as 1832 in Covent Garden in her father's last season as Manager of that theatre.

Samuel Phelps's productions, which span the years from 1844 to 1867, threw overboard, from the performance of 1847 onwards, the last remnants of the spurious D'Avenant version; the music was dropped, and the scene of the murder of Lady Macduff's son came back. But Macbeth was now for the first time killed off the stage,[1] and 5. 3 was cut out. 'Though scenic display', writes Henry Morley in 1856, 'appealed to him more and more, he did not allow it to submerge the drama.' His scenery was of extreme beauty; the illusion of vanishing witches procured by the use of gauze screens of varying thickness was specially praised by *The Times*. Unlike Phelps, Charles Kean in his famous revival of

---

[1] See below p. 88 and note 5. 8. 34.

February 1853, at the Princess's, buried the play under scenery and antiquarian detail; and though not tampering with the text in what he kept, he cut and transposed scenes freely. Once more the operatic excrescences appear, once more the Porter and young Macduff are discarded. Macbeth on the other hand is slain on the stage again as in the Folio. A learned introduction proving the archaeological accuracy of scenery and costumes was issued with his programme. Kean had previously acted Macbeth at the Haymarket in 1840 and 1842; in all his performances his wife played Lady Macbeth.

Henry Irving followed Kean's lead in his free handling of the text, and Phelps's in the matter of devices to obtain illusory effects of dimly appearing and vanishing witches amid prevailing darkness. His revivals at the Lyceum, with Kate Bateman as Lady Macbeth in 1875, and with Ellen Terry in 1888, were not really memorable renderings, though they ran for 80 and 151 nights respectively, and though, as we learn from Ellen Terry's *Memoirs*, 'he always maintained that as Macbeth he did his finest work'. His interpretation of the character as a cowardly, neurotic criminal rather than as a noble warrior ruined did not commend itself, and his voice and manner were adversely criticised. Yet he revived the play again in 1895. The lavish beauty of the castle in I. 6 was variously judged, Fitzgerald regarding it as 'admirably and exactly' corresponding to Duncan's and Banquo's praise, while H. A. Jones declared it contradicted Shakespeare's conception. In 1888 special music by Sullivan took the place of the traditional *Macbeth* music.[1]

---

[1] This was supposed to be Matthew Lock's original music, mentioned by Downes; actually, it is Purcell's, whose setting displaced Lock's at least from the 1688–9 revivals. (See W. J. Lawrence, *Elizabethan Playhouse and Other Studies* (1st ser.), pp. 209–24.)

Irving's and Miss Terry's chief successors in the principal parts were Forbes Robertson with Mrs Patrick Campbell, and Beerbohm Tree with Violet Vanbrugh. Forbes Robertson's Macbeth at the Lyceum in September 1898 was scholarly and impressive, yet not as notable as his Hamlet. 'To our pursuit of the beautiful we are sacrificing the terrible,' writes the dramatic critic of the *Athenaeum*; 'are we unreasonable that we want to be appalled?' Violet Vanbrugh had acted Lady Macbeth to her husband Arthur Bourchier's Macbeth in 1906 and 1909 before she played the part with Tree at His Majesty's from September 1911. Her sleep-walking scene and her invocation to the spirits of evil were much admired. But spectacle was the chief thing dominating Tree's revival. It was left to Benson at the end of the nineteenth century to remember that the play's the thing, and to introduce simple and unobtrusive scenery.

During Benson's direction of the Festivals at Stratford the play was shown ten times between 1896 and 1916. Previous to Benson it had only once been seen there in 1883, when Wainwright and Mrs Charles Calvert used the traditional music, without, however, reverting to the intolerable Restoration text. In the autumn of 1906 Bourchier and his wife put it on three times as visitors to Stratford; and in a special matinee on 5 May 1916 the Old Vic Company substituted for the Bensons, then in France, Ben Greet playing the Doctor, and Mary Anderson Lady Macbeth. Brydges-Adams's management saw the play eight times before the opening of the new Memorial Theatre in 1932, with Edmund Willard, Randall Ayrton, and Wilfrid Walter as successive Macbeths, and Dorothy Massingham as Lady Macbeth.

In London, of the many Macbeths after Beerbohm Tree one can only mention a few. Baliol Holloway with Dorothy Massingham gave the play at the Old Vic in 1926, and Henry Ainley with Sybil Thorndike at the Prince's the same year. At the Court Theatre in 1928 it was acted in modern costume by Eric Maturin and Mary Merrell. Since 1930 it has repeatedly shown John Gielgud in one of his most successful characterisations, both in London and the provinces. In his production in July 1942 in Piccadilly Theatre, he gave the Witches' parts once more to men, and the critic in the *Observer* thought that Ernest Thesiger as leading witch had vindicated the method as the one which should always be followed. Miss ffrangcon-Davies was Lady Macbeth, and Leon Quartermaine Banquo. In 1937, the Old Vic had Laurence Olivier and Judith Anderson in the chief parts, and in 1939 Robert Atkins and Mary Clare played them in the Winter Garden; while since he first played it at the Malvern Festival on 13 October 1937, it has been one of the most successful items in Mr Donald Wolfit's Shakespeare repertory.

The great vogue of the play in America is proved by the theatre records up to 1891 amassed by Professor Odell in his *Annals of the New York Stage* (14 vols.). These show it first played in New York in 1768, and then, from its fifth revival in 1794, in three out of every four years to 1834, and almost every year from 1836 to 1891, usually in several separate productions each year. Of many well-known Macbeths, such as Hamblin, the Wallacks, father and son, and the three Booths, Edwin Forrest played the part most frequently for forty years (1828–68); and Charlotte Cushman, equally famous as Lady Macbeth, ran him close in span of acting years (1836–74) and number of performances. The chief British actors in their visits (Edmund Kean in 1820, Charles and Fanny Kemble in 1833, Charles Kean, 1839–40, and Macready, 1826–7, 1843, and

1848–9) invariably included *Macbeth* in their repertory. Most remarkable of all, on 7 May 1849, New York saw no less than three Macbeths the same night in different theatres (Hamblin, Forrest, and Macready)—an ill-starred concurrence, as it proved, for the rivalry of Forrest and Macready blazed out in disorder which outdid the Covent Garden riot of 1809 (see p. lxxv above) in noise and violence, and forced Macready to suspend the play after the third act. Three days later, a second attempt by Macready provoked new disorder within the theatre, and led to a riot outside in which twenty-two lives were lost.

C. B. YOUNG.

August 1946

P.S. 1950. Dr Percy Simpson, who saw Irving's Macbeth in 1888, disagrees with the references on p. lxxix, which were based on contemporary notices and Austin Brereton's *Life of Irving* (1908), I. 198; II. 134–42. Dr Simpson writes: 'I still remember that performance vividly and I felt (and still feel) that it was a great piece of work. "Neurotic" it certainly was, but there is ample justification for that in the text. Compare the comment on p. lxi on Macbeth's nerves getting more and more out of hand, and the note at 2. 1. 64, S.D. on Irving's exit. I can add a touch there. As Irving pushed open the door at the bottom of the stair, a draft blew it back and the hinges creaked; he started as if someone were coming down to defend Duncan. He brought out, too, to the full, the "astonishing revelation" spoken of in the note on 2. 2. 32.'

TO THE READER

The following is a brief description of the punctuation and other typographical devices employed in the text, which have been more fully explained in the *Note on Punctuation* and the *Textual Introduction* to be found in *The Tempest* volume:

An obelisk (†) implies corruption or emendation, and suggests a reference to the Notes.

A single bracket at the beginning of a speech signifies an 'aside'.

Four dots represent a *full stop* in the original, except when it occurs at the end of a speech, and they mark a long pause. Original *colons* or *semicolons*, which denote a somewhat shorter pause, are retained, or represented as three dots when they appear to possess special dramatic significance. Similarly, significant *commas* have been given as dashes.

Round brackets are taken from the original, and mark a significant change of voice; when the original brackets seem to imply little more than the drop in tone accompanying parenthesis, they are conveyed by commas or dashes.

Single inverted commas (' ') are editorial; double ones (" ") derive from the original, where they are used to draw attention to maxims, quotations, etc.

The reference number for the first line is given at the head of each page. Numerals in square brackets are placed at the beginning of the traditional acts and scenes.

THE TRAGEDY OF
MACBETH

The Scene: Scotland and (in 4.3) England

CHARACTERS IN THE PLAY

DUNCAN, *King of Scotland.*

MALCOLM ⎱ *his sons.*
DONALBAIN ⎰

MACBETH, *at first a general, later King of Scotland.*

BANQUO, *a general.*

MACDUFF
LENNOX
ROSS
MENTEITH ⎰ *noblemen of Scotland.*
ANGUS
CAITHNESS

FLEANCE, *son to Banquo.*

SIWARD, *Earl of Northumberland, general of the English forces.*

YOUNG SIWARD, *his son.*

SETON, *armour-bearer to Macbeth.*

A Boy, son to Macduff.

A Captain.

A Porter.

An Old Man.

An English Doctor.

A Scotch Doctor.

Three Murderers.

LADY MACBETH.

LADY MACDUFF.

A Gentlewoman attending on Lady Macbeth.

The Weird Sisters.

HECATE.

Apparitions.

Lords, Gentlemen, Officers, Soldiers, Attendants, and Messengers.

MACBETH

[1. 1.] *'Thunder and lightning. Enter three Witches'*

1 *Witch.* When shall we three meet again
In thunder, lightning, or in rain?

2 *Witch.* When the hurlyburly's done,
When the battle's lost and won.

3 *Witch.* That will be ere the set of sun.

1 *Witch.* Where the place?

2 *Witch.*   Upon the heath.

3 *Witch.* There to meet with Macbeth.

1 *Witch.* I come, Graymalkin!

2 *Witch.* Paddock calls.

3 *Witch.* Anon!   **10**

All. Fair is foul, and foul is fair:
Hover through the fog and filthy air.

[they vanish in mist

[1. 2.]   *A camp*

'Alarum.' *'Enter King'* DUNCAN, *'*MALCOLM, DONAL-
BAIN, LENNOX, *with attendants, meeting a bleeding
Captain'*

Duncan. What bloody man is that? He can report,
As seemeth by his plight, of the revolt
The newest state.

Malcolm.   This is the sergeant,
Who like a good and hardy soldier fought
'Gainst my captivity...Hail, brave friend!
Say to the king the knowledge of the broil
As thou didst leave it.

Captain.   Doubtful it stood,
As two spent swimmers that do cling together
And choke their art...The merciless Macdonwald
10 (Worthy to be a rebel, for to that
The multiplying villainies of nature
Do swarm upon him) from the Western Isles
Of kerns and gallowglasses is supplied,
And Fortune, on his damnéd quarrel smiling,
Showed like a rebel's whore: but all's too weak:
For brave Macbeth (well he deserves that name)
Disdaining fortune, with his brandished steel,
Which smoked with bloody execution,
Like Valour's minion carvéd out his passage,
20 Till he faced the slave;
   Which ne'er shook hands, nor bade farewell
      to him,
Till he unseamed him from the nave to th' chops,
And fixed his head upon our battlements.
  Duncan. O, valiant cousin! worthy gentleman!
  Captain. As whence the sun 'gins his reflection
Shipwracking storms and direful thunders break;
So from that spring whence comfort seemed to come
Discomfort swells: mark, king of Scotland, mark!
No sooner justice had, with valour armed,
30 Compelled these skipping kerns to trust their heels,
But the Norweyan lord, surveying vantage,
With furbished arms and new supplies of men,
Began a fresh assault.
  Duncan.   Dismayed not this
Our captains, Macbeth and Banquo?
  Captain.   Yes;
As sparrows, eagles; or the hare, the lion.
If I say sooth, I must report they were
As cannons overcharged with double cracks;

So they
Doubly redoubled strokes upon the foe:
Except they meant to bathe in reeking wounds,   40
Or memorize another Golgotha,
I cannot tell:
But I am faint, my gashes cry for help.

  Duncan. So well thy words become thee as thy
    wounds,
They smack of honour both: Go get him surgeons.
                      [attendants help him thence
Who comes here?

'Enter Ross and Angus'

  Malcolm.   The worthy thane of Ross.
  Lennox. What a haste looks through his eyes! So
    should he look
That seems to speak things strange.
  Ross.   God save the king!
  Duncan. Whence cam'st thou, worthy thane?
  Ross.   From Fife, great king,
Where the Norweyan banners flout the sky,   50
And fan our people cold.
Norway himself, with terrible numbers,
Assisted by that most disloyal traitor
The thane of Cawdor, began a dismal conflict,
Till that Bellona's bridegroom, lapped in proof,
Confronted him with self-comparisons,
Point against point, rebellious arm 'gainst arm,
Curbing his lavish spirit: and, to conclude,
The victory fell on us.
  Duncan.   Great happiness!
  Ross. That now   60
Sweno, the Norways' king, craves composition;
Nor would we deign him burial of his men

Till he disbcurséd, at Saint Colme's Inch,
Ten thousand dollars to our general use.

Duncan. No more that thane of Cawdor shall deceive
Our bosom interest: go pronounce his present death,
And with his former title greet Macbeth.

Ross. I'll see it done.

Duncan. What he hath lost, noble Macbeth hath won.

[*they go*

[1. 3.]   *A barren heath*

'*Thunder. Enter the three Witches*'

1 *Witch.* Where hast thou been, sister?

2 *Witch.* Killing swine.

3 *Witch.* Sister, where thou?

1 *Witch.* A sailor's wife had chestnuts in her lap,
And munched, and munched, and munched: 'Give
   me', quoth I.
'Aroint thee, witch!' the rump-fed ronyon cries.
Her husband's to Aleppo gone, master o'th' Tiger:
But in a sieve I'll thither sail,
And, like a rat without a tail,
10 I'll do, I'll do, and I'll do.

2 *Witch.* I'll give thee a wind.

1 *Witch.* Th'art kind.

3 *Witch.* And I another.

1 *Witch.* I myself have all the other,
And the very ports they blow,
All the quarters that they know
I'th' shipman's card.
I will drain him dry as hay:
Sleep shall, neither night nor day
20 Hang upon his pent-house lid;
He shall live a man forbid:

Weary sev'nights nine times nine
Shall he dwindle, peak, and pine:
Though his bark cannot be lost,
Yet it shall be tempest-tost.
Look what I have.

2 *Witch.* Show me, show me.

1 *Witch.* Here I have a pilot's thumb,
Wrecked as homeward he did come.   ['*drum within*'

3 *Witch.* A drum, a drum!   30
Macbeth doth come.

They dance in a ring, whirling faster and faster

All. The Weïrd Sisters, hand in hand,
Posters of the sea and land,
Thus do go, about, about,
Thrice to thine, and thrice to mine,
And thrice again, to make up nine.
Peace! the charm's wound up.

[*they stop suddenly, and a mist hides them*

'*Enter MACBETH and BANQUO*'

Macbeth. So foul and fair a day I have not seen.

Banquo. How far is't called to Forres?   [*the mist
     thins*] What are these,
So withered, and so wild in their attire,   40
That look not like th'inhabitants o'th'earth,
And yet are on't? Live you? or are you aught
That man may question? You seem to understand me,
By each at once her choppy finger laying
Upon her skinny lips: you should be women,
And yet your beards forbid me to interpret
That you are so.

Macbeth.   Speak, if you can: what are you?

1 *Witch.* All hail, Macbeth! hail to thee, thane of
Glamis!

2 *Witch.* All hail, Macbeth! hail to thee, thane of
Cawdor!

50 3 *Witch.* All hail, Macbeth! that shalt be king
hereafter.

Banquo. Good sir, why do you start, and seem to
fear
Things that do sound so fair? I'th' name of truth,
Are ye fantastical, or that indeed
Which outwardly ye show? My noble partner
You greet with present grace and great prediction
Of noble having and of royal hope,
That he seems rapt withal: to me you speak not.
If you can look into the seeds of time,
And say which grain will grow and which will not,
60 Speak then to me, who neither beg nor fear
Your favours nor your hate.

1 *Witch.* Hail!

2 *Witch.* Hail!

3 *Witch.* Hail!

1 *Witch.* Lesser than Macbeth, and greater.

2 *Witch.* Not so happy, yet much happier.

3 *Witch.* Thou shalt get kings, though thou be
none:
So all hail, Macbeth and Banquo!

1 *Witch.* Banquo and Macbeth, all hail!

[*the mist thickens*

70 *Macbeth.* Stay, you imperfect speakers, tell me more:
By Sinel's death I know I am thane of Glamis,
But how of Cawdor? the thane of Cawdor lives
A prosperous gentleman; and to be king
Stands not within the prospect of belief,
No more than to be Cawdor. Say from whence

You owe this strange intelligence, or why
Upon this blasted heath you stop our way
With such prophetic greeting. Speak, I charge you.
                              [*they disappear*

Banquo. The earth hath bubbles, as the water has,
And these are of them: whither are they vanished?   80
  Macbeth. Into the air; and what seemed corporal,
     melted,
As breath into the wind. Would they had stayed!
  Banquo. Were such things here as we do speak about?
Or have we eaten on the insane root
That takes the reason prisoner?
  Macbeth. Your children shall be kings.
  Banquo.   You shall be king.
  Macbeth. And thane of Cawdor too: went it not so?
  Banquo. To th' selfsame tune and words. Who's here?

                'Enter ROSS and ANGUS'

Ross. The king hath happily received, Macbeth,
The news of thy success: and when he reads   90
Thy personal venture in the rebels' fight,
His wonders and his praises do contend
Which should be thine or his: silenced with that,
In viewing o'er the rest o'th' self-same day,
He finds thee in the stout Norweyan ranks,
Nothing afeard of what thyself didst make
Strange images of death. As thick as hail
Came post with post, and every one did bear
Thy praises in his kingdom's great defence,
And poured them down before him.
  Angus.   We are sent   100
To give thee from our royal master thanks,
Only to herald thee into his sight,
Not pay thee.

Ross. And for an earnest of a greater honour,
He bade me, from him, call thee thane of Cawdor:
In which addition, hail, most worthy thane,
For it is thine.

Banquo.   What, can the devil speak true?

Macbeth. The thane of Cawdor lives: why do you
     dress me
In borrowed robes?

Angus.   Who was the thane lives yet,
110 But under heavy judgment bears that life
Which he deserves to lose. Whether he was combined
With those of Norway, or did line the rebel
With hidden help and vantage, or that with both
He laboured in his country's wreck, I know not;
But treasons capital, confessed, and proved,
Have overthrown him.

(*Macbeth.*   Glamis, and thane of Cawdor:
The greatest is behind.—[*aloud*] Thanks for your
     pains—
[*aside to Banquo*] Do you not hope your children shall
     be kings,
When those that gave the thane of Cawdor to me
120 Promised no less to them?

Banquo.   That, trusted home,
Might yet enkindle you unto the crown,
Besides the thane of Cawdor. But 'tis strange:
And oftentimes, to win us to our harm,
The instruments of darkness tell us truths,
Win us with honest trifles, to betray's
In deepest consequence.
Cousins, a word, I pray you.

         [*to Ross and Angus, who move towards him*
(*Macbeth.*   Two truths are told,
As happy prologues to the swelling act

Of the imperial theme. [*aloud*] I thank you, gentle-
　　men.

[*aside*] This supernatural soliciting　　　　　130
Cannot be ill; cannot be good. If ill,
Why hath it given me earnest of success,
Commencing in a truth? I am thane of Cawdor.
If good, why do I yield to that suggestion
Whose horrid image doth unfix my hair,
And make my seated heart knock at my ribs,
Against the use of nature? Present fears
Are less than horrible imaginings:
My thought, whose murder yet is but fantastical,
Shakes so my single state of man that function　140
Is smothered in surmise, and nothing is
But what is not.

　　Banquo.　　　　Look how our partner's rapt.

　(*Macbeth*. If chance will have me king, why, chance
　　may crown me,
Without my stir.

　　Banquo.　　　　New honours come upon him,
Like our strange garments, cleave not to their mould
But with the aid of use.

　(*Macbeth*.　　　　　　Come what come may,
Time and the hour runs through the roughest day.

　　Banquo. Worthy Macbeth, we stay upon your leisure.

　　Macbeth. Give me your favour: my dull brain was
　　wrought
With things forgotten. Kind gentlemen, your pains　150
Are registered where every day I turn
The leaf to read them....Let us toward the king.

　　　　　　　　　　　　　　　[*aside to Banquo*
Think upon what hath chanced; and at more time,
The interim having weighed it, let us speak
Our free hearts each to other.

Banquo.   Very gladly.
Macbeth. Till then, enough....Come, friends.

                      [*they go forward*

[1.4.]   *Forres. A Room in the Palace*
    '*Flourish. Enter King*' DUNCAN, '*MALCOLM,*
      DONALBAIN, LENNOX, and Attendants'

Duncan. Is execution done on Cawdor? Are not
Those in commission yet returned?
    Malcolm.   My liege,
They are not yet come back. But I have spoke
With one that saw him die: who did report
That very frankly he confessed his treasons,
Implored your highness' pardon, and set forth
A deep repentance: nothing in his life
Became him like the leaving it; he died
As one that had been studied in his death,
10 To throw away the dearest thing he owed
As 'twere a careless trifle.
    Duncan.   There's no art
To find the mind's construction in the face:
He was a gentleman on whom I built
An absolute trust.

    '*Enter MACBETH, BANQUO, ROSS, and ANGUS*'

                 O worthiest cousin!
The sin of my ingratitude even now
Was heavy on me. Thou art so far before,
That swiftest wing of recompense is slow
To overtake thee. Would thou hadst less deserved,
That the proportion both of thanks and payment
20 Might have been mine! only I have left to say,
More is thy due than more than all can pay.

Macbeth. The service and the loyalty I owe,
In doing it, pays itself. Your highness' part
Is to receive our duties: and our duties
Are to your throne and state children and servants;
Which do but what they should, by doing every thing
Safe toward your love and honour.

Duncan.   Welcome hither:
I have begun to plant thee, and will labour
To make thee full of growing. Noble Banquo,
That hast no less deserved, nor must be known   30
No less to have done so: let me infold thee,
And hold thee to my heart.

Banquo.   There if I grow,
The harvest is your own.

Duncan.   My plenteous joys,
Wanton in fulness, seek to hide themselves
In drops of sorrow....Sons, kinsmen, thanes,
And you whose places are the nearest, know,
We will establish our estate upon
Our eldest, Malcolm, whom we name hereafter
The Prince of Cumberland: which honour must
Not unaccompanied invest him only,   40
But signs of nobleness, like stars, shall shine
On all deservers....From hence to Inverness,
And bind us further to you.

Macbeth. The rest is labour, which is not used for
       you:
I'll be myself the harbinger, and make joyful
The hearing of my wife with your approach;
So humbly take my leave.

Duncan.   My worthy Cawdor!

(*Macbeth.* The Prince of Cumberland! that is a step
On which I must fall down, or else o'er-leap,
For in my way it lies. Stars, hide your fires!   50

Let not light see my black and deep desires:
The eye wink at the hand; yet let that be
Which the eye fears, when it is done, to see.   [*he goes*
   Duncan. True, worthy Banquo; he is full so valiant,
And in his commendations I am fed;
It is a banquet to me. Let's after him,
Whose care is gone before to bid us welcome:
It is a peerless kinsman.   [*'Flourish.' They go*

[1. 5.]   *Inverness. Before Macbeth's castle*

'*Enter MACBETH's wife alone, with a letter*'

Lady M. [*reads*] 'They met me in the day of success;
and I have learned by the perfect'st report, they have
more in them than mortal knowledge. When I burned
in desire to question them further, they made themselves
air, into which they vanished. Whiles I stood rapt in
the wonder of it, came missives from the king, who all-
hailed me, 'Thane of Cawdor', by which title, before,
these Weïrd Sisters saluted me, and referred me to the
coming on of time, with 'Hail, king that shalt be!' This
10 have I thought good to deliver thee (my dearest partner
of greatness) that thou mightst not lose the dues of
rejoicing, by being ignorant of what greatness is
promised thee. Lay it to thy heart, and farewell.'

Glamis thou art, and Cawdor, and shalt be
What thou art promised: yet do I fear thy nature,
It is too full o'th' milk of human kindness
To catch the nearest way: thou wouldst be great,
Art not without ambition, but without
The illness should attend it: what thou wouldst highly,
20 That wouldst thou holily; wouldst not play false,

And yet wouldst wrongly win: thou'ldst have, great
    Glamis,
That which cries 'Thus thou must do', if thou have it,
And that which rather thou dost fear to do
Than wishest should be undone. Hie thee hither,
That I may pour my spirits in thine ear,
And chastise with the valour of my tongue
All that impedes thee from the golden round,
Which fate and metaphysical aid doth seem
To have thee crowned withal.

An attendant enters

                   What is your tidings?
Attendant. The king comes here to-night.
    Lady M.   Thou'rt mad to say it! 30
Is not thy master with him? who, were't so,
Would have informed for preparation.
    Attendant. So please you, it is true: our thane is
    coming:
One of my fellows had the speed of him;
Who, almost dead for breath, had scarcely more
Than would make up his message.
    Lady M.   Give him tending,
He brings great news. [*attendant goes*] The raven
    himself is hoarse
That croaks the fatal entrance of Duncan
Under my battlements....Come, you spirits
That tend on mortal thoughts, unsex me here,   40
And fill me, from the crown to the toe, top-full
Of direst cruelty! make thick my blood,
Stop up th'access and passage to remorse,
That no compunctious visitings of nature
Shake my fell purpose, nor keep peace between
Th'effect and it! Come to my woman's breasts,

And take my milk for gall, you murd'ring ministers,
Wherever in your sightless substances
You wait on nature's mischief! Come, thick night,
50 And pall thee in the dunnest smoke of hell,
That my keen knife see not the wound it makes,
Nor heaven peep through the blanket of the dark,
To cry 'Hold, hold!'

                   '*Enter* MACBETH'

                  Great Glamis! worthy Cawdor!
Greater than both, by the all-hail hereafter!
Thy letters have transported me beyond
This ignorant present, and I feel now
The future in the instant.

     Macbeth.   My dearest love,
Duncan comes here to-night.

     Lady M.   And when goes hence?
     Macbeth. To-morrow, as he purposes.
     Lady M.   O, never
60 Shall sun that morrow see!
Your face, my thane, is as a book, where men
May read strange matters. To beguile the time,
Look like the time, bear welcome in your eye,
Your hand, your tongue: look like th'innocent flower,
But be the serpent under't. He that's coming
Must be provided for: and you shall put
This night's great business into my dispatch,
Which shall to all our nights and days to come
Give solely sovereign sway and masterdom.
70   *Macbeth.* We will speak further.
     Lady M.   Only look up clear:
To alter favour ever is to fear:
Leave all the rest to me.   [*they go within*

[1. 6.] 'Hautboys.' 'Enter King' DUNCAN, 'MALCOLM,
DONALBAIN, BANQUO, LENNOX, MACDUFF, ROSS,
ANGUS, and attendants'

Duncan. This castle hath a pleasant seat; the air
Nimbly and sweetly recommends itself
Unto our gentle senses.
Banquo.   This guest of summer,
The temple-haunting martlet, does approve,
By his loved mansionry, that the heaven's breath
Smells wooingly here: no jutty, frieze,
Buttress, nor coign of vantage, but this bird
Hath made his pendent bed and procreant cradle:
Where they most breed and haunt, I have observed
The air is delicate.

         '*Enter LADY*' MACBETH

Duncan.   See, see! our honoured hostess!   10
The love that follows us sometime is our trouble,
Which still we thank as love. Herein I teach you
How you shall bid God 'ield us for your pains,
And thank us for your trouble.
Lady M.   All our service
In every point twice done, and then done double,
Were poor and single business to contend
Against those honours deep and broad, wherewith
Your majesty loads our house: for those of old,
And the late dignities heaped up to them,
We rest your hermits.
Duncan.   Where's the thane of Cawdor? 20
We coursed him at the heels, and had a purpose
To be his purveyor: but he rides well,
And his great love (sharp as his spur) hath holp him
To his home before us. Fair and noble hostess,
We are your guest to-night.

Lady M.   Your servants ever
Have theirs, themselves, and what is theirs, in compt,
To make their audit at your highness' pleasure,
Still to return your own.

   Duncan.   Give me your hand:
Conduct me to mine host; we love him highly,
30 And shall continue our graces towards him.
By your leave, hostess.   [*he conducts her into the castle*

[1. 7.] *A court in Macbeth's castle, open to the sky, with
doors to the rear, one on the left the main gate or south
entry, one on the right leading to rooms within, and between
them a covered recess running back, beneath a gallery, to a
third door, through the which when ajar may be seen a flight
of stairs to an upper chamber. A bench with a table before
it against a side wall.*

   '*Hautboys. Torches. Enter a sewer*' *directing* '*divers
servants*' *who pass* '*with dishes and service*' *across the
court. As they come through the door on the right a sound
of feasting is heard within.* '*Then enter* MACBETH' *from
the same door*

   Macbeth. If it were done, when 'tis done, then 'twere
      well
It were done quickly: if th'assassination
Could trammel up the consequence, and catch,
With his surcease, success; that but this blow
Might be the be-all and the end-all....here,
But here, upon this bank and shoal of time,
We'ld jump the life to come. But in these cases
We still have judgement here—that we but teach
Bloody instructions, which being taught return
10 To plague th'inventor: this even-handed justice
Commends th'ingredience of our poisoned chalice

To our own lips. He's here in double trust:
First, as I am his kinsman and his subject,
Strong both against the deed; then, as his host,
Who should against his murderer shut the door,
Not bear the knife myself. Besides, this Duncan
Hath borne his faculties so meek, hath been
So clear in his great office, that his virtues
Will plead like angels, trumpet-tongued, against
The deep damnation of his taking-off: 20
And pity, like a naked new-born babe,
Striding the blast, or Heaven's cherubin, horsed
Upon the sightless couriers of the air,
Shall blow the horrid deed in every eye,
That tears shall drown the wind. I have no spur
To prick the sides of my intent, but only
Vaulting ambition, which o'erleaps itself,
And falls on th'other—

                    'Enter LADY' MACBETH

                         How now, what news?
Lady M. He has almost supped: why have you left
    the chamber?
Macbeth. Hath he asked for me?
Lady M.   Know you not he has? 30
Macbeth. We will proceed no further in this business:
He hath honoured me of late, and I have bought
Golden opinions from all sorts of people,
Which would be worn now in their newest gloss,
Not cast aside so soon.
    Lady M.   Was the hope drunk
Wherein you dressed yourself? hath it slept since?
And wakes it now, to look so green and pale
At what it did so freely? From this time
Such I account thy love. Art thou afeard

40   To be the same in thine own act and valour
As thou art in desire? Wouldst thou have that
Which thou esteem'st the ornament of life,
And live a coward in thine own esteem,
Letting 'I dare not' wait upon 'I would',
Like the poor cat i'th'adage?

    Macbeth.   Prithee, peace:
I dare do all that may become a man;
Who dares do more, is none.

    Lady M.   What beast was't then
That made you break this enterprise to me?
When you durst do it, then you were a man;

50   And, to be more than what you were, you would
Be so much more the man. Nor time nor place
Did then adhere, and yet you would make both:
They have made themselves, and that their fitness
      now
Does unmake you. I have given suck, and know
How tender 'tis to love the babe that milks me—
I would, while it was smiling in my face,
Have plucked my nipple from his boneless gums,
And dashed the brains out, had I so sworn as you
Have done to this.

    Macbeth.   If we should fail?

    Lady M.   We fail?

60   But screw your courage to the sticking place,
And we'll not fail. When Duncan is asleep
(Whereto the rather shall his day's hard journey
Soundly invite him) his two chamberlains
Will I with wine and wassail so convince,
That memory, the warder of the brain,
Shall be a fume, and the receipt of reason
A limbec only: when in swinish sleep
Their drenchéd natures lie as in a death,

What cannot you and I perform upon
Th'unguarded Duncan? what not put upon   70
His spongy officers, who shall bear the guilt
Of our great quell?
   Macbeth.   Bring forth men-children only!
For thy undaunted mettle should compose
Nothing but males. Will it not be received,
When we have marked with blood those sleepy two
Of his own chamber, and used their very daggers,
That they have done't?
   Lady M.   Who dares receive it other,
As we shall make our griefs and clamour roar
Upon his death?
   Macbeth.   I am settled, and bend up
Each corporal agent to this terrible feat.   80
Away, and mock the time with fairest show:
False face must hide what the false heart doth know.
                     [they return to the chamber

[2. 1.] *The same, one or two hours later. 'Enter' from
the back 'BANQUO, and FLEANCE with a torch before him'.
They come forward, leaving the door open behind them*

  Banquo. How goes the night, boy?
  Fleance [*gazing at the sky*]. The moon is down;
     I have not heard the clock.
  Banquo. And she goes down at twelve.
  Fleance.   I take't, 'tis later, sir.
  Banquo. Hold, take my sword....There's husbandry
     in heaven,
Their candles are all out....
              [unclasps his belt with its dagger
            Take thee that too.
A heavy summons lies like lead upon me,

And yet I would not sleep. Merciful powers,
Restrain in me the curséd thoughts that nature
Gives way to in repose! [*he starts*] Give me my sword,

    '*Enter*' (*from the right*) '*MACBETH, and a servant,*
             with a torch'

10 Who's there?

   Macbeth. A friend.

   Banquo. What, sir, not yet at rest? The king's a-bed.
He hath been in unusual pleasure, and
Sent forth great largess to your offices.
This diamond he greets your wife withal,
By the name of most kind hostess; and shut up
In measureless content.

   Macbeth.   Being unprepared,
Our will became the servant to defect,
Which else should free have wrought.

   Banquo.   All's well.
20 I dreamt last night of the three Weird Sisters:
To you they have showed some truth.

   Macbeth.   I think not of them:
Yet, when we can entreat an hour to serve,
We would spend it in some words upon that business,
If you would grant the time.

   Banquo.   At your kind'st leisure.

   Macbeth. If you shall cleave to my consent, when 'tis,
It shall make honour for you.

   Banquo.   So I lose none
In seeking to augment it, but still keep
My bosom franchised and allegiance clear,
I shall be counselled.

   Macbeth.   Good repose the while!
30 *Banquo.* Thanks, sir: the like to you!
               [*Banquo and Fleance go to their chamber*

Macbeth. Go bid thy mistress, when my drink is ready,
She strike upon the bell. Get thee to bed.
　　　　　　　[*the servant goes; he sits at the table*
Is this a dagger which I see before me,
The handle toward my hand? Come, let me clutch thee:
I have thee not, and yet I see thee still.
Art thou not, fatal vision, sensible
To feeling as to sight? or art thou but
A dagger of the mind, a false creation,
Proceeding from the heat-oppresséd brain?
I see thee yet, in form as palpable　　　　　　　　40
As this which now I draw.
Thou marshall'st me the way that I was going,
And such an instrument I was to use!　　　[*he rises*
Mine eyes are made the fools o'th'other senses,
Or else worth all the rest: I see thee still;
And on thy blade and dudgeon gouts of blood,
Which was not so before. There's no such thing:
It is the bloody business which informs
Thus to mine eyes....Now o'er the one half-world
Nature seems dead, and wicked dreams abuse　　50
The curtained sleep; Witchcraft celebrates
Pale Hecate's off'rings; and withered Murder,
Alarumed by his sentinel, the wolf,
Whose howl's his watch, thus with his stealthy pace,
With Tarquin's ravishing strides, towards his design
Moves like a ghost. Thou sure and firm-set earth,
Hear not my steps, which way they walk, for fear
Thy very stones prate of my whereabout,
And take the present horror from the time,
Which now suits with it. Whiles I threat, he lives:　60
Words to the heat of deeds too cold breath gives.
　　　　　　　　　　　　　[*'a bell rings'*
I go, and it is done: the bell invites me.

Hear it not, Duncan, for it is a knell
That summons thee to heaven, or to hell.

> [*he steals out by the open door at back, and
> step by step climbs the stair. A pause*

[2. 2.]   *LADY MACBETH enters from the right,
with a cup in her hand*

Lady M. That which hath made them drunk hath
    made me bold:
What hath quenched them hath given me fire. [*she
    pauses*] Hark! Peace:
It was the owl that shrieked, the fatal bellman,
Which gives the stern'st good-night. He is about it:
The doors are open; and the surfeited grooms
Do mock their charge with snores: I have drugged
    their possets,
That death and nature do contend about them,
Whether they live or die.
  Macbeth [*within*].   Who's there? what, ho!
  Lady M. Alack! I am afraid they have awaked,
10 And 'tis not done: th'attempt and not the deed
Confounds us. Hark! I laid their daggers ready,
He could not miss 'em. Had he not resembled
My father as he slept, I had done't.

> *She turns as if making towards the stair, to find
> MACBETH standing in the door, his arms bathed
> in blood and with two daggers clasped in his left
> hand. He totters forward*

                              My husband!

  Macbeth [*whispers*]. I have done the deed....Didst
    thou not hear a noise?
  Lady M. I heard the owl scream, and the crickets cry.
Did not you speak?
  Macbeth.   When?

Lady M.   Now.

Macbeth.   As I descended?

Lady M. Ay.

Macbeth. Hark!   [*they listen*

Who lies i'th' second chamber?

Lady M.   Donalbain.

Macbeth. This is a sorry sight.   20

         [*stretching forth his right hand*

Lady M. A foolish thought, to say a sorry sight.

Macbeth. There's one did laugh in's sleep, and one
     cried 'Murder!'

That they did wake each other: I stood and heard them:

But they did say their prayers, and addressed them

Again to sleep.

Lady M.   There are two lodged together.

Macbeth. One cried 'God bless us!' and 'Amen' the
     other,

As they had seen me with these hangman's hands:

List'ning their fear, I could not say 'Amen',

When they did say 'God bless us'.

Lady M. Consider it not so deeply.   30

Macbeth. But wherefore could not I pronounce
     'Amen'?

I had most need of blessing, and 'Amen'

Stuck in my throat.

Lady M.   These deeds must not be thought

After these ways; so, it will make us mad.

Macbeth. Methought I heard a voice cry 'Sleep no
     more!

Macbeth does murder sleep'—the innocent sleep,

Sleep that knits up the ravelled sleave of care,

The death of each day's life, sore labour's bath,

Balm of hurt minds, great Nature's second course,

Chief nourisher in life's feast,—   40

Lady M.   What do you mean?

Macbeth. Still it cried 'Sleep no more!' to all the
     house:
'Glamis hath murdered sleep, and therefore Cawdor
Shall sleep no more: Macbeth shall sleep no more!'

   Lady M. Who was it that thus cried? Why, worthy
     thane,
You do unbend your noble strength, to think
So brainsickly of things. Go get some water,
And wash this filthy witness from your hand.
Why did you bring these daggers from the place?
They must lie there: go carry them, and smear
50 The sleepy grooms with blood.

   Macbeth.   I'll go no more:
I am afraid to think what I have done;
Look on't again I dare not.

   Lady M.   Infirm of purpose!
Give me the daggers: the sleeping and the dead
Are but as pictures: 'tis the eye of childhood
That fears a painted devil. If he do bleed,
I'll gild the faces of the grooms withal,
For it must seem their guilt.

             [*she goes up. A knocking heard*

   Macbeth.   Whence is that knocking?
How is't with me, when every noise appals me?
What hands are here? ha! they pluck out mine eyes!
60 Will all great Neptune's ocean wash this blood
Clean from my hand? No; this my hand will rather
The multitudinous seas incarnadine,
Making the green—one red.

      Lady Macbeth returns, closing the inner door

   Lady M. My hands are of your colour; but I shame
To wear a heart so white. [*knocking*] I hear a knocking

At the south entry: retire we to our chamber:
A little water clears us of this deed:
How easy is it then! Your constancy
Hath left you unattended. [*knocking*] Hark! more
    knocking.
Get on your nightgown, lest occasion call us   70
And show us to be watchers: be not lost
So poorly in your thoughts.
    Macbeth. To know my deed, 'twere best not know
        myself.   [*knocking*
Wake Duncan with thy knocking! I would thou
    couldst!   [*they go in*

[2. 3.] *The knocking grows yet louder; a drunken*
                Porter enters the court

    Porter. Here's a knocking indeed! If a man were
porter of hell-gate, he should have old turning the key.
[*knocking*] Knock, knock, knock! Who's there, i'th'
name of Beelzebub? Here's a farmer, that hanged himself on th'expectation of plenty: come in, time-server;
have napkins enow about you, here you'll sweat for't.
[*knocking*] Knock, knock! Who's there, in th'other
devil's name? Faith, here's an equivocator, that could
swear in both the scales against either scale, who committed treason enough for God's sake, yet could not 10
equivocate to heaven: O, come in, equivocator. [*knocking*] Knock, knock, knock! Who's there? Faith, here's
an English tailor come hither, for stealing out of a French
hose: come in, tailor, here you may roast your goose.
[*knocking*] Knock, knock! never at quiet! What are you?
But this place is too cold for hell. I'll devil-porter it no
further: I had thought to have let in some of all pro-
fessions, that go the primrose way to th'everlasting

bonfire. [*knocking*] Anon, anon! I pray you, remember
20 the porter.   [*opens the gate*

'*Enter* Macduff *and* Lennox'

Macduff. Was it so late, friend, ere you went to bed,
That you do lie so late?

Porter. Faith, sir, we were carousing till the second
cock: and drink, sir, is a great provoker of three things.

Macduff. What three things does drink especially
provoke?

Porter. Marry, sir, nose-painting, sleep, and urine.
Lechery, sir, it provokes and unprovokes: it provokes
the desire, but it takes away the performance. Therefore,
30 much drink may be said to be an equivocator with
lechery: it makes him, and it mars him; it sets him on,
and it takes him off; it persuades him, and disheartens
him; makes him stand to, and not stand to: in conclusion, equivocates him in a sleep, and giving him the
lie, leaves him.

Macduff. I believe drink gave thee the lie last night.

Porter. That it did, sir, i'the very throat on me: but
I requited him for his lie, and, I think, being too strong
for him, though he took up my legs sometime, yet I
40 made a shift to cast him.

Macduff. Is thy master stirring?

Macbeth returns, in a dressing gown

Our knocking has awaked him; here he comes.

Lennox. Good-morrow, noble sir.

Macbeth.   Good-morrow, both.

Macduff. Is the king stirring, worthy thane?

Macbeth.   Not yet.

Macduff. He did command me to call timely on him;
I have almost slipped the hour.

Macbeth.　　　　　　　I'll bring you to him.
　　　　　　　　[they move towards the inner door

Macduff. I know this is a joyful trouble to you;
But yet 'tis one.

Macbeth. The labour we delight in physics pain.
This is the door.　　　　　　　　　　*[he points*

Macduff.　　　　I'll make so bold to call,　　　50
For 'tis my limited service.　　　　　*[he goes in*

Lennox. Goes the king hence to-day?

Macbeth. He does: he did appoint so.

Lennox. The night has been unruly: where we lay,
Our chimneys were blown down, and, as they say,
Lamentings heard i'th'air, strange screams of death,
And prophesying with accents terrible
Of dire combustion and confused events
New hatched to th' woeful time. The obscure bird
Clamoured the livelong night: some say, the earth　　60
Was feverous and did shake.

Macbeth.　　　　　　　　'Twas a rough night.

Lennox. My young remembrance cannot parallel
A fellow to it.

MACDUFF *returns*

Macduff. O horror! horror! horror! Tongue, nor
　　heart,
Cannot conceive nor name thee!

Macbeth, Lennox.　　　　　　　What's the matter?

Macduff. Confusion now hath made his master-
　　piece!
Most sacrilegious murder hath broke ope
The Lord's anointed temple, and stole thence
The life o'th' building.

Macbeth.　　　　　　What is't you say? the life?

Lennox. Mean you his majesty?　　　　　70

Macduff. Approach the chamber, and destroy your
   sight
With a new Gorgon: do not bid me speak;
See, and then speak yourselves.
               [*Macbeth and Lennox go up*
                   Awake! awake!
Ring the alarum bell! Murder and treason!
Banquo and Donalbain! Malcolm, awake!
Shake off this downy sleep, death's counterfeit,
And look on death itself! up, up, and see
The great doom's image! Malcolm! Banquo!
As from your graves rise up, and walk like sprites,
80 To countenance this horror!   [*'bell rings'*

     'Enter LADY' MACBETH in a dressing gown

Lady M.   What's the business,
That such a hideous trumpet calls to parley
The sleepers of the house? speak, speak!
Macduff.   O, gentle lady,
'Tis not for you to hear what I can speak:
The repetition, in a woman's ear,
Would murder as it fell.

       'Enter BANQUO' half-clad

           O Banquo! Banquo!
Our royal master's murdered!
Lady M.   Woe, alas!
What, in our house?
Banquo.   Too cruel, any where.
Dear Duff, I prithee, contradict thyself,
And say it is not so.

     MACBETH and LENNOX return

90 *Macbeth.* Had I but died an hour before this chance,

I had lived a blesséd time; for from this instant
There's nothing serious in mortality:
All is but toys: renown and grace is dead,
The wine of life is drawn, and the mere lees
Is left this vault to brag of.

*MALCOLM and DONALBAIN come in haste through
the door on the right*

Donalbain. What is amiss?
Macbeth.　　　　　You are, and do not know't:
The spring, the head, the fountain of your blood
Is stopped—the very source of it is stopped.
Macduff. Your royal father's murdered.
Malcolm.　　　　　　　O, by whom?
Lennox. Those of his chamber, as it seemed, had　100
　　done't:
Their hands and faces were all badged with blood,
So were their daggers, which unwiped we found
Upon their pillows:
They stared and were distracted, no man's life
Was to be trusted with them.
Macbeth. O, yet I do repent me of my fury,
That I did kill them.
Macduff.　　　　Wherefore did you so?
Macbeth. Who can be wise, amazed, temp'rate and
　　furious,
Loyal and neutral, in a moment? no man:
Th'expedition of my violent love　　　　　　110
Outrun the pauser, reason. Here lay Duncan,
His silver skin laced with his golden blood,
And his gashed stabs looked like a breach in nature
For ruin's wasteful entrance: there, the murderers,
Steeped in the colours of their trade, their daggers
Unmannerly breeched with gore: who could refrain,

That had a heart to love, and in that heart
Courage to make's love known?
   Lady M. [*seeming to faint*]   Help me hence, ho!

               MACBETH goes to her

   Macduff. Look to the lady.
   (*Malcolm.*   Why do we hold our tongues,
120 That most may claim this argument for ours?
   (*Donalbain.* What should be spoken here, where our
     fate,
Hid in an auger-hole, may rush and seize us?
Let's away.
Our tears are not yet brewed.
   (*Malcolm.*   Nor our strong sorrow
Upon the foot of motion.   [*enter waiting-women*
   Banquo [*directs them*].   Look to the lady...
                    [*they lead her forth*
And when we have our naked frailties hid,
That suffer in exposure, let us meet,
And question this most bloody piece of work,
To know it further. Fears and scruples shake us:
130 In the great hand of God I stand, and thence
Against the undivulged pretence I fight
Of treasonous malice.
   Macduff.   And so do I.
   All.   So all.
   Macbeth. Let's briefly put on manly readiness.
And meet i'th'hall together.
   All.   Well contented.
         [*all go in but Malcolm and Donalbain*
   Malcolm. What will you do? Let's not consort with
     them:
To show an unfelt sorrow is an office
Which the false man does easy. I'll to England.

Donalbain. To Ireland, I: our separated fortune
Shall keep us both the safer: where we are
There's daggers in men's smiles: the near in blood,   140
The nearer bloody.

Malcolm.   This murderous shaft that's shot
Hath not yet lighted, and our safest way
Is to avoid the aim. Therefore to horse,
And let us not be dainty of leave-taking,
But shift away: there's warrant in that theft
Which steals itself when there's no mercy left.

                                        [*they go*

[2. 4.]   *Before Macbeth's castle. A day*
                 strangely dark

           '*Enter Ross with an Old Man*'

Old Man. Threescore and ten I can remember well,
Within the volume of which time I have seen
Hours dreadful and things strange; but this sore night
Hath trifled former knowings.

Ross. [*looks up*]   Ha, good father,
Thou seest the heavens, as troubled with man's act,
Threatens his bloody stage: by th' clock 'tis day,
And yet dark night strangles the travelling lamp:
Is't night's predominance, or the day's shame,
That darkness does the face of earth entomb,
When living light should kiss it?

Old Man.   'Tis unnatural,   10
Even like the deed that's done. On Tuesday last
A falcon towering in her pride of place
Was by a mousing owl hawked at and killed.

Ross. And Duncan's horses—a thing most strange and
      certain—
Beauteous and swift, the minions of their race,

Turned wild in nature, broke their stalls, flung out,
Contending 'gainst obedience, as they would make
War with mankind.

    Old Man.   'Tis said they eat each other.

    Ross. They did so, to th'amazement of mine eyes,
20 That looked upon't.

MACDUFF comes from the castle

                      Here comes the good Macduff.
How goes the world, sir, now?

    Macduff [*points at the sky*].   Why, see you not?

    Ross. Is't known who did this more than bloody
      deed?

    Macduff. Those that Macbeth hath slain.

    Ross.   Alas, the day!
What good could they pretend?

    Macduff.   They were suborned.
Malcolm and Donalbain, the king's two sons,
Are stol'n away and fled, which puts upon them
Suspicion of the deed.

    Ross.   'Gainst nature still!
Thriftless ambition, that wilt ravin up
Thine own life's means! Then 'tis most like
30 The sovereignty will fall upon Macbeth.

    Macduff. He is already named, and gone to Scone
To be invested.

    Ross.   Where is Duncan's body?

    Macduff. Carried to Colme kill,
The sacred storehouse of his predecessors,
And guardian of their bones.

    Ross.   Will you to Scone?

    Macduff. No cousin, I'll to Fife.

                      Well, I will thither.

Macduff. Well, may you see things well done there:
    adieu!
Lest our old robes sit easier than our new!
  Ross. Farewell, father.
  Old Man. God's benison go with you, and with those   40
That would make good of bad and friends of foes!

                                           [they go

[*Some weeks pass*]

[3. 1.]   *An audience chamber in the palace at*
                        Forres

              Banquo enters

  Banquo. Thou hast it now, King, Cawdor, Glamis, all,
As the weïrd women promised, and I fear
Thou play'dst most foully for't: yet it was said
It should not stand in thy posterity,
But that myself should be the root and father
Of many kings. If there come truth from them—
As upon thee, Macbeth, their speeches shine—
Why, by the verities on thee made good,
May they not be my oracles as well,
And set me up in hope? But hush, no more.   10

'*Sennet sounded. Enter* MACBETH, *as King,* LADY'
MACBETH, *as Queen,* 'LENNOX, ROSS, *Lords, and
attendants*'

  Macbeth. Here's our chief guest.
  Lady M.   If he had been forgotten,
It had been as a gap in our great feast,
And all-thing unbecoming.
  Macbeth. To-night we hold a solemn supper, sir,
And I'll request your presence.

Banquo.   Let your highness
Command upon me, to the which my duties
Are with a most indissoluble tie
For ever knit.

Macbeth. Ride you this afternoon?

Banquo.   Ay, my good lord.

20 *Macbeth.* We should have else desired your good advice
(Which still hath been both grave and prosperous)
In this day's council; but we'll take to-morrow.
Is't far you ride?

Banquo. As far, my lord, as will fill up the time
'Twixt this and supper. Go not my horse the better,
I must become a borrower of the night
For a dark hour or twain.

Macbeth.   Fail not our feast.

Banquo. My lord, I will not.

Macbeth. We hear our bloody cousins are bestowed

30 In England and in Ireland, not confessing
Their cruel parricide, filling their hearers
With strange invention: but of that to-morrow,
When therewithal we shall have cause of state
Craving us jointly. Hie you to horse: adieu,
Till you return at night. Goes Fleance with you?

Banquo. Ay, my good lord: our time does call upon's.

Macbeth. I wish your horses swift and sure of foot;
And so I do commend you to their backs.
Farewell.   [*Banquo goes*

40 Let every man be master of his time
Till seven at night; to make society
The sweeter welcome, we will keep ourself
Till supper-time alone: while then, God be with you!
                        [*all depart but Macbeth and a servant*
Sirrah, a word with you: attend those men
Our pleasure?

Attendant. They are, my lord, without the palace gate.
Macbeth. Bring them before us.   [*the servant goes*
                To be thus is nothing,
But to be safely thus: our fears in Banquo
Stick deep, and in his royalty of nature
Reigns that which would be feared. 'Tis much he dares, 50
And, to that dauntless temper of his mind,
He hath a wisdom that doth guide his valour
To act in safety. There is none but he
Whose being I do fear: and under him
My Genius is rebuked, as it is said
Mark Antony's was by Cæsar. He chid the Sisters,
When first they put the name of king upon me,
And bade them speak to him; then prophet-like
They hailed him father to a line of kings:
Upon my head they placed a fruitless crown,   60
And put a barren sceptre in my gripe,
Thence to be wrenched with an unlineal hand,
No son of mine succeeding. If't be so,
For Banquo's issue have I filed my mind,
For them the gracious Duncan have I murdered,
Put rancours in the vessel of my peace
Only for them, and mine eternal jewel
Given to the common enemy of man,
To make them kings, the seed of Banquo kings!
Rather than so, come Fate into the list,   70
And champion me to th'utterance. Who's there?

      The servant returns 'with two murderers'

Now go to the door, and stay there till we call.
                     [*servant goes out*
Was it not yesterday we spoke together?
1 *Murderer.* It was, so please your highness.
Macbeth.   Well then, now

Have you considered of my speeches? Know
That it was he in the times past which held you
So under fortune, which you thought had been
Our innocent self: this I made good to you
In our last conference; passed in probation with you,
80 How you were borne in hand, how crossed, the
    instruments,
Who wrought with them, and all things else that might
To half a soul and to a notion crazed
Say 'Thus did Banquo'.

   1 *Murderer.*   You made it known to us.
  Macbeth. I did so; and went further, which is now
Our point of second meeting. Do you find
Your patience so predominant in your nature,
That you can let this go? Are you so gospelled,
To pray for this good man, and for his issue,
Whose heavy hand hath bowed you to the grave
90 And beggared yours for ever?

   1 *Murderer.*   We are men, my liege.
  Macbeth. Ay, in the catalogue ye go for men,
As hounds and greyhounds, mongrels, spaniels, curs,
Shoughs, water-rugs, and demi-wolves, are clept
All by the name of dogs: the valued file
Distinguishes the swift, the slow, the subtle,
The housekeeper, the hunter, every one
According to the gift which bounteous nature
Hath in him closed, whereby he does receive
Particular addition, from the bill
100 That writes them all alike: and so of men.
Now, if you have a station in the file,
Not i'th' worst rank of manhood, say't,
And I will put that business in your bosoms,
Whose execution takes your enemy off,
Grapples you to the heart and love of us,

Who wear our health but sickly in his life,
Which in his death were perfect.

  2 *Murderer*.   I am one, my liege,
Whom the vile blows and buffets of the world
Hath so incensed that I am reckless what
I do to spite the world.

  1 *Murderer*.   And I another   110
So weary with disasters, tugged with fortune,
That I would set my life on any chance,
To mend it, or be rid on't.

  Macbeth.   Both of you
Know Banquo was your enemy.

  Both Murderers.   True, my lord.

  Macbeth. So is he mine: and in such bloody distance,
That every minute of his being thrusts
Against my near'st of life: and though I could
With barefaced power sweep him from my sight,
And bid my will avouch it, yet I must not,
For certain friends that are both his and mine,   120
Whose loves I may not drop, but wail his fall
Who I myself struck down: and thence it is
That I to your assistance do make love,
Masking the business from the common eye,
For sundry weighty reasons.

  2 *Murderer*.   We shall, my lord,
Perform what you command us.

  1 *Murderer*.   Though our lives—

  Macbeth. Your spirits shine through you. Within this
      hour at most
I will advise you where to plant yourselves,
Acquaint you with the perfect spy o'th' time,
The moment on't, for't must be done to-night,   130
And something from the palace; always thought
That I require a clearness: and with him—

To leave no rubs nor botches in the work—
Fleance his son, that keeps him company,
Whose absence is no less material to me
Than is his father's, must embrace the fate
Of that dark hour. Resolve yourselves apart;
I'll come to you anon.
   Both Murderers.   We are resolved, my lord.
   Macbeth. I'll call upon you straight; abide within.
                                           [they go
140 It is concluded: Banquo, thy soul's flight,
If it find heaven, must find it out to-night.
                        [he leaves by another door

[3. 2.]   *LADY MACBETH enters with a servant*

   Lady M. Is Banquo gone from court?
   Servant. Ay, madam, but returns again to-night.
   Lady M. Say to the king, I would attend his leisure
For a few words.
   Servant.   Madam, I will.   *[he goes*
   Lady M.   Nought's had, all's spent,
Where our desire is got without content:
'Tis safer to be that which we destroy
Than by destruction dwell in doubtful joy.

MACBETH enters lost in thought

How now, my lord! why do you keep alone,
Of sorriest fancies your companions making,
10 Using those thoughts which should indeed have died
With them they think on? Things without all remedy
Should be without regard: what's done, is done.
   Macbeth. We have scorched the snake, not killed it:
She'll close and be herself, whilst our poor malice
Remains in danger of her former tooth.

But let the frame of things disjoint, both the worlds
    suffer,
Ere we will eat our meal in fear, and sleep
In the affliction of these terrible dreams
That shake us nightly: better be with the dead,
Whom we, to gain our peace, have sent to peace,   20
Than on the torture of the mind to lie
In restless ecstasy. Duncan is in his grave;
After life's fitful fever he sleeps well;
Treason has done his worst: nor steel, nor poison,
Malice domestic, foreign levy, nothing,
Can touch him further.

Lady M.   Come on;
Gentle my lord, sleek o'er your rugged looks,
Be bright and jovial among your guests to-night.

Macbeth. So shall I, love, and so I pray be you:
Let your remembrance apply to Banquo;   30
Present him eminence, both with eye and tongue:
Unsafe the while, that we
Must lave our honours in these flattering streams,
And make our faces vizards to our hearts,
Disguising what they are.

Lady M.   You must leave this.

Macbeth. O, full of scorpions is my mind, dear
    wife!
Thou know'st that Banquo and his Fleance lives.

Lady M. But in them nature's copy's not eterne.

Macbeth. There's comfort yet, they are assailable,
Then be thou jocund: ere the bat hath flown   40
His cloistered flight, ere to black Hecate's summons
The shard-borne beetle with his drowsy hums
Hath rung night's yawning peal, there shall be done
A deed of dreadful note.

Lady M.   What's to be done?

Macbeth. Be innocent of the knowledge, dearest chuck,
Till thou applaud the deed...Come, seeling night,
Scarf up the tender eye of pitiful day,
And with thy bloody and invisible hand
Cancel and tear to pieces that great bond
50 †Which keeps me paled! Light thickens, and the crow
Makes wing to th' rooky wood:
Good things of day begin to droop and drowse,
Whiles night's black agents to their preys do rouse.
Thou marvell'st at my words: but hold thee still;
Things bad begun make strong themselves by ill:
So, prithee, go with me.   [*they go*

[3. 3.] *A steep lane leading through a wood to gates of
the royal park, some way from the palace. The two
murderers come up, with a third*

1 *Murderer.* But who did bid thee join with us?
3 *Murderer.*   Macbeth.
2 *Murderer.* He needs not our mistrust, since he
        delivers
Our offices and what we have to do,
To the direction just.
1 *Murderer.*   Then stand with us.
The west yet glimmers with some streaks of day:
Now spurs the lated traveller apace
To gain the timely inn, and near approaches
The subject of our watch.
3 *Murderer.*   Hark! I hear horses.
Banquo [*at a distance*] Give us a light there, ho!
2 *Murderer.*   Then 'tis he; the rest
10 That are within the note of expectation
Already are i'th' court.
1 *Murderer.*   His horses go about.

3 *Murderer.* Almost a mile: but he does usually—
So all men do—from hence to th' palace gate
Make it their walk.

   *'BANQUO and FLEANCE with a torch' are seen
coming up the lane*

2 *Murderer.*   A light, a light!
3 *Murderer.*   'Tis he.
1 *Murderer.* Stand to't.
Banquo. It will be rain to-night.
1 *Murderer.*   Let it come down.
       *[1 Murderer strikes out the torch; the
others set upon Banquo*

Banquo. O, treachery! Fly, good Fleance, fly, fly, fly!
Thou mayst revenge. O slave!
               [he dies; Fleance escapes
3 *Murderer.* Who did strike out the light?
1 *Murderer.*   Was't not the way?
3 *Murderer.* There's but one down; the son is fled.
2 *Murderer.*   We have lost 20
Best half of our affair.
 1 *Murderer.* Well, let's away, and say how much is
   done.   *[they go*

[3. 4.] *The hall of the palace. At the upper end a dais
with doors to left and right, between which are two thrones
and a table before them, while a longer table, at right
angles, extends down the room*

 *A 'banquet prepared. Enter MACBETH, LADY' MAC-
BETH, 'ROSS, LENNOX, Lords, and attendants'*

 Macbeth. You know your own degrees, sit down: at
   first
And last, the hearty welcome.

Lords.   Thanks to your majesty.

*Macbeth leads Lady Macbeth to the dais; the Lords
sit on either side of the long table, leaving an empty stool
at the head*

Macbeth. Ourself will mingle with society,
And play the humble host:
                    [*Lady Macbeth ascends to her throne*
Our hostess keeps her state, but in best time
We will require her welcome.

Lady M. Pronounce it for me, sir, to all our friends,
For my heart speaks they are welcome.

As Macbeth passes by the door on the left 1 *Murderer
appears thereat. The Lords rise and bow to Lady
Macbeth*

Macbeth. See, they encounter thee with their hearts'
      thanks.
10 Both sides are even: here I'll sit i'th' midst.
                              [*points to the empty stool*
Be large in mirth, anon we'll drink a measure
The table round.
    [*turns to the door*] There's blood upon thy face.
    (*Murderer.* 'Tis Banquo's then.
    (*Macbeth.* 'Tis better thee without than he within.
Is he dispatched?
    (*Murderer.* My lord, his throat is cut, that I did for
      him.
    (*Macbeth.* Thou art the best o'th' cut-throats! Yet
      he's good
That did the like for Fleance: if thou didst it,
Thou art the nonpareil.
    (*Murderer.*   Most royal sir,
20 Fleance is 'scaped.

(*Macbeth.* Then comes my fit again: I had else been
    perfect;
Whole as the marble, founded as the rock,
As broad and general as the casing air:
But now I am cabined, cribbed, confined, bound in
To saucy doubts and fears. But Banquo's safe?
  (*Murderer.* Ay, my good lord: safe in a ditch he
    bides,
With twenty trenchéd gashes on his head;
The least a death to nature.
  (*Macbeth.*   Thanks for that:
There the grown serpent lies; the worm that's fled
Hath nature that in time will venom breed,   30
No teeth for th' present. Get thee gone; to-morrow
We'll hear ourselves again.   [*murderer goes*
  Lady M.   My royal lord,
You do not give the cheer. The feast is sold
That is not often vouched, while 'tis a-making,
'Tis given with welcome: to feed were best at home;
From thence the sauce to meat is ceremony;
Meeting were bare without it.

     ['*The Ghost of Banquo*' *appears,* '*and sits in
            Macbeth's place*'

  Macbeth.   Sweet remembrancer!
Now good digestion wait on appetite,
And health on both!
  Lennox.   May't please your highness sit?
  Macbeth. Here had we now our country's honour
    roofed,   40
Were the graced person of our Banquo present;
Who may I rather challenge for unkindness
Than pity for mischance!
  Ross.   His absence, sir,

Lays blame upon his promise. Please't your highness
To grace us with your royal company?

　　Macbeth. The table's full.

　　Lennox. 　　　　　　　　Here is a place reserved, sir.

　　Macbeth. Where?

　　Lennox. Here, my good lord....What is't that moves
　　　your highness?

　　Macbeth. Which of you have done this?

　　Lords. 　　　　　　　　What, my good lord?

50 *Macbeth.* Thou canst not say I did it: never shake
　　Thy gory locks at me. 　　　　　　[*Lady Macbeth rises*

　　Ross. Gentlemen, rise, his highness is not well.

　　Lady M. [*coming down*] Sit, worthy friends: my lord
　　　is often thus,
And hath been from his youth: pray you, keep seat,
The fit is momentary, upon a thought
He will again be well: if much you note him,
You shall offend him and extend his passion:
Feed, and regard him not. [*aside*] Are you a man?

　　(*Macbeth.* Ay, and a bold one, that dare look on that
60 Which might appal the devil.

　　(*Lady M.* 　　　　　　　　O proper stuff!
This is the very painting of your fear:
This is the air-drawn dagger which, you said,
Led you to Duncan. O, these flaws and starts
(Impostors to true fear) would well become
A woman's story at a winter's fire,
Authorized by her grandam....Shame itself!
Why do you make such faces? When all's done,
You look but on a stool.

　　(*Macbeth.* Prithee, see there! behold! look! lo! how
　　　say you?
70 Why what care I? If thou canst nod, speak too.
If charnel-houses and our graves must send

Those that we bury back, our monuments
Shall be the maws of kites.   [*the Ghost vanishes*

(*Lady M.*   What! quite unmanned in folly?
(*Macbeth.* If I stand here, I saw him.
(*Lady M.*   Fie, for shame!
(*Macbeth* [*paces to and fro*]. Blood hath been shed ere
     now, i'th'olden time,
Ere humane statute purged the gentle weal;
Ay, and since too, murders have been performed
Too terrible for the ear: the time has been,
That, when the brains were out, the man would die,
And there an end: but now they rise again,   80
With twenty mortal murders on their crowns,
And push us from our stools....This is more strange
Than such a murder is.
     Lady M. [*touches his arm*] My worthy lord,
Your noble friends do lack you.
     Macbeth.   I do forget...
Do not muse at me, my most worthy friends;
I have a strange infirmity, which is nothing
To those that know me. Come, love and health to all;
Then I'll sit down. Give me some wine, fill full.

          [*as he raises his cup, the Ghost reappears*
               in the seat behind him

I drink to th' general joy o'th' whole table,
And to our dear friend Banquo, whom we miss;   90
Would he were here! to all, and him we thirst,
And all to all!
     Lords [*drinking*]. Our duties, and the pledge.
     Macbeth [*turns to his seat*]. Avaunt! and quit my sight!
     let the earth hide thee!
               [*drops the cup*]
Thy bones are marrowless, thy blood is cold;

Thou hast no speculation in those eyes
Which thou dost glare with!

    Lady M.   Think of this, good peers,
But as a thing of custom: 'tis no other;
Only it spoils the pleasure of the time.

    Macbeth. What man dare, I dare:
100 Approach thou like the ruggéd Russian bear,
The armed rhinoceros, or th'Hyrcan tiger,
Take any shape but that, and my firm nerves
Shall never tremble: or be alive again,
And dare me to the desert with thy sword;
If trembling I inhabit then, protest me
The baby of a girl. Hence, horrible shadow!
Unreal mock'ry, hence!   *[the Ghost vanishes*
                     Why, so; being gone,
I am a man again. Pray you, sit still.

    Lady M. You have displaced the mirth, broke the
        good meeting,
110 With most admired disorder.

    Macbeth.   Can such things be,
And overcome us like a summer's cloud,
Without our special wonder? You make me strange
Even to the disposition that I owe,
When now I think you can behold such sights,
And keep the natural ruby of your cheeks,
When mine is blanched with fear.

    Ross.   What sights, my lord?

    Lady M. I pray you, speak not; he grows worse and
        worse;
Question enrages him: at once, good night.
Stand not upon the order of your going,   *[they rise*
120 But go at once.

    Lennox.   Good night, and better health
Attend his majesty!

Lady M.   A kind good night to all!

                                        [*they leave*

Macbeth. It will have blood; they say, blood will
     have blood:
Stones have been known to move and trees to speak;
Augures and understood relations have
By maggot-pies and choughs and rooks brought forth
The secret'st man of blood....What is the night?

   Lady M. Almost at odds with morning, which is
     which.

   Macbeth. How say'st thou, that Macduff denies his
     person
At our great bidding?

   Lady M.   Did you send to him, sir?

   Macbeth. I hear it by the way; but I will send: 130
There's not a one of them but in his house
I keep a servant fee'd....I will to-morrow
(And betimes I will) to the Weïrd Sisters:
More shall they speak; for now I am bent to know,
By the worst means, the worst. For mine own good
All causes shall give way: I am in blood
Stepped in so far that, should I wade no more,
Returning were as tedious as go o'er:
Strange things I have in head that will to hand,
Which must be acted ere they may be scanned.   140

   Lady M. You lack the season of all natures, sleep.

   Macbeth. Come, we'll to sleep. My strange and
     self-abuse
Is the initiate fear that wants hard use:
We are yet but young in deed.   [*they go*

[3. 5.   *A heath*   ]

'*Thunder. Enter the three Witches*',
                    meeting HECATE

  1 *Witch.* Why, how now, Hecat, you look angerly.
  Hecate. Have I not reason, beldams as you are,
Saucy and overbold? How did you dare
To trade and traffic with Macbeth
In riddles and affairs of death;
And I, the mistress of your charms,
The close contriver of all harms,
Was never called to bear my part,
Or show the glory of our art?
10 And, which is worse, all you have done
Hath been but for a wayward son,
Spiteful and wrathful, who (as others do)
Loves for his own ends, not for you.
But make amends now: get you gone,
And at the pit of Acheron
Meet me i'th' morning: thither he
Will come to know his destiny.
Your vessels and your spells provide,
Your charms and every thing beside.
20 I am for th'air; this night I'll spend
Unto a dismal and a fatal end.
Great business must be wrought ere noon:
Upon the corner of the moon
There hangs a vap'rous drop profound;
I'll catch it ere it come to ground:
And that distilled by magic sleights
Shall raise such artificial sprites
As by the strength of their illusion
Shall draw him on to his confusion.

He shall spurn fate, scorn death, and bear　　　30
His hopes 'bove wisdom, grace, and fear:
And you all know security
Is mortals' chiefest enemy.

> '*Music and a song*': '*Come away, come away*,' &c.
> 　*A cloud descends*

Hark, I am called: my little spirit, see,
Sits in a foggy cloud, and stays for me.

> 　　　　　　　　　　[*she flies away on the cloud*

⎡ 1 *Witch*. Come, let's make haste; she'll soon be back

⎣ 　again. 　　　　*They vanish* 　　　　　　　　⎤

[3. 6.] 　　　*A castle in Scotland*

'*Enter* LENNOX *and another Lord*'

Lennox. My former speeches have but hit your
　　thoughts,
Which can interpret farther: only I say
Things have been strangely borne. The gracious
　　Duncan
Was pitied of Macbeth: marry, he was dead:
And the right valiant Banquo walked too late—
Whom you may say (if't please you) Fleance killed,
For Fleance fled: men must not walk too late.
Who cannot want the thought, how monstrous
It was for Malcolm and for Donalbain
To kill their gracious father? damnéd fact! 　　　10
How it did grieve Macbeth! did he not straight,
In pious rage, the two delinquents tear,
That were the slaves of drink and thralls of sleep?
Was not that nobly done? Ay, and wisely too;
For 'twould have angered any heart alive

To hear the men deny't. So that, I say,
He has borne all things well: and I do think
That, had he Duncan's sons under his key
(As, an't please heaven, he shall not) they should find
20 What 'twere to kill a father; so should Fleance.
But, peace! for from broad words, and 'cause he failed
His presence at the tyrant's feast, I hear,
Macduff lives in disgrace. Sir, can you tell
Where he bestows himself?
    Lord.   The son of Duncan
(From whom this tyrant holds the due of birth)
Lives in the English court, and is received
Of the most pious Edward with such grace
That the malevolence of fortune nothing
Takes from his high respect. Thither Macduff
30 Is gone to pray the holy king, upon his aid
To wake Northumberland and warlike Siward,
That by the help of these (with Him above
To ratify the work) we may again
Give to our tables meat, sleep to our nights;
Free from our feasts and banquets bloody knives;
Do faithful homage and receive free honours:
All which we pine for now. And this report
Hath so exasperate the king that he
Prepares for some attempt of war.
    Lennox.   Sent he to Macduff?
40 *Lord.* He did: and with an absolute 'Sir, not I',
The cloudy messenger turns me his back,
And hums, as who should say, 'You'll rue the time
That clogs me with this answer'.
    Lennox.   And that well might
Advise him to a caution, t'hold what distance
His wisdom can provide. Some holy angel
Fly to the court of England and unfold

His message ere he come, that a swift blessing
May soon return to this our suffering country
Under a hand accursed!

Lord.　　　　　　　　　I'll send my prayers with him.

　　　　　　　　　　　　　　　　　　　[they go

[4. 1.] *A cavern and in the midst a fiery pit with a boiling
cauldron above it. 'Thunder', as the Weird Sisters rise,
one after the other, from the flames*

　1 *Witch.* Thrice the brinded cat hath mewed.
　2 *Witch.* Thrice and once the hedge-pig whined.
　3 *Witch.* Harpier cries:— 'Tis time, 'tis time.
　1 *Witch.* Round about the cauldron go:
In the poisoned entrails throw.

　　　　　　　　　　　　[they move leftwards about it

Toad, that under cold stone
Days and nights has thirty-one
Sweltered venom sleeping got,
Boil thou first i'th' charméd pot!

　All. Double, double toil and trouble;　　　　10
Fire burn and cauldron bubble.

　　　　　　　　　　　　　　　[they stir the cauldron

　2 *Witch.* Fillet of a fenny snake,
In the cauldron boil and bake:
Eye of newt and toe of frog,
Wool of bat and tongue of dog,
Adder's fork and blind-worm's sting,
Lizard's leg and howlet's wing,
For a charm of powerful trouble,
Like a hell-broth boil and bubble.

　All. Double, double toil and trouble;　　　　20
Fire burn and cauldron bubble.　　　　*[they stir*

3 *Witch.* Scale of dragon, tooth of wolf,
Witch's mummy, maw and gulf
Of the ravined salt-sea shark,
Root of hemlock digged i'th' dark,
Liver of blaspheming Jew,
Gall of goat and slips of yew
Slivered in the moon's eclipse,
Nose of Turk and Tartar's lips,
30 Finger of birth-strangled babe
Ditch-delivered by a drab,
Make the gruel thick and slab:
Add thereto a tiger's chaudron,
For th'ingredience of our cauldron.
　　All. Double, double toil and trouble;
Fire burn and cauldron bubble.　　　　　[*they stir*

　2 *Witch.* Cool it with a baboon's blood,
Then the charm is firm and good.

⌈　　'*Enter* HECATE *and the other three Witches*'　　⌉

　Hecate. O, well done! I commend your pains,
40 And every one shall share i'th' gains:
　　　　　And now about the cauldron sing,
　　　　　Like elves and fairies in a ring,
　　　　　Enchanting all that you put in.

⌊ '*Music and a song: Black spirits, &c.*'　 *Hecate goes* ⌋

　2 *Witch.* By the pricking of my thumbs,
Something wicked this way comes:
Open, locks,
Whoever knocks!

　　　A door flies open, showing MACBETH *without*

　Macbeth [*enters*]. How now, you secret, black, and
　　midnight hags!
What is't you do?

All.   A deed without a name.

Macbeth. I conjure you, by that which you profess   50
(Howe'er you come to know it) answer me:
Though you untie the winds and let them fight
Against the churches; though the yesty waves
Confound and swallow navigation up;
Though bladed corn be lodged and trees blown
          down;
Though castles topple on their warders' heads;
Though palaces and pyramids do slope
Their heads to their foundations; though the treasure
Of Nature's germens tumble all together,
Even till destruction sicken; answer me   60
To what I ask you.

1 *Witch.*   Speak.

2 *Witch.*   Demand.

3 *Witch.*   We'll answer.

1 *Witch.* Say if th'hadst rather hear it from our
          mouths,
Or from our masters.

Macbeth.   Call 'em, let me see 'em!

1 *Witch.* Pour in sow's blood, that hath eaten
          Her nine farrow; grease that's sweaten
          From the murderer's gibbet throw
          Into the flame.

All.   Come, high or low;
          Thyself and office deftly show.

'*Thunder. First Apparition, an armed head*' *like
          Macbeth's, rises from the cauldron*

Macbeth. Tell me, thou unknown power—

1 *Witch.*   He knows thy thought:
Hear his speech, but say thou nought.   70

1 *Apparition.* Macbeth! Macbeth! Macbeth! beware
 Macduff,
Beware the thane of Fife. Dismiss me. Enough.

           ['*descends*'

Macbeth. Whate'er thou art, for thy good caution
 thanks;
Thou hast harped my fear aright. But one word more—
 1 *Witch.* He will not be commanded: here's another,
More potent than the first.

   '*Thunder. Second Apparition, a bloody child*'

2 *Apparition.* Macbeth! Macbeth! Macbeth!
Macbeth. Had I three ears, I'ld hear thee.
2 *Apparition.* Be bloody, bold, and resolute: laugh to
 scorn
80 The power of man; for none of woman born
Shall harm Macbeth.   ['*descends*'
 Macbeth. Then live, Macduff: what need I fear of
 thee?
But yet I'll make assurance double sure,
And take a bond of fate: thou shalt not live,
That I may tell pale-hearted fear it lies,
And sleep in spite of thunder.

  '*Thunder. Third Apparition, a child crowned, with
    a tree in his hand*'

          What is this,
That rises like the issue of a king,
And wears upon his baby-brow the round
And top of sovereignty?
 All.   Listen, but speak not to't.
90 3 *Apparition.* Be lion-mettled, proud, and take no care
Who chafes, who frets, or where conspirers are:
Macbeth shall never vanquished be until

Great Birnam wood to high Dunsinane hill
Shall come against him.   ['*descend*'
 Macbeth.   That will never be;
Who can impress the forest, bid the tree
Unfix his earth-bound root? Sweet bodements! good.
Rebellious dead, rise never, till the wood
Of Birnam rise, and our high-placed Macbeth
Shall live the lease of nature, pay his breath
To time and mortal custom. Yet my heart   100
Throbs to know one thing; tell me, if your art
Can tell so much: shall Banquo's issue ever
Reign in this kingdom?
 All.   Seek to know no more.
 Macbeth. I will be satisfied: deny me this,
And an eternal curse fall on you! Let me know....

     '*Hautboys*' *play as the cauldron descends*

Why sinks that cauldron? and what noise is this?
 1 *Witch*. Show!
 2 *Witch*. Show!
 3 *Witch*. Show!
 All. Show his eyes, and grieve his heart;   110
Come like shadows, so depart.

'*A show of eight kings*', *who pass one by one across the
back of the cavern as Macbeth speaks, the* '*last with a
glass in his hand*'; *Banquo's Ghost following*

 Macbeth. Thou art too like the spirit of Banquo:
     down!
Thy crown does sear mine eye-balls. And thy hair,
Thou other gold-bound brow, is like the first.
A third is like the former. Filthy hags!
Why do you show me this?—A fourth? Start, eyes!
What, will the line stretch out to th' crack of doom?

Another yet? A seventh? I'll see no more:
And yet the eighth appears, who bears a glass
120 Which shows me many more; and some I see
That two-fold balls and treble sceptres carry.
Horrible sight!....Now I see 'tis true,
For the blood-boltered Banquo smiles upon me,
And points at them for his. What, is this so?
[1 *Witch*. Ay, sir, all this is so. But why
Stands Macbeth thus amazedly?
Come, sisters, cheer we up his sprites,
And show the best of our delights.
I'll charm the air to give a sound,
130 While you perform your antic round:
That this great king may kindly say
[Our duties did his welcome pay.]

'*Music. The Witches dance, and vanish*'

Macbeth. Where are they? Gone? Let this per-
    nicious hour
Stand aye accursèd in the calendar
Come in, without there!

'*Enter* LENNOX'

Lennox.   What's your grace's will?
Macbeth. Saw you the Weïrd Sisters?
Lennox.   No, my lord.
Macbeth. Came they not by you?
Lennox.   No indeed, my lord.
Macbeth. Infected be the air whereon they ride,
And damned all those that trust them! I did hear
140 The galloping of horse. Who was't came by?
    Lennox. 'Tis two or three, my lord, that bring you
      word
Macduff is fled to England.

Macbeth.   Fled to England!

Lennox. Ay, my good lord.

(*Macbeth.* Time, thou anticipat'st my dread exploits:
The flighty purpose never is o'ertook
Unless the deed go with it. From this moment
The very firstlings of my heart shall be
The firstlings of my hand. And even now
To crown my thoughts with acts, be it thought and
    done:
The castle of Macduff I will surprise,   150
Seize upon Fife, give to th'edge o'th' sword
His wife, his babes, and all unfortunate souls
That trace him in his line. No boasting like a fool;
This deed I'll do before this purpose cool.
But no more sights! [*aloud*] Where are these gentlemen?
Come, bring me where they are.   [*they go*

[4. 2.]   *Fife. Macduff's castle*

'*Enter* MACDUFF'S *Wife, her Son, and* ROSS'

L. Macduff. What had he done, to make him fly the
    land?

Ross. You must have patience, madam.

L. Macduff.   He had none:
His flight was madness: when our actions do not,
Our fears do make us traitors.

Ross.   You know not
Whether it was his wisdom or his fear.

L. Macduff. Wisdom! to leave his wife, to leave his
    babes,
His mansion and his titles, in a place
From whence himself does fly? He loves us not;

He wants the natural touch: for the poor wren,
10 The most diminutive of birds, will fight,
Her young ones in her nest, against the owl.
All is the fear and nothing is the love;
As little is the wisdom, where the flight
So runs against all reason.

   Ross.   My dearest coz,
I pray you, school yourself. But, for your husband,
He is noble, wise, judicious, and best knows
The fits o'th' season. I dare not speak much further,
But cruel are the times, when we are traitors
And do not know ourselves; when we hold rumour
20 From what we fear, yet know not what we fear,
But float upon a wild and violent sea,
†Each way and none. I take my leave of you:
Shall not be long but I'll be here again:
Things at the worst will cease, or else climb upward
To what they were before. My pretty cousin,
Blessing upon you!

   L. Macduff. Fathered he is, and yet he's fatherless.
   Ross. I am so much a fool, should I stay longer
It would be my disgrace and your discomfort.
30 I take my leave at once.   [*he hurries forth*
   L. Macduff.   Sirrah, your father's dead,
And what will you do now? How will you live?
   Son. As birds do, mother.
   L. Macduff.   What, with worms and flies?
   Son. With what I get, I mean, and so do they.
   L. Macduff. Poor bird! thou'ldst never fear the net
     nor lime,
The pitfall nor the gin.
   Son. Why should I, mother? Poor birds they are not
     set for.
My father is not dead, for all your saying.

L. Macduff. Yes, he is dead: how wilt thou do for
　　a father?

Son. Nay, how will you do for a husband?

L. Macduff. Why, I can buy me twenty at any market. 40

Son. Then you'll buy 'em to sell again.

L. Macduff. Thou speak'st with all thy wit, and yet
　　i'faith

With wit enough for thee.

Son. Was my father a traitor, mother?

L. Macduff. Ay, that he was.

Son. What is a traitor?

L. Macduff. Why, one that swears and lies.

Son. And be all traitors that do so?

L. Macduff. Every one that does so is a traitor, and
　　must be hanged. 　　　　　　　　　　　　　　50

Son. And must they all be hanged that swear and lie?

L. Macduff. Every one.

Son. Who must hang them?

L. Macduff. Why, the honest men.

Son. Then the liars and swearers are fools; for there
are liars and swearers enow to beat the honest men
and hang up them.

L. Macduff. Now God help thee, poor monkey! But
how wilt thou do for a father?

Son. If he were dead, you'ld weep for him: if you 60
would not, it were a good sign that I should quickly
have a new father.

L. Macduff. Poor prattler, how thou talk'st!

'*Enter a* MESSENGER'

Messenger. Bless you, fair dame! I am not to you
　　known,

Though in your state of honour I am perfect.

I doubt some danger does approach you nearly.

If you will take a homely man's advice,
Be not found here; hence, with your little ones.
To fright you thus, methinks I am too savage;
70 To do worse to you were fell cruelty,
Which is too nigh your person. Heaven preserve you!
I dare abide no longer.   [*he goes*
    L. Macduff.   Whither should I fly?
I have done no harm. But I remember now
I am in this earthly world; where to do harm
Is often laudable, to do good sometime
Accounted dangerous folly: why then, alas,
Do I put up that womanly defence,
To say I have done no harm?

'*Enter* MURDERERS'

                   What are these faces?
    Murderer. Where is your husband?
80 *L. Macduff.* I hope in no place so unsanctified
Where such as thou mayst find him.
    Murderer.   He's a traitor.
    Son. Thou liest, thou †shag-haired villain.
    Murderer.   What, you egg!   [*stabs him*
Young fry of treachery!
    Son.   He has killed me, mother:
Run away, I pray you.   [*dies*

       [*Lady Macduff hurries forth* '*crying murder*',
          pursued by the Murderers

[4. 3.] *England. Before the palace of King Edward the
    Confessor.* MALCOLM *and* MACDUFF *come forth*

    Malcolm. Let us seek out some desolate shade, and
      there
Weep our sad bosoms empty.

Macduff.   Let us rather
Hold fast the mortal sword, and like good men
Bestride our down-fall'n birthdom: each new morn
New widows howl, new orphans cry, new sorrows
Strike heaven on the face, that it resounds
As if it felt with Scotland and yelled out
Like syllable of dolour.
   Malcolm.   What I believe, I'll wail;
What know, believe; and what I can redress,
As I shall find the time to friend, I will.   10
What you have spoke, it may be so perchance.
This tyrant, whose sole name blisters our tongues,
Was once thought honest: you have loved him well;
He hath not touched you yet. I am young, but some-
      thing
You may deserve of him through me; and wisdom
To offer up a weak, poor, innocent lamb,
T'appease an angry god.
   Macduff. I am not treacherous.
   Malcolm.   But Macbeth is.
A good and virtuous nature may recoil
In an imperial charge. But I shall crave your pardon; 20
That which you are, my thoughts cannot transpose:
Angels are bright still, though the brightest fell:
Though all things foul would wear the brows of
      grace,
Yet grace must still look so.
   Macduff.   I have lost my hopes.
   Malcolm. Perchance even there where I did find my
      doubts.
Why in that rawness left you wife and child,
Those precious motives, those strong knots of love,
Without leave-taking? I pray you,
Let not my jealousies be your dishonours,

30 But mine own safeties: you may be rightly just,
Whatever I shall think.

Macduff.   Bleed, bleed, poor country!
Great tyranny, lay thou thy basis sure,
For goodness dares not check thee: wear thou thy
          wrongs,
The title is affeered! Fare thee well, lord:
I would not be the villain that thou think'st
For the whole space that's in the tyrant's grasp,
And the rich East to boot.

Malcolm.   Be not offended:
I speak not as in absolute fear of you:
I think our country sinks beneath the yoke,
40 It weeps, it bleeds, and each new day a gash
Is added to her wounds. I think withal
There would be hands uplifted in my right;
And here from gracious England have I offer
Of goodly thousands. But for all this,
When I shall tread upon the tyrant's head,
Or wear it on my sword, yet my poor country
Shall have more vices than it had before,
More suffer and more sundry ways than ever,
By him that shall succeed.

Macduff.   What should he be?
50 *Malcolm.* It is myself I mean: in whom I know
All the particulars of vice so grafted
That, when they shall be opened, black Macbeth
Will seem as pure as snow, and the poor state
Esteem him as a lamb, being compared
With my confineless harms.

Macduff.   Not in the legions
Of horrid hell can come a devil more damned
In evils to top Macbeth.

Malcolm.   I grant him bloody,

Luxurious, avaricious, false, deceitful,
Sudden, malicious, smacking of every sin
That has a name: but there's no bottom, none,　60
In my voluptuousness: your wives, your daughters,
Your matrons and your maids, could not fill up
The cistern of my lust, and my desire
All continent impediments would o'erbear
That did oppose my will. Better Macbeth,
Than such an one to reign.

Macduff.　　　　　　　　Boundless intemperance
In nature is a tyranny; it hath been
Th'untimely emptying of the happy throne,
And fall of many kings. But fear not yet
To take upon you what is yours: you may　70
Convey your pleasures in a spacious plenty,
And yet seem cold, the time you may so hoodwink:
We have willing dames enough; there cannot be
That vulture in you, to devour so many
As will to greatness dedicate themselves,
Finding it so inclined.

Malcolm.　　　　　　　With this there grows
In my most ill-composed affection such
A stanchless avarice that, were I king,
I should cut off the nobles for their lands,
Desire his jewels and this other's house,　80
And my more-having would be as a sauce
To make me hunger more, that I should forge
Quarrels unjust against the good and loyal,
Destroying them for wealth.

Macduff.　　　　　　　　This avarice
Sticks deeper; grows with more pernicious root
Than summer-seeming lust: and it hath been
The sword of our slain kings: yet do not fear;
Scotland hath foisons to fill up your will

Of your mere own. All these are portable,
90 With other graces weighed.
 Malcolm. But I have none. The king-becoming
  graces,
 As justice, verity, temp'rance, stableness,
 Bounty, perseverance, mercy, lowliness,
 Devotion, patience, courage, fortitude,
 I have no relish of them, but abound
 In the division of each several crime,
 Acting it many ways. Nay, had I power, I should
 Pour the sweet milk of concord into hell,
 Uproot the universal peace, confound
100 All unity on earth.
 Macduff.   O Scotland! Scotland!
 Malcolm. If such a one be fit to govern, speak:
 I am as I have spoken.
 Macduff.   Fit to govern!
 No, not to live. O nation miserable!
 With an untitled tyrant bloody-sceptred,
 When shalt thou see thy wholesome days again,
 Since that the truest issue of thy throne
 By his own interdiction stands accurst,
 And does blaspheme his breed? Thy royal father
 Was a most sainted king; the queen that bore thee
110 Oft'ner upon her knees than on her feet,
 Died every day she lived. Fare thee well!
 These evils thou repeat'st upon thyself
 Hath banished me from Scotland. O my breast,
 Thy hope ends here!
 Malcolm.   Macduff, this noble passion,
 Child of integrity, hath from my soul
 Wiped the black scruples, reconciled my thoughts
 To thy good truth and honour. Devilish Macbeth
 By many of these trains hath sought to win me

Into his power; and modest wisdom plucks me
From over-credulous haste: but God above   120
Deal between thee and me! for even now
I put myself to thy direction, and
Unspeak mine own detraction; here abjure
The taints and blames I laid upon myself,
For strangers to my nature. I am yet
Unknown to woman, never was forsworn,
Scarcely have coveted what was mine own,
At no time broke my faith, would not betray
The devil to his fellow, and delight
No less in truth than life: my first false speaking   130
Was this upon myself: what I am truly
Is thine and my poor country's to command:
Whither indeed, before thy here-approach,
Old Siward, with ten thousand warlike men,
Already at a point, was setting forth:
Now we'll together, and the chance of goodness
Be like our warranted quarrel! Why are you silent?
 Macduff. Such welcome and unwelcome things at
  once
'Tis hard to reconcile.

   'A Doctor' comes from the palace

 Malcolm. Well, more anon. Comes the king forth,
  I pray you?   140
 Doctor. Ay, sir: there are a crew of wretched souls
That stay his cure: their malady convinces
The great assay of art; but at his touch,
Such sanctity hath heaven given his hand,
They presently amend.
 Malcolm. I thank you, doctor. [*the Doctor goes*
 Macduff. What's the disease he means?
 Malcolm.   'Tis called the evil:

A most miraculous work in this good king,
Which often, since my here-remain in England,
I have seen him do. How he solicits heaven,
150 Himself best knows: but strangely-visited people,
All swoln and ulcerous, pitiful to the eye,
The mere despair of surgery, he cures,
Hanging a golden stamp about their necks,
Put on with holy prayers: and 'tis spoken,
To the succeeding royalty he leaves
The healing benediction. With this strange virtue
He hath a heavenly gift of prophecy,
And sundry blessings hang about his throne
That speak him full of grace.

Ross approaches

 Macduff.   See who comes here.
160 *Malcolm.* My countryman; but yet I know him not.
 Macduff. My ever gentle cousin, welcome hither.
 Malcolm. I know him now: good God, betimes
  remove
The means that makes us strangers!
 Ross.   Sir, amen.
 Macduff. Stands Scotland where it did?
 Ross.   Alas, poor country,
Almost afraid to know itself! It cannot
Be called our mother, but our grave; where nothing,
But who knows nothing, is once seen to smile;
Where sighs and groans and shrieks that rend the
  air,
Are made, not marked; where violent sorrow seems
170 A modern ecstasy: the dead man's knell
Is there scarce asked for who, and good men's lives
Expire before the flowers in their caps,
Dying or ere they sicken.

Macduff.   O, relation
Too nice, and yet too true!
  Malcolm.   What's the newest grief?
  Ross. That of an hour's age doth hiss the speaker;
Each minute teems a new one.
  Macduff.   How does my wife?
  Ross. Why, well.
  Macduff.   And all my children?
  Ross.   Well too.
  Macduff. The tyrant has not battered at their peace?
  Ross. No, they were well at peace, when I did
    leave 'em.
  Macduff. Be not a niggard of your speech: how
    goes't?   180
  Ross. When I came hither to transport the tidings
Which I have heavily borne, there ran a rumour
Of many worthy fellows that were out;
Which was to my belief witnessed the rather,
For that I saw the tyrant's power a-foot.
Now is the time of help: your eye in Scotland
Would create soldiers, make our women fight,
To doff their dire distresses.
  Malcolm.   Be't their comfort
We are coming thither: gracious England hath
Lent us good Siward and ten thousand men;   190
An older and a better soldier none
That Christendom gives out.
  Ross.   Would I could answer
This comfort with the like! But I have words,
That would be howled out in the desert air,
Where hearing should not latch them.
  Macduff.   What concern they?
The general cause? or is it a fee-grief
Due to some single breast?

Ross.   No mind that's honest
But in it shares some woe, though the main part
Pertains to you alone.
　　Macduff.   If it be mine,
200 Keep it not from me, quickly let me have it.
　　Ross. Let not your ears despise my tongue for ever,
Which shall possess them with the heaviest sound
That ever yet they heard.
　　Macduff.   Humh! I guess at it.
　　Ross. Your castle is surprised; your wife and babes
Savagely slaughtered: to relate the manner,
Were, on the quarry of these murdered deer,
To add the death of you.
　　Malcolm.   Merciful heaven!
What, man! ne'er pull your hat upon your brows;
Give sorrow words: the grief that does not speak
210 Whispers the o'er-fraught heart and bids it break.
　　Macduff. My children too?
　　Ross.   Wife, children, servants, all
That could be found.
　　Macduff.   And I must be from thence!
My wife killed too?
　　Ross.   I have said.
　　Malcolm.   Be comforted:
Let's make us med'cines of our great revenge,
To cure this deadly grief.
　　Macduff. He has no children. All my pretty ones?
Did you say all? O, hell-kite! All?
What, all my pretty chickens and their dam
At one fell swoop?
220　*Malcolm.* Dispute it like a man.
　　Macduff.   I shall do so;
But I must also feel it as a man:
I cannot but remember such things were,

That were most precious to me. Did heaven look on,
And would not take their part? Sinful Macduff,
They were all struck for thee! naught that I am,
Not for their own demerits, but for mine,
Fell slaughter on their souls: heaven rest them now!
  Malcolm. Be this the whetstone of your sword:
    let grief
Convert to anger; blunt not the heart, enrage it.
  Macduff. O, I could play the woman with mine eyes, 230
And braggart with my tongue! But, gentle heavens,
Cut short all intermission; front to front
Bring thou this fiend of Scotland and myself;
Within my sword's length set him; if he 'scape,
Heaven forgive him too!
  Malcolm.   This tune goes manly.
Come, go we to the king, our power is ready,.
Our lack is nothing but our leave. Macbeth
Is ripe for shaking, and the Powers above
Put on their instruments. Receive what cheer you may;
The night is long that never finds the day.   [*they go* 240

[5. 1.] *Dunsinane. A room in the castle.* '*Enter a*
    Doctor of Physic, and a Waiting Gentlewoman'

  Doctor. I have two nights watched with you, but can
perceive no truth in your report. When was it she last
walked?

  Gentlewoman. Since his majesty went into the field,
I have seen her rise from her bed, throw her night-gown
upon her, unlock her closet, take forth paper, fold it,
write upon't, read it, afterwards seal it, and again return
to bed; yet all this while in a most fast sleep.

  Doctor. A great perturbation in nature, to receive at
once the benefit of sleep and do the effects of watching! 10

In this slumbry agitation, besides her walking and other actual performances, what, at any time, have you heard her say?

Gentlewoman. That, sir, which I will not report after her.

Doctor. You may to me, and 'tis most meet you should.

Gentlewoman. Neither to you nor any one, having no witness to confirm my speech.

'*Enter LADY*' MACBETH, '*with a taper*'

Lo you, here she comes! This is her very guise, and
20 upon my life fast asleep. Observe her, stand close.

Doctor. How came she by that light?

Gentlewoman. Why, it stood by her: she has light by her continually, 'tis her command.

Doctor. You see, her eyes are open.

Gentlewoman. Ay, but their sense are shut.

Doctor. What is it she does now? Look, how she rubs her hands.

Gentlewoman. It is an accustomed action with her, to seem thus washing her hands: I have known her
30 continue in this a quarter of an hour.

Lady M. Yet here's a spot.

Doctor. Hark, she speaks! I will set down what comes from her, to satisfy my remembrance the more strongly.

Lady M. Out, damnéd spot! out, I say! One: two: why, then 'tis time to do't. Hell is murky! Fie, my lord, fie! a soldier, and afeard? What need we fear who knows it, when none can call our power to accompt? Yet who would have thought the old man to have had so much blood in him?

40 *Doctor.* Do you mark that?

Lady M. The Thane of Fife had a wife; where is she now? What, will these hands ne'er be clean? No more o'that, my lord, no more o'that: you mar all with this starting.

Doctor. Go to, go to; you have known what you should not.

Gentlewoman. She has spoke what she should not, I am sure of that: heaven knows what she has known.

Lady M. Here's the smell of the blood still: all the perfumes of Arabia will not sweeten this little hand. 50 Oh! oh! oh!

Doctor. What a sigh is there! The heart is sorely charged.

Gentlewoman. I would not have such a heart in my bosom, for the dignity of the whole body.

Doctor. Well, well, well,—

Gentlewoman. Pray God it be, sir.

Doctor. This disease is beyond my practice: yet I have known those which have walked in their sleep who have died holily in their beds.   6c

Lady M. Wash your hands, put on your night-gown, look not so pale: I tell you yet again, Banquo's buried; he cannot come out on's grave.

Doctor. Even so?

Lady M. To bed, to bed: there's knocking at the gate: come, come, come, come, give me your hand: what's done, cannot be undone: to bed, to bed, to bed.

[*she goes out*

Doctor. Will she go now to bed?

Gentlewoman. Directly.

Doctor. Foul whisp'rings are abroad: unnatural deeds 70 Do breed unnatural troubles: infected minds To their deaf pillows will discharge their secrets: More needs she the divine than the physician: God, God forgive us all! Look after her, Remove from her the means of all annoyance,

And still keep eyes upon her. So, good night:
My mind she has mated and amazed my sight:
I think, but dare not speak.

 Gentlewoman.   Good night, good doctor.

                 [they go

[5. 2.] *The country near Dunsinane.* 'Drum and
Colours. Enter MENTEITH, CAITHNESS, ANGUS, LENNOX,
Soldiers'

 Menteith. The English power is near, led on by
   Malcolm,
His uncle Siward and the good Macduff.
Revenges burn in them: for their dear causes
Would to the bleeding and the grim alarm
Excite the mortified man.

 Angus.   Near Birnam wood
Shall we well meet them, that way are they coming.

 Caithness. Who knows if Donalbain be with his
   brother?

 Lennox. For certain, sir, he is not: I have a file
Of all the gentry: there is Siward's son,

10 And many unrough youths, that even now
Protest their first of manhood.

 Menteith.   What does the tyrant?

 Caithness. Great Dunsinane he strongly fortifies:
Some say he's mad; others, that lesser hate him,
Do call it valiant fury: but, for certain,
He cannot buckle his distempered cause
Within the belt of rule.

 Angus.   Now does he feel
His secret murders sticking on his hands;
Now minutely revolts upbraid his faith-breach;
Those he commands move only in command,

Nothing in love: now does he feel his title   20
Hang loose about him, like a giant's robe
Upon a dwarfish thief.

  Menteith.   Who then shall blame
His pestered senses to recoil and start,
When all that is within him does condemn
Itself for being there?

  Caithness.   Well, march we on,
To give obedience where 'tis truly owed:
Meet we the med'cine of the sickly weal,
And with him pour we, in our country's purge,
Each drop of us.

  Lennox.   Or so much as it needs
To dew the sovereign flower and drown the weeds.   30
Make we our march towards Birnam.

                            ['*exeunt, marching*'

[5. 3.] *Dunsinane. A court in the castle.* '*Enter*
     MACBETH, Doctor, and Attendants'

  Macbeth. Bring me no more reports, let them fly all:
Till Birnam wood remove to Dunsinane
I cannot taint with fear. What's the boy Malcolm?
Was he not born of woman? The spirits that know
All mortal consequence have pronounced me thus:
'Fear not, Macbeth, no man that's born of woman
Shall e'er have power upon thee'. Then fly, false thanes,
And mingle with the English epicures:
The mind I sway by and the heart I bear
Shall never sag with doubt nor shake with fear.   10

           A '*servant*' *enters*

The devil damn thee black, thou cream-faced loon!
Where got'st thou that goose look?

Servant. There is ten thousand—

Macbeth.   Geese, villain?

Servant.   Soldiers, sir.

Macbeth. Go prick thy face and over-red thy fear,
Thou lily-livered boy. What soldiers, patch?
Death of thy soul! those linen cheeks of thine
Are counsellors to fear. What soldiers, whey-face?

Servant. The English force, so please you.

Macbeth. Take thy face hence.   [*servant goes*

      Seton!— [*brooding*] I am sick at heart,
20 When I behold—Seton, I say!—This push
Will cheer me ever, or disseat me now.
I have lived long enough: my way of life
Is fall'n into the sere, the yellow leaf,
And that which should accompany old age,
As honour, love, obedience, troops of friends,
I must not look to have; but, in their stead,
Curses, not loud but deep, mouth-honour, breath
Which the poor heart would fain deny and dare not.
Seton!

     SETON enters

30 *Seton.* What's your gracious pleasure?

Macbeth.   What news more?

Seton. All is confirmed, my lord, which was
 reported.

Macbeth. I'll fight, till from my bones my flesh be
 hacked.
Give me my armour.

Seton.   'Tis not needed yet.

Macbeth. I'll put it on.
Send out moe horses, skirr the country round,
Hang those that talk of fear. Give me mine armour....

      [*Seton goes to fetch it*
How does your patient, doctor?

Doctor.   Not so sick, my lord,
As she is troubled with thick-coming fancies,
That keep her from her rest.
  Macbeth.   Cure her of that:
Canst thou not minister to a mind diseased,   40
Pluck from the memory a rooted sorrow,
Raze out the written troubles of the brain,
And with some sweet oblivious antidote
†Cleanse the stuffed bosom of that perilous stuff
Which weighs upon the heart?
  Doctor.   Therein the patient
Must minister to himself.

*Seton returns with armour and an armourer, who
presently begins to equip Macbeth*

  Macbeth. Throw physic to the dogs, I'll none of it.
Come, put mine armour on; give me my staff;
Seton, send out; doctor, the thanes fly from me;
Come, sir, dispatch.—If thou couldst, doctor, cast   50
The water of my land, find her disease,
And purge it to a sound and pristine health,
I would applaud thee to the very echo,
That should applaud again.—Pull't off, I say.—
What rhubarb, senna, or what purgative drug,
Would scour these English hence? Hear'st thou
    of them?
  Doctor. Ay, my good lord; your royal preparation
Makes us hear something.
  Macbeth.   Bring it after me.
I will not be afraid of death and bane
Till Birnam forest come to Dunsinane.   60
          [he goes; Seton follows with armourer
  Doctor. Were I from Dunsinane away and clear,
Profit again should hardly draw me here.   *[he goes*

[5. 4.] *Country near Birnam.* '*Drum and Colours.*
Enter MALCOLM, SIWARD, MACDUFF, SIWARD'S *Son*,
MENTEITH, CAITHNESS, ANGUS', LENNOX, ROSS, '*and*
Soldiers, marching'

Malcolm. Cousins, I hope, the days are near at hand
That chambers will be safe.

Menteith.   We doubt it nothing.

Siward. What wood is this before us?

Menteith.   The wood of Birnam.

Malcolm. Let every soldier hew him down a bough,
And bear't before him: thereby shall we shadow
The numbers of our host, and make discovery
Err in report of us.

Soldier.   It shall be done.

Siward. We learn no other but the confident tyrant
Keeps still in Dunsinane, and will endure
10 Our setting down before't.

Malcolm.   'Tis his main hope:
For where there is advantage to be gone,
Both more and less have given him the revolt,
And none serve with him but constrainéd things
Whose hearts are absent too.

Macduff.   Let our just censures
Attend the true event, and put we on
Industrious soldiership.

Siward.   The time approaches,
That will with due decision make us know
What we shall say we have and what we owe.
Thoughts speculative their unsure hopes relate,
20 But certain issue strokes must arbitrate:
Towards which advance the war.

                              ['*exeunt, marching*'

[5. 5.] *Dunsinane. The court of the castle as before.*
‘Enter MACBETH, SETON, *and Soldiers with Drum*
and Colours’

Macbeth. Hang out our banners on the outward walls;
The cry is still ‘They come’: our castle’s strength
Will laugh a siege to scorn: here let them lie
Till famine and the ague eat them up:
Were they not forced with those that should be ours,
We might have met them dareful, beard to beard,
And beat them backward home.

                              [‘*a cry within of women*’
                                   What is that noise?
Seton. It is the cry of women, my good lord.   [*goes*
(*Macbeth.* I have almost forgot the taste of fears:
The time has been, my senses would have cooled   10
To hear a night-shriek, and my fell of hair
Would at a dismal treatise rouse and stir
As life were in’t: I have supped full with horrors;
Direness, familiar to my slaughterous thoughts,
Cannot once start me.

                     SETON *returns*

                     Wherefore was that cry?
Seton. The queen, my lord, is dead.
Macbeth. She should have died hereafter;
There would have been a time for such a word.
To-morrow, and to-morrow, and to-morrow,
Creeps in this petty pace from day to day,   20
To the last syllable of recorded time;
And all our yesterdays have lighted fools
The way to dusty death. Out, out, brief candle!
Life’s but a walking shadow, a poor player
That struts and frets his hour upon the stage,

And then is heard no more: it is a tale.
Told by an idiot, full of sound and fury,
Signifying nothing.

'Enter a messenger'

Thou com'st to use thy tongue; thy story quickly.
30 *Messenger.* Gracious my lord,
I should report that which I say I saw,
But know not how to do't.
     Macbeth.   Well, say, sir.
     Messenger. As I did stand my watch upon the hill,
I looked toward Birnam, and anon methought
The wood began to move.
     Macbeth.   Liar and slave!
     Messenger. Let me endure your wrath, if't be not so:
Within this three mile may you see it coming.
I say, a moving grove.
     Macbeth.   If thou speak'st false,
Upon the next tree shalt thou hang alive,
40 Till famine cling thee: if thy speech be sooth,
I care not if thou dost for me as much.
†I pall in resolution, and begin
To doubt th'equivocation of the fiend
That lies like truth: 'Fear not, till Birnam wood
Do come to Dunsinane'; and now a wood
Comes toward Dunsinane. Arm, arm, and out!
If this which he avouches does appear,
There is nor flying hence nor tarrying here.
I 'gin to be aweary of the sun,
50 And wish th'estate o'th' world were now undone.
Ring the alarum bell! Blow, wind! come, wrack!
At least we'll die with harness on our back.
                              [they hurry forth

[5. 6.] *Dunsinane. Before the castle gate.* '*Drum and Colours. Enter* MALCOLM, SIWARD, MACDUFF, *and their army, with boughs*'

Malcolm. Now near enough: your leavy screens throw
    down,
And show like those you are. You, worthy uncle,
Shall with my cousin your right noble son
Lead our first battle: worthy Macduff and we
Shall take upon's what else remains to do,
According to our order.
Siward.   Fare you well.
Do we but find the tyrant's power to-night,
Let us be beaten, if we cannot fight.
Macduff. Make all our trumpets speak; give them all
    breath,
Those clamorous harbingers of blood and death.   10

     They go forward, their trumpets sounding.

[5. 7.]   *MACBETH comes from the castle*

Macbeth. They have tied me to a stake; I cannot fly,
But bear-like I must fight the course. What's he
That was not born of woman? Such a one
Am I to fear, or none.

       Young SIWARD *comes up*

Young Siward. What is thy name?
Macbeth.   Thou'lt be afraid to hear it.
Young Siward. No; though thou call'st thyself a
    hotter name
Than any is in hell.

Macbeth.   My name's Macbeth.

Young Siward. The devil himself could not pronounce a title

More hateful to mine ear.

Macbeth.   No, nor more fearful.

10 *Young Siward.* Thou liest, abhorréd tyrant, with my
sword

I'll prove the lie thou speak'st.

        [*they 'fight, and young Siward' is 'slain'*

Macbeth.   Thou wast born of woman.

But swords I smile at, weapons laugh to scorn,
Brandished by man that's of a woman born.

*He passes on and presently a sound of more fighting
is heard. MACDUFF comes up*

Macduff. That way the noise is. Tyrant, show thy
face!

If thou beest slain and with no stroke of mine,
My wife and children's ghosts will haunt me still.
I cannot strike at wretched kerns, whose arms
Are hired to bear their staves; either thou, Macbeth,
Or else my sword with an unbattered edge

20 I sheathe again undeeded. There thou shouldst be;
By this great clatter, one of greatest note
Seems bruited. Let me find him, fortune!
And more I beg not. [*he follows Macbeth. 'Alarums'*

MALCOLM and old SIWARD come up

Siward. This way, my lord; the castle's gently
rendered:

The tyrant's people on both sides do fight,
The noble thanes do bravely in the war,
The day almost itself professes yours,
And little is to do.

Malcolm.   We have met with foes
That strike beside us.
    Siward.   Enter, sir, the castle
                 [*they pass in at the gate.* '*Alarum*'

[5. 8.]   *MACBETH returns*

  Macbeth. Why should I play the Roman fool, and die
On mine own sword? whiles I see lives, the gashes
Do better upon them.

     MACDUFF returns, following him

  Macduff.   Turn, hell-hound, turn.
  Macbeth. Of all men else I have avoided thee:
But get thee back, my soul is too much charged
With blood of thine already.
    Macduff.   I have no words:
My voice is in my sword, thou bloodier villain
Than terms can give thee out! [*they* '*fight*'. '*Alarum*'
    Macbeth.   Thou losest labour.
As easy mayst thou the intrenchant air
With thy keen sword impress as make me bleed: 10
Let fall thy blade on vulnerable crests,
I bear a charméd life, which must not yield
To one of woman born.
    Macduff.   Despair thy charm,
And let the angel whom thou still hast served
Tell thee, Macduff was from his mother's womb
Untimely ripped.
  Macbeth. Acccurséd be that tongue that tells
      me so,
For it hath cowed my better part of man!
And be these juggling fiends no more believed,
That palter with us in a double sense,   20

That keep the word of promise to our ear,
And break it to our hope. I'll not fight with thee.
  Macduff. Then yield thee, coward,
And live to be the show and gaze o'th' time.
We'll have thee, as our rarer monsters are,
Painted upon a pole, and underwrit,
'Here may you see the tyrant'.
  Macbeth.   I will not yield,
To kiss the ground before young Malcolm's feet,
And to be baited with the rabble's curse.
30 Though Birnam wood be come to Dunsinane,
And thou opposed, being of no woman born,
Yet I will try the last. Before my body
I throw my warlike shield: lay on, Macduff,
And damned be him that first cries 'Hold, enough'.
      [*they fight to and fro beneath the castle wall,
        until at length* '*Macbeth*' *is* '*slain*'

[5. 9.]   *Within the castle.*

'*Retreat and flourish. Enter, with Drum and Colours,*
  MALCOLM, SIWARD, ROSS, *Thanes and Soldiers*'

  Malcolm. I would the friends we miss were safe
    arrived.
  Siward. Some must go off: and yet, by these I see,
So great a day as this is cheaply bought.
  Malcolm. Macduff is missing, and your noble son.
  Ross. Your son, my lord, has paid a soldier's debt:
40 He only lived but till he was a man,
The which no sooner had his prowess confirmed
In the unshrinking station where he fought,
But like a man he died.
  Siward.   Then he is dead?

Ross. Ay, and brought off the field: your cause of
    sorrow
Must not be measured by his worth, for then
It hath no end.

Siward.   Had he his hurts before?

Ross. Ay, on the front.

Siward.   Why then, God's soldier be he!
Had I as many sons as I have hairs,
I would not wish them to a fairer death:
And so his knell is knolled.

Malcolm.   He's worth more sorrow, 50
And that I'll spend for him.

Siward.   He's worth no more.
They say he parted well and paid his score:
And so God be with him! Here comes newer comfort.

     '*Enter* MACDUFF, *with* MACBETH'S *head*'
               on a pole

Macduff. Hail, king! for so thou art. Behold, where
    stands
Th'usurper's curséd head: the time is free:
I see thee compassed with thy kingdom's pearl,
That speak my salutation in their minds;
Whose voices I desire aloud with mine:
Hail, king of Scotland!

All.   Hail, king of Scotland! ['*flourish*'

Malcolm. We shall not spend a large expense of time 60
Before we reckon with your several loves,
And make us even with you. My thanes and kinsmen,
Henceforth be earls, the first that ever Scotland
In such an honour named. What's more to do,
Which would be planted newly with the time,
As calling home our exiled friends abroad
That fled the snares of watchful tyranny,

Producing forth the cruel ministers
Of this dead butcher and his fiend-like queen,
70 Who, as 'tis thought, by self and violent hands
Took off her life; this, and what needful else
That calls upon us, by the grace of Grace
We will perform in measure, time, and place:
So thanks to all at once, and to each one,
Whom we invite to see us crowned at Scone.

[*flourish*]. *They march away*

THE COPY FOR *MACBETH*, 1623

'One of the worst printed of all the plays'[1] is the verdict of the Cambridge editors of 1865 on the F. *Macbeth*; and, enlarging upon this in their 'Clarendon' text seven years later, they observe that it was probably 'printed from a transcript of the author's MS., which was in great part not copied from the original but written to dictation';[2] while in both editions they insist upon the irregularity of the verse lineation. Modern experts are less pessimistic. '*Macbeth* is doubtless printed from a prompt-copy'[3] declared Sir Edmund Chambers in 1930. Dr Greg, expanding this in 1942, notes that 'the directions are normal and reveal the hand of the book-keeper though some probably originated with the author'.[4] Expanding it still further, I would add that, as we have two authors to deal with in *Macbeth*,[5] the F. stage-directions, while basically Shakespeare's, are likely to contain additions and alterations by Middleton, together with some by the book-keeper, who had of course the final word. A couple of duplicated directions are illuminating in this connexion. At 2. 3. 80, it seems pretty clear that the author, here probably Shakespeare, wrote 'Bell rings. Enter Lady', that the prompter added 'Ring the Bell' on his own account in the margin, and that these three words, happening to stand opposite to half a line of verse at the end of Macduff's speech, were taken by the F. compositor as completing the line and set up accordingly. In 3. 5 again F. reads *Musicke and a Song*

[1] *Cambridge Shakespeare*, ed. by W. G. Clark and W. Aldis Wright, VII, p. viii.

[2] *Macbeth*, 'Clarendon Shakespeare', p. v.

[3] *William Shakespeare*, i, 471.

[4] *The Editorial Problem in Shakespeare*, p. 147.

[5] See pp. xxii–xlii above.

at l. 33 and *Sing Within. Come away, come away, &c.* at l. 35, where the directions are obviously alternative, one being the prompter's. And, since scene 3. 5 is an interpolation by Middleton, this duplication is evidence that the prompter went through the MS. after Middleton had finished with it. An interesting direction standing at the beginning of Middleton's addition in 4. 1 and I think to be credited to him, is *Enter Hecat, and the other three Witches*, which F. prints at l. 38 and which, as W. J. Lawrence points out, almost certainly implies a dance of six witches such as we find in the cauldron scene of *The Witch*.[1] Directions, again, that cannot be Shakespeare's, but might belong to either of the other two scribes, are the absurd *Hoboyes and Torches* at the head of 1. 6, the one sunlit scene of the play, and, at 4. 1. 111, *A Shew of eight Kings, and Banquo last, with a glasse in his hand*, which runs counter to l. 119 of the text. Lastly, the double F. direction at 5. 8. 34:

> *Exeunt fighting. Alarums.*
> *Enter Fighting, and Macbeth slaine.*

which has been cited by most editors, including myself,[2] as marking the end of the play in an alternative and shorter version, merely provides, as I show in the Notes, for a prolonged contest between two skilled stage-swordsmen, culminating in the death of the tyrant in full view of the audience.

A prompt-book, with a second dramatist intervening between Shakespeare and the book-keeper, is not likely to retain many traces of Shakespeare's original MS., such as we often seem to catch sight of in the spellings, misprints, speech-headings, etc., of the 'good' quarto or

---

[1] Lawrence, *Shakespeare's Workshop*, p. 38. See above, p. xxvii and note 4. 1. 38 below.

[2] v. Introd. to *Macbeth* ('Folio Facsimiles'), based upon the findings of previous editors.

folio texts. And in point of fact I have not found more than one probable example.[1] Yet, though the Cambridge editors are almost certainly correct in diagnosing a transcript, for their theory of dictation I can see no evidence whatever.[2] They speak of 'blunders of the ear and not of the eye', but give no examples. A number of errors, it is true, seem more likely to be due to a transcriber than a compositor, four obvious cases of which are: 1. 2. 13 Gallowgrosses (for 'gallowglasses': F 2); 1. 2. 14 quarry (for 'quarrel': Hanmer); 1. 3. 97–8 tale Can (for 'hail Came': Rowe); 4. 1. 97 Rebellious dead (for 'Rebellion's head': Theobald). But mistakes of this kind, a kind of which the F. *Hamlet* provides not a few instances, are best explained as the blunders of actors which have been inadvertently reproduced by a scribe familiar with the play on the stage.[3] Indeed, relying upon this explanation, I have not hesitated to follow the Cambridge editors in accepting all the four emendations printed in brackets, though every F. reading has of course found its last-ditch defender. Incidentally, since on the evidence of F. *Hamlet*, such a theatre scrivener as I postulate, or the actor whose tricks he reproduces, will be particularly prone to anticipations or repetitions,[4] I strongly suspect the famous corruption in 5. 3. 44—

> Cleanse the stuffed bosom of that perilous stuff—

is due to him, while it is possible that the seeming tautology in 3. 2. 50–1,

> ...the crow
> Makes wing to th' rooky wood,

should be set down to an actor's account also.

---

[1] v. Note 1. 4. 1—an *a:o* error.

[2] Except perhaps at 3. 3. 7.

[3] v. *Manuscript of Shakespeare's 'Hamlet'*, App. C (v) (3) and (4) and p. 64.

[4] *Ibid.* p. 55.

All this means that I take the copy for F. *Macbeth* to have been, not the prompt-book as Chambers and Greg assume, but a transcript therefrom, probably made for the printers in 1622 or 1623. It means also, if we may argue again from the F. *Hamlet*, that *Macbeth*, printed from a transcript of a transcript, itself contaminated by Middleton, must contain a pretty large number of departures from Shakespeare's original.[1] Most of these were, no doubt, trivial variants or small vulgarisations, though others, such as the (to my mind) obvious instances just cited, would be serious. Yet we are never likely to know the extent of the damage, and with editors, as with other folk, ignorance is bliss. Thus my obelisks are happily few, and I think we heirs of Shakespeare should congratulate ourselves that matters are not much worse. We may suspect a little roughness or discoloration here and there as we peer through our microscopes, but put them away and stand back, as we should in looking at a masterpiece intended for the theatre, and the play overwhelms us with its stupendous perfection. In any case, the verdict of the Cambridge editors, cited at the outset of this note, seems entirely unwarranted.

What clearly troubled them most of all was the mis-division of the verse, and much of this should undoubtedly be laid at the door of scribal transmission. But (i) not only is it most evident in the second scene, as one might expect, but it grows noticeably less as the play goes forward, so that the process of abridgement which probably affected the first half most, and in which Shakespeare was involved, no doubt accounts for it in part; and (ii) the F. compositors must take their share also since they have obviously been monkeying with the verse-lining at places, as in other F. texts, in order

---

[1] *The Manuscript of Shakespeare's 'Hamlet'*, § XVII.

to fill up their columns.[1] On the other hand, the F. spacing-out seems at times to be dramatically significant, i.e. to come from the prompt-book, where it warns the actor to break off, it may be for some action, it may be for a dramatic pause of considerable length; in which case it becomes a form of punctuation.[2]

And that F. was set up from a transcript of good acting copy seems to be shown by the punctuation proper, which, though hardly likely to be Shakespeare's own, may be based on his, and is in any case very fair of its kind. The copy must have been fully, even perhaps over-fully, pointed, though the compositor goes astray in not a few instances, sometimes because he is confused by a word in his copy, as he was at 1. 6. 8–9. This punctuation is not, of course, modern, but rhythmical and dramatic, and needs to be interpreted, as with Mr Percy Simpson's help it generally can be.[3]

It may be noted here that F 1 (1623) was not only followed by F 2 (1632) and F 3 (1664) but by a Q (1673), which is in the main (cf. note 3. 5. 33, S.D.) a reprint of the F 3 text and is quite distinct from D'Avenant's version of 1674, described on p. lxxiii.

---

[1] E.g. the last 10 ll. of 2. 2 are printed as 14 ll. in F. probably because the compositor miscalculated the space required for the prose in 2. 3.

[2] Cf. Simpson, *Shakespearian Punctuation,* pp. 69–70; note 3. 4. 48 below, and the broken line, 1. 5. 60.

[3] See notes 1. 2. 57; 1. 7. 5; 2. 2. 63; 3. 1. 105, 133.

NOTES

All significant departures from F. are recorded; the name of the text or edition in which the accepted reading first appeared being placed in brackets. Square brackets about an author's name denote a general acknowledgement; round brackets mean that his actual words are quoted. Line-numeration for references to plays not yet issued in this edition is that found in Bartlett's *Concordance* and the *Globe Shakespeare*.

F. stands for the First Folio (1623); G. for Glossary; O.E.D. for the *Oxford English Dictionary*; S.D. for stage-direction; Sh. for Shakespeare and Shakespearian; Hol. for Holinshed; common words (e.g. prob. = probably), together with names of characters and well-known editors, are also abbreviated where convenient.

The following is a list of other books cited with abridged titles: Adams = *The Globe Playhouse* by J. C. Adams, 1943; Apperson = *English Proverbs and Proverbial Phrases* by G. L. Apperson, 1929; *Bas. Dor.* = *Basilikon Doron* by James I, 1599 (cited from *The Political Works of James I* by C. H. McIlwain, 1918); Boece = Hector Boece, *Chroniklis of Scotland* trans. by John Bellenden (cited from reprint of 1821); Bradley = *Shakespearean Tragedy* by A. C. Bradley, 1904; Camb. = *The Cambridge Sh.* ed. by Aldis Wright, 1891; Cap. = the ed. of Edward Capell, 1768; Chambers, *Eliz. St.* = *The Elizabethan Stage* by E. K. Chambers, 1923; Chambers, *Wm. Sh.* = *William Shakespeare: a Study of Facts and Problems* by E. K. Chambers, 1930; Clar. = the ed. of W. G. Clark and Aldis Wright (The Clarendon Sh.), 1872; Coleridge = *Coleridge's Shakespearean Criticism* ed. by T. M. Raysor, 1930; Craig = *Sh.: A Historical and Critical Study of Twenty-one Plays* by Hardin Craig,

1931; Cunliffe = *Influence of Seneca on Eliz. Tragedy* by J. W. Cunliffe, 1893; Curry = *Sh.'s Philosophical Patterns* by W. C. Curry, 1937; D*æm.* = D*æmonologie* by James I, 1597 (cited from rep. by G. B. Harrison, 'Bodley Quartos', 1924); Darm. = ed. by James Darmesteter, Paris, 1887; Dav. = D'Avenant's *Macbeth*, 1674 (cited from rep. in Furness, q.v.); Draper = '*Macbeth* as a compliment to James I' by J. W. Draper (*Englische Studien*, 72 Bd, 207–20); E.K.C. = ed. by E. K. Chambers, 1893 (*Warwick Sh.*); Fordun = Fordun's *Chronicle of the Scottish Nation* (trans., ed. W. F. Skene, 1872); Franz = *Die Sprache Shakespeares* (4th ed.) by W. Franz, 1939; French = *Shakespeareana Genealogica* by G. R. French, 1869; Furness = the ed. by H. H. Furness, 1873 (New Variorum); Gr. = the ed. by H. J. C. Grierson and J. C. Smith, Oxford, 1914; Greg = *The Editorial Problem in Sh.* by W. W. Greg, 1942; Harington = *Nugae Antiquae* by Sir John Harington, ed. T. Park, 1804; Hol. = *The Scottish Chronicle* by Raphael Holinshed (rep. in 2 vols. 1805 from *The Chronicles of England, Scotland, and Ireland*, 1577); J. = the ed. by Samuel Johnson, 1765; Jonson = *Ben Jonson* ed. by C. H. Herford and Percy Simpson, 1925; K. = the ed. by G. L. Kittredge, 1939; K. *Witchcraft* = *Witchcraft in Old and New England* by G. L. Kittredge, 1929; James I, see *Bas. Dor.* and *Dæm.*; Lawrence, see *Pre-R. Stud.* and *Sh.'s Work.*; McKerrow = *The Works of Nashe*, ed. R. B. McKerrow, 1904–10; McIlwain = *The Political Works of James I*, ed. by C. H. McIlwain, 1918; Madden = *Diary of M. William Silence* by D. H. Madden, 1907; Mal. = ed. by Malone and Boswell, 1821; Masefield = *A 'Macbeth' Production* by John Masefield, 1945; Middleton = *Works of Thomas Middleton* ed. by A. H. Bullen, 1885–6; Moulton = *Sh. as a Dramatic Artist* by R. G. Moulton, 1901; MSH = *The Manuscript of Sh.'s 'Hamlet'* by J. Dover

Wilson, 1934; *Newes* = *Newes from Scotland*, 1591 (cited from repr. by G. B. Harrison, 'Bodley Head Quartos', 1924); *Pre-R. Stud.* = *Pre-Restoration Stage Studies* by W. J. Lawrence, 1927; *R.E.S.* = *The Review of English Studies*; Ridley = the ed. by M. R. Ridley in *The New Temple Sh.*; Schmidt = *Sh.-Lexicon* by A. Schmidt (3rd ed.), 1902; Scot = *The Discoverie of Witchcraft* by Reginald Scot, 1584; *Sh. Eng.* = *Sh.'s England*, Oxford, 1917; *Sh.'s Work.* = *Sh.'s Workshop* by W. J. Lawrence, 1928; Simpson = *Sh.'s Punctuation* by Percy Simpson, 1911; Spalding = *Eliz. Demonology* by T. A. Spalding, 1880; Sprague = *Sh. and the Actors* by A. C. Sprague, 1944; Spurgeon = *Sh.'s Imagery* by C. Spurgeon, 1925; Steev. = the ed. by George Steevens, 1773; Stewart = *The Buik of the Croniclis of Scotland* by William Stewart (ed. by W. B. Turnbull, Rolls Series, 1858); Stoll = *Sh. Studies* by E. E. Stoll, 1927; Theo. = the ed. by Lewis Theobald, 1734; Tieck = *Sh.s dramatische Werke* v. Schlegel und Tieck, 1839; Ver. = the ed. by A. W. Verity, 1901.

Names of the Characters. List first given by Rowe. Most names were taken by Sh. from Hol. and have since been modernised by edd. For *Seton* see note 5. 3. 29 S.D. *Lady Macbeth* is given no name in Hol., Boece or Stewart; she is Gruock in Wyntoun and Gruach in Hailes's *Annals of Scotland*, 1779, ii, 332.

Acts and Scenes. Divided throughout in F., which is followed by most edd. except for 5. 8, first introduced by Pope. I follow Pope also and begin a ninth scene at 5. 8. 34 (see note). *Punctuation.* See p. 91.

Stage-directions. See pp. 87–8. I only cite those in F. which call for special comment. For the rest see my facsimile of the text (Faber's 'Folio Facsimiles').

Lineation. See pp. 87, 90–1. I have generally followed the verse-division of the *Cambridge Sh.* It would have overweighted the Notes to record F. variants.

I. I.

S.D. F. 'Thunder and Lightning. Enter three Witches.' Camb. locates in 'A desert place'. Locality best undefined; 'at or near hell-gate' is what the contemp. staging suggested, with its 'thunder and lightning' (which concealed the noise of the trap), its evil creatures springing from the 'cellarage' beneath, the eerie cries of the familiars 'off', and the 'fog and filthy air' with which the scene closes and into which the creatures melt 'as breath into the wind' (1. 3. 82). Cf. note l. 12 below; Adams, 114, 120–3; *Pre-R. Stud.* 130, 139. The three beings are also undefined. Sh. calls them 'Weird Sisters' throughout; they are 'witches' only in the S.Ds. Cf. Introd. pp. xix–xxii.

1. *again* (Hanmer) F. 'againe?'. The uncertain pointing and careless distribution of speeches in this scene suggest hasty transcription.

2. *In thunder...rain?* 'Witches and demons were supposed to be particularly active in boisterous weather ...often thought to be caused by their spells' (K.). Cf. 1. 3. 10–25, 4. 1. 52–8.

8–10. *I come...Anon!* Answers to their attendant demons, who cry with the scream of a cat, the croak of a toad, and some third voice belonging to the spirit called 'Harpier' or 'Harpy' at 4. 1. 3; v. G. 'Graymalkin', 'Paddock'. The cat-familiar in Middleton's *Witch* (3. 3. 62) is called 'Malkin'. Cf. Introd. p. xxvii.

9–12. *Paddock...air* (Hunter) F. prints 'Padock calls anon: faire...faire,/Houer...ayre' and assigns to '*All*' which 'can scarcely be right either in distribution or punctuation' (Clar.). The sisters, hitherto speaking in turn, will naturally answer their spirits in turn. F. uses numeral prefixes (1, 2, 3), which might easily get displaced.

11. *Fair*...*fair* Cf. Satan's 'Evil, be thou my good', *Par. Lost*, iv, 110 [Ver.].

12. *Hover* Rowe 'They rise from the stage and fly away' [S.D.]; but *Macbeth* is hardly late enough for free levitation, of which Ariel in *The Tempest* is prob. earliest example at Globe (v. Adams, 338–9). No doubt they left by trap, after vanishing first into the 'fog', a stage-effect found in use as early as *c.* 1580 (v. Adams, 121–2) and freely employed by Sh. in *M.N.D.* Cf. note 1. 3. 38 below. Such fogs or mists were produced apparently by burning resin and could be used to conceal groups of persons or to produce 'darkness' (cf. Jonson, *Catiline*, 1. 1. 310 ff.).

I. 2.

For the problems raised by the style, misdivisions and broken lines of this sc. v. Introd. pp. xxiv–xxvi and p. 90.

S.D. Capell and mod. edd. read 'A camp near Forres', deduced from Hol. and 1. 3. 39. But the battle, in which Malc. and the bleeding captain have just been engaged, takes place in Fife (v. l. 49), nearly 100 miles off. As there is no mention of Forres in this scene, K. James would prob. not have noticed any inconsistency.

S.D. F. 'Alarum within. Enter King Malcolme, Donalbaine, Lenox, with attendants, meeting a bleeding Captaine.' Most edd. read 'Sergeant' for 'Captain'; but F. is better, since in the 16th c. 'Sergeant-major' was the title of a commissioned officer in the army; cf. *Sh. Eng.* i, 117 and note l. 3 below. The 'alarum' (v. G.) was sounded by trumpet. 'within' = 'off'.

3. *sergeant* Three syllables. I.e. sergeant-major (v. previous note). Hol. speaks of 'a sergeant at armes', i.e. an officer of the bodyguard, whom the rebels slew when the King sent him to summon them to his presence.

5. *'Gainst...friend!* The metre is imperfect; perhaps the speech was orig. longer.

my captivity: Malc.'s presence at the battle was prob. suggested by Hol.'s reference to Macdowald's capture and slaughter of another Malcolm.

9. *Macdonwald* 'Macdowald' in Hol. Spelling perhaps influenced by 'Donwald', the name of the murderer of King Duff. Cf. Introd. p. xii.

10. *to that* to fill such a role; (or) in addition to that.

11. *The...nature* the ever-increasing villainies of his nature. The phrase foreshadows Macb.'s development. Cf. note 1. 4. 11–14.

12–13. *from...supplied* is reinforced by Irish troops from the Hebrides.

gallowglasses (F2) F. 'Gallowgrosses'.

14. *quarrel* (Hanmer and mod. edd.) F. 'Quarry'. Hol. 'rebellious quarell'.

15. *Showed...whore* i.e. deceived him by bringing him success at first. Cf. *K. John*, 3. 1. 54–6, and *Arcadia* (1590) ed. Feuillerat, p. 424; 'Amphialus (following his fawning fortune) laid on so thicke', etc.

all's too weak Fortune and Macdonwald together are unable to stand up to Macb.

16. *name* i.e. the name 'brave'.

17. *Disdaining fortune* i.e. despite the initial success of the rebels (cf. ll. 14–15).

19. *Valour's minion* i.e. Macb., who confronts Fortune's minion. Cf. 'Bellona's bridegroom' (l. 55) and *K. John*, 2. 1. 390–4.

20. *Till he faced the slave* Most edd. think this irregular line points to mutilation, 'which would also account for the difficulty in the next line' (E.K.C.).

21. *Which* seems to refer to Macb. 'Perhaps some lines have been cut here' (E.K.C.).

shook hands...him i.e. let him go. A grim jest; 'shaking hands', the politest form of parting (cf. *Ham.*

1. 5. 128), being contrasted with Macb.'s actual leave-taking.

22. *from the nave...chops* Cf. Introd. p. xli, Middleton, *Chaste Maid*, 3. 2. 195, ''Life, rip my belly up to the throat then!' and v. G. 'nave'.

25. *reflection* v. G.

26. *break* Not found in F.; supplied by Pope from 'breaking', which F 2 reads.   28. *swells* v. G.

29—33. *No sooner...assault.* For the three separate campaigns in Hol., here combined into one battle, v. Introd. p. xiii.

No sooner justice...fresh assault Cf. Hol. 'Thus was justice and law restored againe...by the diligent means of Makbeth. Immediatelie whereupon word came that Sueno King of Norway was arrived in Fife with a puissant armie.'

31. *surveying vantage* seeing his opportunity.

32. *furbished* (Rowe) F. 'furbufht'.

33—4. *Dismayed...Banquo* (Pope) As prose in F.

38. *So they* (Steevens) F. prints with l. 39.

39. *Doubly redoubled* Cf. *Ric. II*, 1. 3. 80.

41. *memorize...Golgotha* i.e. make the battlefield famous as a second 'place of the skull'. Cf. *Ric. II*, 4. 1. 144.

42—3. *I cannot...help* (Rowe) F. 'I cannot... faint/My...helpe.' The whole speech (34—43), a number of verse-scraps which follow each other in awkward sequence, seems the ruin of a longer one. Perhaps 'As...cracks', which now reads oddly after 'I must report they were', was orig. the first half of the correspondence of which 'So they...foe' was the second.

45. S.D. F. 'Enter Roffe and Angus'—giving no exit for the Captain. Steev. and most mod. edd. omit Angus, who does not speak. But 'We are sent' (1. 3. 100) indicates his presence here [E.K.C.].

47. *a haste* Perhaps this superfluous 'a' was added by the transcriber.

48. *seems...strange* Cf. 1. 5. 28, where 'to seem' also = 'to look as if about to'.

50–1. *Where...cold* i.e. where our people are now panic-stricken by the Norse invasion.

54. *Cawdor* v. Introd. pp. xxv–xxvi.

began Pope read ''gan' and there is undoubtedly a superfluous syllable after the second foot. Cf. note l. 47.

55. *Bellona's bridegroom* i.e. Mars = Macb. Cf. Chapman, *Iliad*, v, 590, 'Before him marcht great Mars himselfe, matcht with his femall mate, | The drad Bellona'. I owe this parallel to Dr Percy Simpson.

proof v. G.

56. *self-comparisons* i.e. showed himself as good as the other in every way.

57. *point, rebellious* (F.) All edd. (except K. and Ridley) follow Theo. who read 'point rebellious,'. Simpson (p. 13) writes: 'By thus deserting F. they have obliterated a characteristic feature of Sh.'s style', and cites *K. John*, 2. 1. 390; *Ric. II*, 1. 1. 15–16; *Hen. V*, 5. 2. 30–1. K. points out that 'rebellious arm' refers (of course) to Sweno's.

58. *lavish* v. G. *and to conclude* This sudden conclusion again suggests abridgement.

60–1. *That...composition* (Steev.) F. divides 'King,/Craues'. Steev. conj. 'That...composition' to be the orig. line disturbed by the addition of Sweno 'injudiciously thrust into the text'—which seems likely. The name had not been mentioned before.

63. *Saint Colme's Inch* i.e. Inchcolm (St Columba's Isle) in the Firth of Forth.

64. *Ten thousand dollars* Hol. does not name the sum: Sh. expresses it in 16th-c. currency.

66. *bosom interest* confidence and affection.

present Another extra-metrical word; cf. notes ll. 47, 54.

69. *noble* F. 'Noble'. The capital may suggest emphasis. See Introd. p. liii.

1. 3.

F. S.D. 'Thunder. Enter the three Witches.' The thunder suggests entry from below (cf. note 1. 1. 2). Cap. reads 'A heath'—cf. 'this blasted heath' (l. 77). Hol. speaks of Macb. and Ban. meeting the witches 'in the middes of a launde', or glade, while 'passing through the woodes and fieldes', but the illustration in Hol. ed. i (v. frontispiece above) suggests a 'blasted heath'.

2. *Killing swine* Witches were commonly accused of blasting their neighbours' swine.

4. *A sailor's wife* In 1601 a sailor's wife at Dartmouth deposed before the J.P. that a witch had brought disasters to her husband at sea (cf. K. *Witchcraft*, pp. 12–14).

5. *munched* F. 'mouncht'. A normal sp.

6. *rump-fed* i.e. pampered or 'fat-rumped' (K.; who cites *Troil.* 5. 2. 55–6) v. G.

7. *o'th' Tiger* Cf. *Tw. Nt.* 5. 1. 61. A common name for a ship.

8. *sieve* Witches, doing everything by contraries, were wont by magic to put to sea in sieves. *Newes* (p. 13) tells of 200 witches who did so at one time on the Firth of Forth.

9. *like a rat* So as to creep on board. Cf. *Dæm.* p. 39, which speaks of witches 'being transformed in the likenesse of a little beast or foule'.

without a tail Such transformations were often incomplete, e.g. the cloven hoof which gives the Devil away.

10. *do* Most edd. assume that she gnaws a hole in the hull. But this contradicts l. 24. What she will 'do' is left mysterious, until she unfolds her scheme of making 'the voyage one long torture' (K.).

11. *give...wind* The gift was 'kind', because 'Witches for gold will sell a man a wind' (Nashe, *Summer's Last Will*, 1. 12. 20; McKerrow, iii, 272).

Cf. Middleton, *Changeling*, 1. 1. 17: 'If you could buy a gale amongst the witches.'

14. *the other* the other winds.

15. *ports* Supposed corrupt, because misunderstood. 'Ports' is the subject. Having all winds at command, 1 Witch will cause a contrary wind to blow from every port the ship should touch at on its voyage home from Aleppo, and thus not only tempest-toss it, but keep it at sea without water or victuals for nine weary weeks. K. James's bark was tempest-tossed and much delayed by contrary winds in 1589 owing to witchcraft (*Newes*, p. 17).

18–21. *I will* (Pope) F. 'Ile'. *drain...forbid* Through thirst and the spells she would put upon him.

forbid=under a curse (*interdictus*). Coleridge's *Ancient Mariner* owes much to these lines.

20. *pent-house lid* v. G. and Dekker, *Gull's Hornbook*, ch. III: 'The two eyes are the glass windows...having goodly penthouses of hair to overshadow them.'

28–9. *a pilot's thumb*, etc. A powerful charm against her enemy. Cf. note 4. 1. 23.

32. *Weïrd* (Theo.) F. 'weyward'. Also at 1. 5. 8; 2. 1. 20. Poss. a mistranscription of 'weyard', the sp. found at 3. 1. 2; 3. 4. 133; 4. 1. 136, perhaps representing the stage pronunciation. Hol. prints 'weird'. The term (<A.S. 'wyrd'=fate) was already used in 8th c. for the Parcae, as it is by Gavin Douglas (*Aeneis*, Bk. i. Cap. 1, 30) and Surrey (*Aeneis*, iv, 581). Cf. Introd. pp. xix–xxii and head-note 1. 1.

hand in hand Cf. *Newes*, p. 13, 'they...tooke handes...and daunced this reill or short daunce, singing all with one voice'. Cf. note 4. 1. 5.

33. *posters...land* Cf. *Dæm.* p. 38 [Witches] 'carryed by the force of the Spirite which is their conductor, either aboue the earth or aboue the Sea swiftlie'.

35–6. *Thrice...nine* i.e. three rounds apiece.

37. *the charm's wound up* i.e. to deal with Macb.

38. *So foul and fair* A dramatically ironical echo of
I.I.II. On the surface: 'fair' because of victory (cf. Hol.
i. 339, where the Scots give thanks to God 'that had sent
them so faire a day ouer their enemies'); 'foul' because
of the 'fog', which has sprung up to conceal the witches,
from which they then appear and into which they
vanish at l. 78. Cf. ll. 81–2, note I. I. 12; I. 5. 4, 'they
made themselves air into which they vanished', and
Dæm. 39: 'May he [the Devil] not...thicken and
obscure so the aire, that is next about them [witches] by
contracting it strait together, that the beames of any
other mans eyes cannot pearce thorow the same, to see
them?'

39. *Forres* (Pope 'Foris') F. 'Soris'. On the Moray
Firth, halfway between Nairn and Elgin.

40–2. *So withered, and so wild...on't?* 'In strange
and wild apparell, resembling creatures of an elder world'
(Hol.). Ed. i reads 'ferly' for 'wild'; ed. ii omits 'an'.

43. *question* speak to. Cf. *Ham.* I. I. 45; I. 4. 43.
Spirits might not speak unless first addressed.

44–5. *her choppy...lips* They refuse to speak to him,
but reply directly to Macb. (Bradley, p. 380).

46. *beards* Cf. *MWW*, 4. 2. 188–9, and Spalding,
p. 99.

48–50. *All hail...hereafter* Almost verbatim from
Hol.

Glamis! Rightly one syllable, but treated as two
by Sh.

51. *start* Coleridge (i, 68) sees here a sign that
Macb.'s mind has been 'rendered temptable by previous
dalliance of the fancy with ambitious thoughts'. Cf.
Introd. pp. l, lv and I. 5. 19–26.

53. *fantastical* imaginary.

58. *look...time* Cf. *Wint.* 4. 4. 475–6; *2 Hen. IV;*

3. 1. 82–6, 4. 1. 58–60 (note); Introd. p. lxiii and
Curry, ch. 11. The *seeds of time* are the creative 'germens'
or virtues of Nature from which springs the future.

70. *Stay* The rising mist warns him that they are
about to depart.

71. *Sinel's* i.e. Finel or Finlaech (mod. Finlay),
Macb.'s father. 'Finele' in Fordun (iv, ch. 44, p. 180),
was mis-transcribed 'Synele' by Boece, and so the name
reached Hol. Cf. Introd. p. x above.

72–3. *the thane of Cawdor...gentleman* Cf. Introd.
pp. xxv–xxvi.

79. *bubbles* illusions; cf. O.E.D. and *A.Y.L.* 2. 7.
152, 'the bubble reputation'. Ban. is interested in the
phenomenon, Macb. enthralled by the prophecies. In
Hol. both men treat the apparitions as 'some vaine
fantasticall illusion' and laugh at the prophecies.

82. *As breath* Coleridge (i. 69) suggests 'the
appropriateness of the simile...in a cold climate'. It is
also apt to a Scotch mist. Cf. l. 38 note.

84. *insane* i.e. causing insanity. Plutarch relates in
his *Life of Antony* how, left without provisions in the
Parthian war, the Roman soldiers tasted of roots 'among
the which there was one that...made them out of their
wits' [Mal.].

86. *Your...kings* He wishes to hear the prophecy
again from Ban.'s lips.

88. *To...words.* Spoken lightly, quibbling upon
Macb.'s 'went' in a musical sense (v. O.E.D. 'go' 9a).

91. *personal venture* Cf. 1. 2. 16 ff.

92–3. *His wonders...or his* i.e. he lacks words to
express at once his own astonishment and your praises,
which struggle with each other for utterance.

96–7. *Nothing afeard...death* A character-clue;
cf. ll. 137–8.   97. *death.* *As* (Pope) F. 'death, as'.

97–8. *hail | Came* (Rowe) F. 'Tale | Can'. Most
edd. follow Rowe. J. defends F. and explains 'As thick

as tale' 'as fast as they could be counted'. But 'thick as hail' is a common prov. form, from which 'thick as tale' would sound a forced departure; 'poured them down' (l.100) continues the image of 'hail' (cf. *K. John*, 4. 2. 109); and 'tale' is the kind of queer misprint we find in this text (cf. p. 89).

108–9. *The thane...robes?* (Cap.) F. divides 'liues:/Why'. Cf. Introd. p. xxv.

111–14. *Which...He...know not* (Mal.) F. mis-lines, which suggests adaptation. Cf. Introd. p. xxv.

111. *combined* leagued.

113. *vantage,* F. 'vantage;'

120. *trusted home* credited implicitly. He speaks 'in a free, off-hand, even jesting manner' (Bradley, p. 381), citing Hol. 'Banquo jested with him', etc.

121. *enkindle you unto* 'excite you to hope for' (Bradley, p. 381). He warns him against false hopes, not false deeds.

126. *In...consequence* in matters of vital moment.

127. *Two truths* That 'Sinel's death', though known to Macb., had not become common knowledge was perhaps made clear in the unabridged 1. 2. After the prophecy of 1 Witch Hol. adds in brackets 'for he had latelie entered into that dignitie and office by the death of his father Sinell'; Boece says nothing of the fulfilment of this prophecy; and Stewart explains that Macb. hears next day of his father's death.

128. *swelling* v. G. and *Hen. V*, 1. Pro. 1. 4.

131. *If ill* (Rowe) F. prints with l. 132.

135. *horrid image* At l. 139 we learn what it is he sees: himself murdering Duncan. Cf. Introd. p. lv. This and what follows prepare us for 'the air-drawn dagger', etc.

unfix my hair Cf. 5. 5. 11–13 and *Ham.* 3. 4. 121.
hair (Rowe) F. 'Heire'.

137. *of nature* i.e. of his nature. Cf. ll. 95–7, which

shew his attitude towards 'present fears', i.e. dangers he can actually see.

139. *whose* i.e. in which.

fantastical Cf. l. 53.

140. *single* feeble; cf. 1. 6. 16. A reference to himself as a microcosm or 'little kingdom' (cf. *Cæs.* 2. 1. 67–8), which J. and others discover, seems pointless in the context.

140–2. *function...not* i.e. the normal operations of the mind are spell-bound and only what is imaginary seems to exist.

142. *Look...rapt* Ban. is amused by Macb.'s abstraction, which he explains as the effect of the new honours.

145. *our strange garments* new clothes ('our' is indefinite).

their mould i.e. the body; v. G.

146–7. *Come...roughest day* The fatalistic couplet expresses a 'mind made up' to dismiss the subject from his thought (Moulton, p. 135). Yet the lie in 'my dull brain...forgotten' (149–50), and 'the promising courtesies of a usurper in intention' (Coleridge, i, 70) that follow, reveal a guilty conscience. We learn, too, from 1. 5. 2 that he at once makes enquiries about the credentials of the Weird Sisters.

151. *registered* i.e. 'within the book and volume of my brain' (*Ham.* 1. 5. 103).

155. *Very gladly* Spoken with 'free heart' enough.

1. 4.

S.D. The heading is from Cap. and the entry adapts F. 'Flouriſh. Enter King, Lenox, Malcolme, Donalbaine, and Attendants.'

1. *Are not* (F2) F. 'Or not'—an *o* : *a* error, v. MSH, 110.

2. *in commission* charged with the duty, i.e. Ross and Angus; v. 1. 2. 65–7.

11–14. *There's…trust.* Cf. note 1. 2. 11. Immediately preceding the welcoming 'O *worthiest* cousin', this is a fine stroke of dramatic irony, underlined by Duncan's eager generosity of praise and his use of 'the familiar and affectionate *thou*' (K.).

19. *proportion* v. G.

21. *all* i.e. all I have.

22–7. *The service…honour* (Pope) '*Reasoning* instead of joy; effort; stammering repetition of "duties"' (Coleridge, i. 70 n.). That Duncan finds it a little chilling is, I think, shown by the fact that the torrent of his affection turns aside and flings itself upon Ban.

27. *safe toward* 'with sure regard to' (Clar.).

28. *plant* v. G.

29. *growing* Develops the image in 'plant'. Ban. (ll. 32–3) extends it to the vine clinging to the elm (v. G. 'grow'); 'the harvest' meaning fruit (cf. *Cymb.* 5. 5. 263).

33–5. *joys…sorrow* Cf. *Rom.* 3. 2. 102–4; *Wint.* 5. 2. 47–50; *Ado*, 1. 1. 20–2.

35 ff. *Sons, kinsmen* etc. The change is very abrupt (cf. Bradley, p. 468 and Introd. p. xxvi), though the advancement of the thanes naturally turns Dunc.'s thoughts to the succession, the public establishment of which will give occasion for the bestowal of favours upon 'all deservers'. Moreover, the announcement that follows is clearly the true occasion of the Council meeting; Macb.'s arrival an unforeseen accident. The impression received is of a loyal and happy court and of a monarch overflowing with benevolence.

39. *Prince of Cumberland* 'As it were to appoint him his successor in the kingdome immediatlie after his deceasse' (Hol.). For the old custom of succession

which this violated, though Sh. knew nothing about it, v. Introd. p. viii.

42. *Inverness* i.e. Macb.'s castle. But this fact and the reason for the K.'s visit must surely have been made clear in the longer text; cf. Bradley, p. 468 and Introd. p. xxvi above.

43. *bind...you* 'lay us under deeper obligations' (Ver.).

44–7. *The rest* etc. 'The same language of effort' (Coleridge, i, 71).

rest=leisure.

make joyful 'Duncan does not know what will be the nature of L. Macb.'s joy' (E.K.C.).

48–53. *The Prince...to see* On this solil. Coleridge (i. 71) notes 'Messiah—Satan', i.e. he compares ll. 35–53 with *Par. Lost*, v, 600–71.

48. *step* (*a*) promotion for Malc., (*b*) obstacle before Macb. Duncan has 'signed his own death-warrant'; Chance will *not* crown Macb. 'without his stir' [K.].

50. *Stars...fires!* The 'conscia sidera' of *Aen.* iv, 519 [Gr.]. Cf. 1. 5. 49 ff.

54. *so* i.e. as you have made him out. Ban. has been praising Macb. 'aside'—evidence that so far he is quite unsuspicious (cf. Bradley, p. 382).

1. 5.

S.D. Camb. heads 'Inverness, Macbeth's castle'. This is the first of six scenes at Inverness; 1. 6 is clearly before the castle gates and ll. 37–9 below suggest 'before' for 1. 5 also.

2. *I have...report* Cf. note 1. 3. 146–7.

4–5. *they made...air* Cf. note 1. 3. 38.

6. *missives* messengers.

10. *deliver* v. G.

10–11. *my dearest...greatness* The first of several
tender words to his wife. Coleridge (i. 72) contrasts her
speech, which shows 'no wifely joy at the return of her
husband; no retrospection on the dangers he had
escaped'. But ll. 53–7 explain that. 'Her ambition' is
'for her husband and herself; there was no distinction
to her mind' (Bradley, p. 377).

16. *human kindness* A cardinal expression, much
discussed; 'kind' meaning either 'natural' or 'tender'
elsewhere in Sh. But since 'milk' (fig.) generally means
'gentleness' (cf. l. 47; 4. 3. 98; *Lear*, 1. 4. 364 'milky
gentleness') 'the milk of human kindness' must imply a
tender and gentle disposition or (to L. Macb.'s mind)
a weak sentimentality. And this evidence, coming from
her, cannot be set aside, as Bradley is inclined to do
(p. 351). Cf. Introd. p. li above.

19. *illness* v. G.
should＝which should.

21–4. *thou'ldst have...undone* A disputed passage,
F. having no inverted commas. Discussion turns
mainly on the placing of these; Pope and most edd.
making 'Thus...undone' the quotation, though none
seems able to explain the text thus pointed. Ver. and
Ridley alone have seen that 'thou'ldst have' has two
objects, (i) 'that which...have it' (i.e. the crown),
and (ii) 'that which...undone' (i.e. the murder).

24. *undone. Hie* F. 'undone High'.

26. *chastise* whip (cf. *Hen. V*, 1. 1. 29).

27. *the golden round* Cf. 4. 1. 88 and 2. *Hen. IV*,
4. 5. 36.

28–9. *seem...crowned* look like having you
crowned. Cf. 1. 2. 48.

29 S.D. F. 'Enter Meſſenger'. Cap. 'Enter an
Attendant'. Camb. reverts to F., but Cap. is right:
Macb.'s courier being 'almost dead for breath', one of his
'fellows', i.e. a servant of the castle, delivers the message.

30. *it!* F. 'it.' A long pause for amazement and recovery.

37. *The raven...hoarse* The messenger 'may well want breath and such a message would add hoarseness to the raven' (J.).

39. *my* Significant, though not to be over-stressed as it is by some actresses. All critics have noticed the effect of the metrical pause before 'Come' and the tremendous lines that follow. Cf. the still longer pause at l. 60.

39 ff. *Come, you spirits* For this invocation v. Introd. pp. lvi–lvii.

40. *mortal thoughts* 'murderous designs' (J.). Mal. cites Nashe, *Pierce Penilesse* (McKerrow, i, 230. 19–24) who speaks of a kind of devils 'called the spirits of reuenge, & the authors of massacres', who 'incense men to rapines, sacriledge, murther, wrath, furie, and all manner of cruelties'. Cf. *Lucr.* ll. 909–10.

42. *make thick my blood* Cf. *Wint.* 1. 2. 171 and *K. John*, 3. 3. 42–7.

43. *remorse* pity.

44. *visitings of nature* e.g. such as she repudiates at 1. 7. 54–8 and admits at 2. 2. 12–13.

45–6. *keep peace...it* intervene between my cruel purpose and its fulfilment.

46. *it* F. 'hit'.

47. *take...for* change...to.

47–9. *murd'ring ministers...nature's mischief!* The 'spirits' of ll. 39 ff., whom Nashe (*op. cit.*) describes as 'seedesmen of mischief'; v. G. 'sightless', 'mischief'.

51. *my keen knife* i.e. she intends to do the deed herself. Cf. ll. 66–7, 72, and Introd. p. xxxvii.

52. *blanket* The homely word, which has offended many, including J. (v. *Rambler*, No. 168) and Coleridge (i. 73), implies a 'sleeping world' (Clar.). Cf. *Lucr.* ll. 788, 801 and *1 Hen. VI*, 2. 2. 2; *3 Hen. VI*, 4. 2. 22.

54. *hereafter* i.e. that followed. She avoids the title. Note 'the half-spoken thoughts (l. 59), the euphemisms (l. 66), the significant pauses (l. 60)' [E.K.C.]. At l. 60 they gaze into each other's eyes and acknowledge the 'deed' as the child of both.

61. *my thane* Almost as expressive as the 'my' in l. 39; she knows that he is now hers, smiles as she completes the sentence, and then at once becomes practical.

62. *beguile the time* deceive the world.

64–5. *th'innocent...under't* Prov. v. Apperson, 583; from Virgil, *Ecl*. iii, 93, 'latet anguis in herba'. Cf. pp. xxxvii, lvii, and *Caes*. 2. 1. 224–5.

67. *great business* Cf. 'great quell', 1. 7. 72. She speaks as if going into battle.

my dispatch Cf. note l. 51 and Introd. p. xxxvii.

70. *We...further*. He is appalled at her frankness and drops his eyes as he speaks.

clear cheerfully Cf. 3. 2. 27–8.

71. *To alter...fear* i.e. That hang-dog look would almost make one think you were afraid of something.

72. *Leave...me* Cf. Introd. p. lvii.

1. 6.

The F. S.D. begins 'Hoboyes, and Torches', the latter most inappropriate to one of the few sunlit scenes in *Macbeth*; cf. note l. 3, Bradley, p. 334, and Note on Copy, p. 88.

3. *gentle* Proleptic; cf. 3. 4. 76. 'Intimates the peaceable delight of a fine day' (J.).

3–10. *This guest...delicate* Ban. little suspects that the martins are building above the gate of hell; cf. 'temple-haunting' = fond of churches, and Bradley, p. 382; while for 'martin' as symbolising illusion see Spurgeon, pp. 187–90.

4. *martlet* (Rowe) F. 'Barlet'. Cf. *Merch.* **2. 9. 28.**
approve v. G.

5. *By his...mansionry* 'by the fact that he has
chosen this as a favourite site for his mansions. "Mansionry"...is collective, implying many nests—as
explained in the graphic details that follow' (K.).

mansionry (Theo.) F. 'mansonry'; Pope 'masonry'.

6. *Smells...frieze* Perhaps a word has dropped out
here.   7. *coign of vantage* 'convenient corner' (J.).

8–9. *cradle:...haunt,* (Rowe) F. 'Cradle,...
haunt:'

9. *most* (Rowe) F. 'muſt'.

11–14. *The love...your trouble* i.e. just as I am
grateful for the love of those subjects who pester me at
times with their attentions, so I ask you to give thanks
for the love which prompts this present tiresome visit—
'an elegantly punctilious mode of saying that regard for
Macb. and his wife is the cause of his visit' (Elwin *ap.*
Furness).

14–18. *All our service...house* Cf. Stewart,
36,061–6 [Donwald speaks]:

'Wes neuir none of hie or low degre,
'With sic ane prince so weill louit as he,
'Gettand of him so mony riche reward;
'Wes neuir one of all the kingis gard,
'Rewardit wes so weill among thame all.
'"Suppois"', he said, '"*that my seruice be small.*"'

16. *single* Cf. **1. 3. 140.** Coleridge (i. 73) detects
'laboured rhythm and hypocritical over-much' in this
speech. Hypocrisy, no doubt; but it could (and I think
should) be spoken very charmingly. Cf. Introd. p. liii
above.

20. *rest your hermits* we shall always offer prayers
for you (v. G. 'hermit' and cf. *Gent.* **1. 1. 18**). A
reply to his 'you shall bid God 'ild us'.

22. *purveyor* v. G.

26. *theirs...compt* their own servants, themselves, and all they possess in trust for you.

29. *host; we* F. 'Hoſt we'.

31. *By...hostess* What sovereign grace!

1.7.

S.D. F. 'Ho-boyes. Torches. Enter a Sewer, and diuers Seruants with Diſhes and Seruice ouer the Stage. Then enter Macbeth.' The 'Torches' (cf. head-note 1.6) are here appropriate, since it is now night, towards the end of an elaborate supper, which began about 7 p.m. (v. 3. 1. 41). The 'Sewer' (v. G.), etc. are, I assume from l. 29, removing empty dishes and leaving the chamber; all but the 'banquet' (i.e. wine and dessert) being over. My locality-direction covers all four scenes, 1. 7 to 2. 3 (which are continuous), in the context of the Globe playhouse. The stair at the back is a private one leading direct to Duncan's bedroom. Beyond that lies the 'second chamber' in which his sons sleep, and to which we must imagine an outer door leading to passages and a main staircase, since both Lady M. and the sons find their way down without using the visible stair at the back. Cf. 2. 2 S.D. and 2. 3. 95 S.D. 'A court open to the sky' is needed for 2. 1.

1–28. *If it were done...th'other* Macb.'s visual imagination here finds its supreme expression. The speech begins with a simple proposition (cf. *Ham*. 3. 1. 56), out of thirteen words twelve being monosyllables; works up to a passionate climax, and then tails off into a jog-trot commonplace ending with an unfinished sentence. Cf. Introd. pp. lvii–lviii.

3. *trammel up* i.e. catch in a net from which nothing can escape, and which thus gives perfect security; v. G.

4. *his surcease* his death (cf. *Lucr*. l. 1766). Other

interpretations are: its (i.e. the consequence's) cessation; and its (i.e. the assassination's) accomplishment. But simplest is best; we are in the theatre.

5. *end-all....here*, F. 'end all. Heere,' Hanmer and most edd. 'end-all here,' Hanmer's reading marks the gram. construction, the F. period a dramatic pause. 'That but this blow' to 'end-all' is a complete thought in itself, or might have been, had not the thought of 'the life to come' followed, to give it new point and direction. Cf. Simpson, pp. 82–3 for a defence of F. on metrical grounds. Ridley reads 'end-all, here.'

6. *bank and shoal* (Theo.) F. 'Bank and Schoole'— 'schoole'=a 17th-c. sp. of 'shoal'. Perhaps, after '"a babbled o' green fields', Theo.'s most brilliant elucidation. Accept it, and we see life as a 'narrow bank in the ocean of eternity' (J.); reject it, and the image shrinks to the limits of a dusty class-room with Macb. seated upon a 'bank' or bench.

7. *jump...come* Cf. Introd. p. lviii.

8–12. *that we...own lips* Cf. Seneca, *Hercules Furens*, ll. 735–6:

> Quod quisque fecit, patitur: auctorem scelus
> Repetit suoque premitur exemplo nocens.

10. *this* Mason's conj. 'thus' is attractive.

11. *ingredience* (F.) Pope and subs. edd. (except Darm. and K.) 'ingredients'. Cf. 4. 1. 34 above; *Oth.* 2. 3. 311; Middleton, *Chaste Maid*, 5. 2. 25; and O.E.D. 'ingredience'. v. G.

12–20. *He's here...taking-off* Note Sh.'s cunning introduction of expository matter.

17–18. *borne...office* Cf. Introd. p. xiii; v. G. 'faculties', 'clear'.   17. *meek*, F. 'meek;'.

19. *angels, trumpet-tongued* Suggests the Last Judgement and so leads on to the apocalyptic imagery that follows.

21. *And pity* Cf. note 1. 5. 16.

naked new-born babe Supreme symbol of pity and tenderness.

22. *the blast* i.e. (*a*) of the trumpet, v. l. 19; (*b*) the tempest of horror and indignation aroused by the deed. Only a man full of 'human kindness' would imagine a world so pitiful; the real world is otherwise.

22–3. *Heaven's cherubim...air* This and 'striding the blast' are inspired by Ps. xviii. 10: 'He rode upon the cherubims, and did fly; he came flying upon the wings of the wind' (Book of Common Prayer). Cf. also *2 Hen. IV*, Ind. 4, and *Cymb.* 3. 4. 38.

cherubim (Jennens etc.) F. 'Cherubin'—a minim error.

24. *blow...eye* i.e. make the whole world see it.

25. *tears...wind* i.e. the rain of men's tears of pity will check the storm of their anger. Sh. is fond of using storm, and the rain that descends as the storm abates, to symbolise the agitation and tears of human passion. *Lear* is an essay on this theme, already simply expressed in *Lucr.* ll. 1788–90:

> This windy tempest [i.e. fury], till it blew up rain,
> Held back his sorrow's tide to make it more;
> At last it rains and busy winds give o'er.

25–8. *I have no spur...th'other—* The 'spur' image leads on to a second image from horsemanship; vaulting into one's saddle being a much admired feat of Sh.'s day (cf. *1 Hen. IV*, 4. 1. 107; *Hen. V*, 5. 2. 143). Macb.'s ambition to vault into the royal seat at one bound only means, he says, that he will come a cropper by teaching 'bloody instructions' to others.

28. *th'other—* (Rowe) F. 'th'other.' 'Side' is obviously understood, but its repetition after 'sides' (l. 26) would sound awkward; for which technical reason and for the dramatic reason that Macb. is exhausted by his

passion, Sh. makes him end with an unfinished sentence; a weary gesture supplying the gap.

32–5. *He hath...so soon* Clear indication that so far he only contemplates an open and acknowledged assassination. Cf. Introd. pp. lviii–lix.

34. *would* should. Cf. 5. 5. 17, 'should'(=would).

35–45. *Was the hope...th'adage* She 'chastises' (1. 5. 26) him first by accusing him of cowardice, a reproach which 'cannot be borne by any man from a woman without great impatience' (J.), least of all by one whose whole reputation is based on courage.

35–6. *drunk...slept* Cf. *K. John*, 4. 2. 116–17.

37. *green and pale* As a man looks the morning after a drinking-bout.

39. *Such* 'so great in promise, so poor in performance' (Gr.).

43. *a coward* Cf. Introd. p. xviii n. 1 and Stewart, 39,793–6:

> Than scho begonth to flyt
> With him that tyme, and said he had the wyit,
> So cowartlie that durst nocht tak on hand,
> For to fulfill as God had gevin command.

45. *th'adage* 'The cat would eat fish but would not wet her feet', Apperson, p. 88.

46–7. *I dare...is none* Cf. Introd. p. l.

47. *do more* (Rowe) F. 'no more'. Perhaps a copyist error; v. p. 90.

is none i.e. must be superhuman or devilish, which it suits Lady M. to interpret as subhuman.

47–59. *What beast...done to this.* Cf. Introd. pp. xxxiv–xxxviii.

54. *I have given suck* Cf. note 4. 3. 216, and Eckermann, *Convers. with Goethe*, April 18, 1827: 'Whether this be true or not does not appear; but the lady says it, and she must say it, in order to give emphasis to her speech.' Hol. says nothing of children and it is most unlikely that Sh. had Gruoch's son (v. p. viii above) in mind.

55. *me*— (Rowe) F. 'me,'.

56–8. *I would...brains out* This, 'though usually thought to prove a merciless and unwomanly nature, proves the direct opposite.... Had she regarded [such an act] with savage indifference, there would have been no force in the appeal' (Coleridge, ii. 271). And that she misrepresents herself is shown by 2. 2. 12–13. If she could not kill an old man who looked like her father, she certainly could not have killed her own child. Yet, as we hear the words in the theatre, we think: 'A woman, yes; but what a woman to utter such sentiments!'

59. *We fail?* (F.) A scornful echo of his question. Mrs Siddons, having tried 'We fail?' and 'We fail!' decided in favour of 'We fail.'—a resolute acceptance of the possibility and its consequences. But the F. pointing is in general too good to be deserted lightly. Cf. p. 91.

60. *screw...place* Cf. *Tw. Nt.* 5. 1. 121–2; *Cor.* 1. 8. 11. Alluding to the screwing up of a string to the required musical pitch. She contemptuously likens him and his moods to a fiddle; yet how true the image is! He has all the 'tenseness of a violin string stretched' (Masefield, p. 41).

63–8. *two chamberlains...as in death* Drawn from Hol. (Chronicle of King Duff); v. G. 'chamberlain', 'wassail', 'convince'.   68. *lie* (F 2) F. 'lyes'.

65–7. *memory...limbec only* Memory was placed by the old physiologists at the base of the skull, like a guard to protect the reason from vapours etc., rising from the body. But wine and wassail converted memory itself to alcoholic vapour (cf. *Ant.* 2. 1. 24) and the brain into a still; v. G. 'receipt', 'limbec', 'drenched'.

72. *our great quell* She speaks proudly and coins a

sb. from a verb which suggests the suppression of something disagreeable. To her the deed is a glorious one. Cf. note 1. 5. 67.

73. *mettle* v. G. The same word as 'metal'.

77–9. *Who dares...death?* Cf. note 2. 3. 118 and Stewart, cited above p. xviii.   78. *roar* F. 'rore,'.

79–80. *bend...agent to* strain every faculty of mind and body for. Cf. 'unbend', 2. 2. 46 above and *Hen. V*, 3. 1. 16.

81–2. *Away...know* Cf. 1. 5. 64–5. He echoes her advice, a 'symbol of their relative positions' (Ver.).

show: F. 'fhow,'

2. 1.

S.D. F. 'Enter Banquo and Fleance, with a Torch before him.' 'Torch' implies a torch-bearer. Enough time has elapsed between 1. 7 and 2. 1 for Dunc. to get to bed and Ban. and Fl. to come from attending him thither, themselves on the way to bed.

2–5. *The moon...all out* 'The stars *have* hid their fires' (Gr.); cf. 1. 4. 51; 1. 5. 49–53.

4. *husbandry* thrift.

4–5. *take my sword...that too* He begins disarming for bed. By 'that too' some suppose 'helmet', others 'shield', is meant, but he would have taken neither to the K.'s bedroom, whereas belt and dagger naturally follow sword and it is not *he* who will need a dagger in this scene!

7. *I would not sleep* etc. At l. 20 we learn that he had 'dreamt last night of the Weïrd Sisters', after a fashion he evidently does not wish to repeat, and his words at once recall them to the mind of the audience and deepen the sense of imminent evil. Cf. ll. 50–1.

7–9. *Merciful powers...repose!* He prays to 'that order of angels' which is 'concerned especially with the

restraint and coercion of demons' (cf. note 4. 3. 238–9):
for it is to demons he (and Sh.'s audience) would ascribe
unholy visions in sleep (cf. Curry, p. 81). Ban.'s
dreams are far less terrible than Macb.'s; cf. 3. 2. 18.
But that he, of all men, should be thus visited shows how
dense is the atmosphere of evil about the castle; cf. the
dream of the prince who cries 'murder' (2. 2. 22).

12–17. *The king's...content*. This, revealing that
they have just come from the K.'s bedroom, reveals also
that it can be reached by the stair visible at the back.

13–14. *pleasure, and*/*Sent* (Jennens) F. 'Pleaſure,/
And ſent'.

14. *offices* servants' quarters.

16. *shut up* concluded the day; cf. O.E.D. 'shut'
19g.

17–19. *Being...wrought* Our hospitality would have
been more liberal had we not been unprepared. The
laboured phrasing betrays an unquiet mind.

22–3. *we...We* Not the 'royal we' (Clar.) but
'you and I'.

an hour to serve a convenient hour.

25. *If you...'tis* 'If you will espouse my interests
when the time comes' (K.). Macb. intends Ban. to
suppose he refers to Dunc.'s death in the course of
nature and Ban. does so suppose it; for that, I agree with
K., is the purport of his reply (ll. 26–9). Bradley's idea
that 'Ban. fears a treasonable proposal' (pp. 383–4) is
unnecessary. Cf. Introd. p. xiv.

31. *my drink* night-cap or 'posset' (2. 2. 6).

32. *strike upon the bell* The preconcerted signal
(cf. l. 62).

33 ff. *Is this a dagger* etc. Macb. is to wait for the
bell; and to wait is to sit. As he sits, he is suddenly
arrested by something before him on the table [E.K.C.].
The audience see from the first that it is 'a dagger of
the mind', but this only dawns upon Macb. gradually.

At l. 34 he fails to clutch it; at l. 42 it seems to rise into the air and move towards *the door*; at l. 46 it begins to drip blood. He then frees himself from the vision; but he is even more 'settled' (1.7.79), and moves forward involuntarily, absorbed 'into the midnight world of secrecy, darkness and wickedness' (Masefield, p. 41). Cf. Sprague, 238 ff. for Irving and others in this speech.

41. *As this...draw* He draws it to compare reality with vision, but when his eye returns to the table the vision has gone. For a second he seems puzzled, but immediately after sees it floating in the air before him and pointing towards the K.'s room, whereupon he rises with the cry 'thou marshall'st me' etc.; a muted cry, since the whole action is as if in trance.

44–5. *Mine eyes...rest* Either the eyes are fooled, while the other senses apprehend correctly, or else their perception is keener than that of all the rest put together.

48. *informs* takes shape (O.E.D. and most edd.). K. explains 'gives [false] information' and cites Dav. 'that thus informs my eye-sight'.

49–60. *Now o'er...with it* Cf. *Lucr.* ll. 162 ff.:

> Now stole upon the time the dead of night,
> When heavy sleep had closed up mortal eyes;
> No comfortable star did lend his light,
> No noise but owls' and wolves' death-boding cries.

49. *half-world* (Camb.) F. 'halfe world'.

50. *abuse* deceive.

51. *curtained* Formerly men slept in four-post beds with the curtains drawn.

Witchcraft (Rowe and edd. 'now witchcraft'). Note the pause after 'sleep'. Cf. p. lxi.

52. *Hecate's* F. 'Heccats', v. G. A dissyllable. Cf. 3. 2. 41.

off'rings rituals (such as we witness in 4. 1).

53. *Alarumed* Like a soldier roused to arms in the night.

54. *watch* Either watchman (cf. 2. 2. 3) or time-piece (cf. *2 Hen. IV*, 3. 1. 17).

55. *strides* (Pope) F. 'fides'. Cf. *Lucr.* 365: 'Into. the chamber wickedly he stalks.'

56. *sure* (Cap.) F. 'fowre'. Cf. *Ps.* xciii. 2: 'the round world so sure that it cannot be moved' (Book of Common Prayer).

57. *which way they* (Rowe) F. 'which they may'.

58. *Thy very stones prate* Cf. *Luke* xix. 40: 'The stones would...cry out.'

59–60. *take...with it* i.e. by breaking this silence. Cf. 2.2.2, 11, 19. Macb. speaks as if watching himself in a dream.

60–1. *Which...gives* 63–4. *Hear...hell.* Many believe these couplets to be interpolations (cf. p. xxiv). But Hamlet speaks similar ones in a similar situation (*Ham.* 3. 2. 401–2; 3. 3. 95–6). Cf. also note 2. 2. 56–7. Jests and jingles were felt to be a relief at moments of great dramatic tension. For 'words... gives' (sing. verb + plur. subj.) cf. Franz, pp. 565–74.

64. S.D. For Irving's exit ('his feet, as it were', feeling 'for the ground, as if he were walking with difficulty a step at a time on a reeling deck') cf. Sprague, p. 241, and Simpson cited p. lxxxii, P.S.

2. 2.

2. *Hark!* Repeated l. 11 and by Macb. l. 19 Indicates nervous strain.

Peace She reproves herself.

3. *fatal bellman* Cf. *Lucr.* 165, 'owls'...death-boding cries' (cited 2. 1. 49–60).

4. *it:* (Rowe) F. 'it,'

6. *snores:* (edd.) F. 'Snores.'

charge duty (of guarding the K.).

7–8. *That death...die.* Based on Hol.; cf. note
1. 7. 63–8 above.

8. S.D. from Steev. and mod. edd. F. 'Enter
Macbeth'. Tieck reads '*Macb.* (der oben erscheint)'
and E.K.C. '*Enter Macbeth above, for a moment.*' Both
imagine him on the upper stage. But the cry from an
unseen is far more effective than from a seen Macb.;
ll. 16–17 tell us he utters it as he 'descended' the stair;
and F.'s S.D. means no more than that the player is to
speak.

10. *th'attempt and...deed* (Camb. after Hunter)
F. 'th' attempt, and...deed,' in which the commas
emphasise the words they follow; cf. Simpson, 26–30
and note 2. 2. 63 below. The sense is: an unsuccessful
attempt will ruin us.

12–13. *Had he...done't* Cf. Introd. pp. xxxviii,
lvii. She is impatient and anxious. What *is* happening?
She must go and see.

13. S.D. For the blood cf. 5. 1. 38–9 and 18th-c.
stage-tradition. Garrick and others carried a dagger in
each hand, but one hand should be free to spread at
l. 20; Lady M. first notices the daggers at l. 48 (v. note).
'Don't look at each other' is a MS. note in Irving's
copy of the play at this point. Cf. Sprague, pp. 241–4.

14. *I have...noise* The inconsequence marks the
breakdown of all control. N.B. Never once does he say
how the deed was done or speak of the victim. Cf.
ll. 51–2.

15. *scream* F. 'ſchreame'. Also at 2. 3. 56.

16. *Did not you speak?* The 'you' is scornful. His
'when?' shows he has forgotten all about his cry at l. 8.
Hunter, Furness, E.K.C. and other edd. reverse the
speakers, and spoil a fine point.

19. *i' th' second chamber* Cf. head-note 1. 7.

20. S.D. Pope 'Looking on his hands'. Cf. note, l. 13,
S.D.

22. *There's one* there was one.

25. *There...lodged together* i.e. there's nothing in that; the two princes are sleeping in the same room. Some, even Bradley (p. 355), take 'two' for the drugged grooms!

27. *hangman's hands* In Sh.'s day hanging, which included drawing and quartering, was a butcher's job.

32. *I had...blessing* That he feels he 'needs', or even speaks of, God's blessing on his deed is an astonishing revelation of his state of mind. Cf. *Lucrece*, ll. 341–3:

> So from himself impiety hath wrought,
> That for his prey to pray he doth begin,
> As if the heavens should countenance his sin.

33–4. *These deeds...mad* 'This idea of the effect of obsession on sanity is firmly fixed in Sh.'s psychology' (Craig). Cf. *Oth.* 3. 3. 326–9. An adumbration of 5. 1.

35–6. *I heard a voice...murder sleep* As Furness (p. 359) first noted, this famous speech was suggested to Sh. by the following passage in Hol.'s chronicle of King Kenneth (who had slain his nephew secretly):

> A voice was heard, as he was in bed in the night time to take his rest, uttering unto him these or the like woordes in effect: 'Thinke not Kenneth that the wicked slaughter... by thee contriued is kept secret from the knowledge of the eternall God'...the King with this voice being striken into great dread and terror, passed that night without anie sleepe comming in his eies.

35. *Sleep no more* One of the leading motifs of *Macbeth*. Cf. 3. 2. 17–22; 3. 4. 141; 4. 1. 85–6; 5. 1; and Middleton Murry, *Shakespeare* (1936), pp. 332 ff.

36. *murder sleep*' F. supplies no inverted commas; J. first closed the quotation at these words.

37–40. *Sleep...life's feast* Eliz. sonneteers were fond of ringing the changes on the theme of 'care-charmer sleep'. Mal. thought Sh. had in mind the opening lines of Sidney's sonnet (*A. & S.* xxxix, ed. 1591) which set the fashion:

> Come sleepe, O sleepe, the certain knot of peace,
> The bathing place of wits, the balme of woe.

Cf. 'balm of hurt minds', 'bath', 'knits'. But, as **Gr.** points out, Seneca, *Hercules Furens*, ll. 1065–7:

> tuque, o domitor
> Somne malorum, requies animi,
> Pars humanae melior vitae,

also offers a close parallel, which may well be Sh.'s source; cf. Introd. p. xliii, n. 1.

37. *sleave* 'a tender filament of silk obtained by separating a thicker thread' (O.E.D.), and therefore very easily tangled.

39. *second course* i.e. second race or career (after 'the death of each day's life'). But it then suggests 'feast' (l. 40), in which the 'second course' was the most sustaining. Steev. cites Chaucer, *Squire's Tale* (l. 347), 'The norice of digestioun, the slepe'.

40. *What...mean?* She tries to bring him to his senses.

43. *no more:* The F. pause implies hesitation. 'He does not dare to say the word king' (Gr.).

45. *unbend* Cf. 1. 7. 79.

47. *witness* tell-tale.

48. *these daggers* Noticing them for the first time.

54–5. *'tis the eye...devil* K. cites *Lucr.* l. 245, 'Shall by a painted cloth be kept in awe'; and Steev., Webster's imitation: *White Devil*, 3. 2. 151, 'Terrify babes, my Lord, with painted devils'.

56–7. *gild...guilt* A common jest with Sh., here put to ghastly use. Cf. 'golden blood', 2. 3. 112 (note).

57. S.D. F. 'Knocke within', i.e. from the tiring-house upon one of the side doors to the main stage.

De Quincey's essay, 'On the knocking at the gate in *Macbeth*', explains the secret of the extraordinary effect of this knocking immediately after the murder: we have been looking into hell, 'and the re-establishment of the goings-on of the world in which we live, first makes us profoundly sensible of the awful parenthesis that had suspended them'.

59–63. *What hands are here...one red* See l. 20, which he has forgotten! Miss Byrne (*Library*, June 1932, pp. 31–2) cites many Eliz. parallels. All, like this, prob. derive from Seneca, *Hercules Furens*, ll. 1323–9:

> Quis Tanais aut quis Nilus aut quis Persica
> Violentus unda Tigris aut Rhenus ferox
> Tagusque hibera turbidus gaza fluens,
> Abluere dextram poterit? Arctoum licet
> Maeotis in me gelida transfundat mare,
> Et *tota Tethys per meas currat manus,*
> Haerebit altum facinus.

The words in italics come very near ll. 60–1 and have (C. B. Young notes privately) no close parallel in Jasper Heywood's trans. 1581. Young also compares 'haerebit', etc. with 5. 2. 17. But Cunliffe (84) cites an even closer parallel from *Hippolytus*, ll. 723–6:

> Quis eluet me Tanais...
> Non ipse toto magnus oceano pater
> Tantum expiavit sceleris.

62. *The...incarnadine* The long latinised words, preceded and followed by monosyllables give the effect of a boundless ocean.

63. *the green—one red* (Steev.) F. 'the Greene one, Red'. Simpson, though not citing this, shows (p. 27) that a F. comma often follows the stressed word, and quotes *Ant.* 2. 6. 65–6 (F.), 'I have heard that Iulius Cæfar, grew fat with feafting there'.

S.D. F. 'Enter Lady'. For the closing of the door v. 2. 3. 50 (note).

66. *At the south entry* Thus she actualises what seems to him something 'metaphysical'.

67–8. *A little water...then!* Contrast 5. 1. 42, 49–50.

68–9. *Your constancy...unattended* you have lost your nerve.

73. *To know...myself* better be lost in thought than look my deed in the face. 'To know'=in knowing, i.e. if I must know.

2. 3.

1–20. *Here's...remember the porter.* Coleridge (i. 75, 77–8) found this speech 'disgusting' and wrote it off as 'an interpolation of the actors', but J. W. Hales (*New Sh. Soc. Trans.* 22 May 1874; Hales, *Notes and Essays,* 1884, pp. 273 ff.) proved it a necessary point of the play and steeped in dramatic irony. The three sinners have all been brought to Hell (like Macbeth) through some 'vaulting ambition that o'erleaps itself'.

2. *have old...key* have plenty of key-turning; cf. *2 Hen. IV,* 2. 4. 19.

4–5. *hanged...plenty* Hoarding his corn in order to sell it at famine prices, he finds himself ruined by the promise of a good harvest. Mal. referred this to 1606, when corn was very cheap. But it was only slightly less so in 1605 and 1607, and 'the suicide of a disappointed engrosser of corn was an old notion' (v. Chambers, *Wm. Sh.* i, 474; *Sh. Eng.* i, 39–40).

5. *come in time* Darm. suggests that since in ll. 11, 14 we have 'come in, equivocator', 'come in, tailor', Sh. here wrote 'come in, time' with some word (omitted by compositor or transcriber) relating to his miscalculating the 'time'. My guess is 'come in, time-server',

an epithet appropriate to all farmers, who must serve
Time in its changes of season and caprices of weather,
and to this farmer in its special sense of one who adapts
his conduct to the time with an eye to the main chance;
while, inasmuch as 'server' also means waiter at table,
it links together the otherwise unrelated words 'napkins' and 'farmer'. See my 'Note on the Porter in
Macbeth'. (*Edinburgh Bib. Soc. Trans.* (1947), ii, pt 4,
pp. 413–16.)

6. *napkins* for use at table or as handkerchiefs;
cf. *Ham.* 5. 2. 286, 'Here, Hamlet, take my napkin,
rub thy brows'.

8. *an equivocator* See Introd. pp. xxviii–xxx. E. E.
Kellett (*Suggestions*, p. 64) thinks that a remembrance
of Garnet's alias, 'Mr Farmer', may have prompted
Sh. to introduce 'equivocator' after 'farmer'.

13. *for stealing...French hose* i.e. the tailor, who
has for years stolen cloth in the cutting out of the
ampler garments of his customers, tries the trick once too
often in the making of French hose which, as fashion
changed, became so close-fitting that any loss of cloth
would be instantly detected. Mal. again tried to associate
this with 1606, not convincingly; v. G. 'French hose'.

14. *roast your goose* heat your smoothing-iron.
O.E.D. gives no instance of 'cook one's goose'
(='do for' oneself) earlier than 1851 (v. 'cook', vb.
4 b), but that meaning would be very apt here.

18–19. *primrose way...bonfire* Cf. *Ham.* 1. 3. 50;
All's Well, 4. 5. 53–5.

19–20. *remember the porter* To the audience,
perhaps holding out his hand or his hat, for coins. The
porter-scene gives the Clown his only 'fat' in the play;
but he might hope for largesse from two kings. Cf.
Introd. p. xxviii.

23–4. *second cock* i.e. about 3 a.m.; cf. *Rom.* 4. 4. 3.
Macd.'s question (ll. 21–2) implies that it is now morning.

It was shortly after midnight at 2. 1. 3 and there has been no break since. But Sh. deals in dramatic, not clock, time.

30. *be an equivocator with* i.e. play fast and loose with.

34. *in a sleep* i.e. by a dream (Elwin *ap.* Furness).

36. *gave thee the lie* laid you low.

40. *cast* v. G.

47. *this...trouble* i.e. putting up the K. and his retinue.

49. *physics pain* v. G. 'physic' and cf. *Temp.* 3. 1. 1–2; *Cymb.* 3. 2. 34.

50. *this is the door* Obviously now shut; cf. note 2. 2. 63 S.D.

51. *my limited service* Ban. had 'served' last night; it was now Macd.'s turn; v. G. 'limited'.

53. *He does:* Cf. note 2. 2. 43.

54–61. *The night...did shake* Len. here and the old man in 2. 4 fill in the background of portents and prodigies, cosmic and social, which, according to the belief of that age, accompanied the violent death of princes. Cf. *Caes.* 2. 2. 31.

58. *dire...events* disastrous tumult and disorderly occurrences.

59. *New hatched...time* Cf. *2 Hen. IV*, 3. 1. 86. Perhaps 'hatched' suggested to Sh. 'the obscure bird' (=the owl, cf. *Caes.* 1. 3. 26). Cf. Kellett, *Suggestions*, p. 65.

60–1. *the earth...shake* Cf. *1 Hen. IV*, 3. 1. 14–16.

68. *The Lord's...temple* Combines 1 *Sam.* xxiv. 10, 'the Lord's anointed' (of a king) with 2 *Cor.* vi. 16, 'the temple of the living God' (of every Christian). Macd. uses 'the very terms of the theory of Divine Right' (Draper, p. 215).

74. *the alarum bell* the great bell of the castle (and the Globe theatre). Cf. G., note l. 80, 5. 5. 51, and Adams, pp. 371–2.

78. *The great doom's image* Cf. *Lear*, 5. 3. 264.
The idea is developed in ll. 79–80.

80. *countenance* v. G. After *horror*! in F. Macd.
adds 'Ring the Bell', which Theo. and most 18th-c. edd.
omitted as an intrusive S.D., noting that if it were part
of the text, Lady M.'s speech would begin with a
broken line. Camb. followed F., but Bald (*RES*, IV,
429) and Chambers (*Wm. Sh.* i, 471) agree with Theo.
Cf. note l. 74 and pp. 87–8 on double S.D.s.

81. *hideous trumpet* Cf. *Oth.* 2. 3. 175. The bell is
like a trumpet calling to parley.

84. *repetition* v. G.

87. *What, in our house?* A 'mistake in acting'
(Bradley, p. 369); and Ban. seems to reprove her. K. calls
it 'a natural expression from an innocent hostess'.

89. S.D. F. 'Enter Macbeth, Lenox, and Roſſe'.
Cap. first omitted Ross, who cannot have been in the
K.'s chamber. Cf. also 2. 4. 22 f.

90–5. *Had I but died...brag of* 'This is...meant
to deceive, but it utters at the same time his profoundest
feeling' (Bradley, p. 359). Cf. 5. 5. 19–28.

95. *vault* v. G.

S.D. For Malc. and Don.'s ignorance of a murder
in a room next to theirs v. 1. 7 S.D. (head-note).

101. *badged* v. G.

106. *fury* frenzy.

111–18. *Here lay...love known?* 'Forced and
unnatural metaphors' (J.).

112. *golden blood* Gold is often called red in Sh.
(cf. 2. 2. 56–7) and other early writers. Cf. *Sir Patrick
Spens*, 'gude red gowd' and O.E.D. 'red' 3a (=gold).

113–14. *breach...entrance* Cf. *2 Hen. IV*, 4. 4.
118–20; *Library*, June 1945, p. 5; and Sidney's
Arcadia, bk. 3, ch. 12, 'battering down the walls of
their armour, making breaches almost in every place,
for troupes of wounds to enter'.

116. *Unmannerly breeched* indecently clothed. With this oxymoron Macb.'s hyperbole topples to absurdity. Cf. *Tw. Nt.* 3. 4. 251, 'strip your sword stark naked'.

118. S.D. 'seeming to faint' Rowe added this, and 18th-c. edd. agreed. Anticipated by the Germans Horn (1823) and Bodenstedt (1871), the actress Helen Faucit (1885) declared the faint real, and since Bradley (pp. 374, 484–6) agreed, the idea has been generally accepted. In view of everything Lady M. has said and done hitherto, I cannot see how any actress, Faucit or another, could persuade *an audience* of this reality, while Sh. almost certainly took the suggestion from Donwald's pretended 'swoun' in Stewart's *Croniclis* (v. Introd. p. xviii). Since she warns us beforehand what to expect (v. 1. 7. 78–9), Lady M. prob. comes to and screams at intervals; Macb. is too busy, no doubt, cutting her lace (cf. *Ant.* 1. 2. 71), etc., for speech (hence his silence, which some find puzzling); and, while this convenient diversion is being played, Malc. and Donal. have their word apart.

120. *argument* theme.

122. *auger-hole* v. G. Cf. Scot, 1, iv, 'they [witches] can go in and out at awger holes', a superstition referred to also by Ben Jonson, *Masque of Queens* (Jonson, vii, 298, top).

124–5. *Our tears...motion* Both 'our's are emphatic and 'brewed' is sarcastic, referring to the facile distraction of Macb. and his lady. Cf. *Tit. And.* 3. 2. 38.

125. *Upon...motion* 'yet begun to act' (K.).

126. *our naked frailties* All but Macd. and Len. are 'in night-gowns [dressing-gowns] with bare throats and legs' (Clar.).

127. *exposure*, F. 'expoſure;'.

129. *scruples* v. G.

131. *pretence* v. G.

133–4. *Let's...together* He ignores Ban.'s resolute words, but covers his silence with a light, almost kindly, note.

manly readiness 'The garb, and with it the spirit, of action' (Gr.).

140. *the near in blood* i.e. Macb. Cf. 1. 7. 13; 3. 1. 29; and *Ric. III*, 2. 1. 92. But they suspect every one. *near* = nearer, v. G.

141. *The nearer bloody* the more likely to murder us.

144. *dainty* v. G.

145. *shift* v. G.

145–6. *there's warrant...itself* quibble on 'steal'. Cf. *All's Well*, 2. 1. 33–4.

2. 4.

S.D. Theo. 'The outside of Macbeth's castle'.

1–20. *Threescore...upon't.* Cf. note 2. 3. 54–61. Sh. found the darkness, the cannibal horses and the owl that killed the falcon in Hol.'s account of K. Duff's murder.

4. *Ah* F. 'Ha'.

5–10. *Thou seest...kiss it?* Cf. Seneca, *Aga-memnon*, ll. 726–7:

> fugit lux alma et obscurat genas
> Nox alta et aether obditus tenebris latet.

5. *Thou seest the* (F.) Edd. 'Thou see'st, the'.

6. *Threatens* (F.) Rowe and edd. 'Threaten'.

his bloody stage Cf. *A.Y.L.* 2. 7. 139 f.; *Son.* 15, 3–4.

7. *travelling* (F 3) F. 'trauailing'. Prob. both senses intended. In the old astron. the sun was a planet.

8. *predominance* Astrol. term (gen. used of a planet). 'Is night triumphant in the deed of darkness...or is

day ashamed to look upon it?' (Clar.). Cf. *Lear*, 1. 2.
134; *Troil*. 2. 3. 138.

12. *towering...place* i.e. at her full pitch (*c.* 150
yards up). Cf. *Lucr*. l. 506, and Madden, p. 201.

13. *mousing* i.e. that hunts close to the ground.
'The mousing owl and the rebellious horses symbolise'
the traitor who struck the K. (E.K.C.).

15. *minions...race* of the finest pedigree.

16. *Turned...nature* became 'wild beasts'.
Cannibalism betokens the extreme limit of 'wildness'.
Cf. *Troil*. 1. 3. 124.

20. S.D. 'Macd. comes from the meeting referred
to at 2. 3. 126–34. He has been forced to accept
Macb.'s account of the murder and his election, but he
is full of suspicions and will not confide in Ross'
(E.K.C.).

21. *How goes...now?* Ross is all agog for the news.

27. *'Gainst nature still!* Cf. ll. 10–11, 15–18.

28. *wilt* (Warb.) F. 'will'.

29. *life's* (Pope) F. 'liues'.

life's means Either (i) that which gave them life,
their father; or (ii) their livelihood, their 'prospects of
succeeding to the throne' (K.).

31. *Scone* abbey, 2½ miles from Perth, where
Scotland's kings, from Kenneth II to James VI, were
crowned.

33. *Colme-kill* or I-Colm-kill (=the island cell of
Columba), the ancient name of Iona, the royal burial-
ground of Scotland.

36. *Fife* his own castle; cf. 3. 4. 128 f.

thither i.e. to Scone.

38. *Lest...new!* Lest we find we have changed for
the worse. Uttered, I think, *sotto voce*, and referring
back to 'invested' (l. 32). 'Adieu' is parenthetical.

40–1. *God's...foes!* The couplet is both feeble and
obscure (E.K.C., Ver. and K. all give different

interpretations). I suspect that Sh. ended the scene with 'God's benison go with you', which completes Ross's line. Cf. Introd. p. xxiv.

3. 1.

S.D. Cap. read 'Foris' (see 1. 3. 39; 1. 4) and Theo. 'An apartment in the Palace'. Some weeks (K. thinks 'months') have passed: Malc. is in England and Donal. in Ireland; Macb. seems firmly established.

2. *weïrd* F. 'weyard'.

3. *Thou play'dst..for't* Cf. 1. 5. 20–1.

7. *shine* are brilliantly manifest.

10. S.D. 'Sennet' v. G.

13. *all-thing* v. G.

14. *solemn supper* state banquet.

19, 23, 35. 'How naturally Macb. drops these murderous questions! He has progressed far in dissimulation since the last scene' (Gr.) And his handling of both Ban. and the murderers shows him as skilful a 'politician' as Claudius in *Hamlet*. Cf. Masefield, p. 50, and Introd. p. xli above.

22. *we'll take to-morrow* to-morrow will serve; cf. l. 32. Sinister touch.

25. *Go not...better* 'unless my horse goes too fast to make that necessary. The idiom was common from the 13th to the 17th c.' (K.).

28. *I will not* 'Perhaps the most striking' instance of irony in the play (Bradley, p. 340).

34. *Craving...jointly* How gracious!

38. *commend...backs* A friendly jest: 'recommend you to the hospitality of their saddles'.

40–3. *Let every man.. with you!* Deft courtesy, concluding on an almost fatherly note (designed to clear the chamber for the murderers).

41. *night;...welcome,* (Theo.) F. 'Night,...wel-come:'.

43. *God be with you* Pronounced 'God bye you', and often so written in Qq.

47–8. *nothing, But to be* i.e. nothing without being F. 'nothing, But to be' Theo. etc. 'nothing; But to be'.

48. *in Banquo* with regard to Ban.

49. *Stick deep* v. G. Like thorns.

royalty of nature A compliment to James I's ancestor (cf. Introd. p. xv).

50–3. *'Tis much...safety* Bradley (p. 386) reads this as an expression of fear that Ban. is plotting to assassinate him. Cf. l. 62, 'wrenched'.

52–3. *wisdom...safety* i.e. discretion, which is the better part of valour.

54–6. *under him...Cæsar* A link with *Ant.* (2. 3. 18–22) which derives from North's *Plutarch*: 'For thy demon, said he (that is to say, the good angell and spirit that keepeth thee) is afraid of his.'

58. *him; then* (edd.) F. 'him. Then'.

59. *kings:* (edd.) F. 'Kings.'

64. *filed my mind* Cf. 3. 2. 18–22. Does he refer to conscience? Cf. Introd. pp. lxi–lxii and G. 'file'.

66. *Put...peace* Cf. *Ps.* xi, 6; *Isa.* li, 17. 'Rancours' (v. G.) suggest his fears of assassination.

67. *mine...jewel* my immortal soul. At 1. 7. 7 he spoke differently.   69. *seed* (Pope) F. 'Seedes'.

71. *champion...utterance* challenge me to the death; v. G.

S.D. The murderers 'are not assassins by profession, as is clear from what follows, but soldiers whose fortunes, acc. to Macb., have been ruined by Ban.'s influence' (Clar.). Cf. Masefield, p. 50.

77. *under fortune* 'beneath your deserts' (Gr.).

79. *passed...you* 'proved to you in detail point by point' (Clar.).

80. *borne in hand* v. G. 'bear'.   82. *notion* v. G.

87–8. *so gospelled To pray* such Sunday-school boys as to pray. Cf. *Matth.* v. 44.

91. *in the catalogue* in a mere list.

94. *valued file* price-list, catalogue which defines qualities.

98. *closed* Prob.='set' (like a jewel). Cf. O.E.D. 'close' vb. 3 b.

99. *addition* v. G.

from the bill as distinct from his place in the list.

105. *Grapples...heart* Cf. *Ham.* 1. 3. 63.

heart and (Pope) F. 'heart; and'. The semicolon emphasises 'heart'; v. Simpson, p. 63.

106. *wear...life* i.e. find life dangerous while he lives.

109. *Hath* (F.) Rowe and edd. 'Have'. Cf. 4. 3. 113 and Franz, pp. 565–74.

115. *distance* enmity, v. G.

117. *near'st of life* vitals.

119. *it, yet* (edd.) F. 'it; yet'.

bid...avouch it say it is my humour.

126. *lives—* So F.

127. *spirits* i.e. of hatred and revenge.

129. *the perfect spy o'th' time* Obscure. J. and others take it as referring to 3 Murd. in 3. 3 to whom Macb. delivers detailed instructions. Others again explain as 'the knowledge, or espial, of the perfect time to act' (E.K.C.); 'spy' lit.='espial, observation' (K.). I agree with J. and suggest that a line or two, making the reference clear, has been cut after l. 129. Cf. note, l. 137 and Introd. p. xxvi.

132. *a clearness* Cf. Hol. 'that in time to come he might clear himself if anie thing were laid to his charge'

133. *To leave...work* i.e. to make a clean job of it. F. gives no brackets, but prints 'Worke:' which marks an emphatic pause (Simpson, p. 67).

137. *Resolve...apart* This and l. 139, which suggest that they go out to return shortly, also suggest that the sc. was once longer, perhaps for a conversation between Macb. and the mysterious 3 Murd. Cf. note 3. 3 S.D.

140–1. *It is...to-night* Cf. 2. 1. 63–4.

3. 2.

S.D. Lady M. enters from the inner stage, 'disillusioned and weary for want of sleep' (Bradley, pp. 374–5).

6–7. *'Tis safer...joy* Amplified by Macb. in ll. 19–26.

10. *Using* v. G. and *Per.* 1. 2. 3–7.

12. *without regard* ignored.

what's done, is done Contrast 5. 1. 67, 'what's done, cannot be undone'.

13. *scorched* (F. and Dav.) slashed; cf. *Err.* 5. 1. 183 (misinterpreted in my notes). Theo.'s emendation 'scotched' was accepted by all until 1914, when O.E.D. showed that 'scorch'='slash with a knife' in 16th and 17th c.

15. *tooth* Cf. 3. 4. 31 and *Lear*, 1. 4. 310.

16. *let...disjoint* let the whole universe go to pieces; v. Introd. pp. lxii ff. For 'frame' (a carpenter's) cf. *1 Hen. IV*, 3. 1. 16 and *Ham.* 2. 2. 302. Macb. includes the heavens in his 'frame', as does Milton in *Par. Lost*, viii, 15–16. Cf. *Masque of Queens*, ll. 147–9 (Jonson, vii, 289).

18. *these terrible dreams* The context (v. ll. 24–6) shows that he dreams he is being murdered; the reverse of the 'horrid image' of 1. 3. 135–9 (v. note). Cf. Introd. p. lxi and note 2. 1. 7–9.

21. *lie* Suggests the rack.

22–6. *Duncan...further!* Cf. *Tit. And.* 1. 1. 150–6.

30–1. *apply...eminence* v. G. Ban. is 'chief guest' (3. 1. 11).

32–3. *Unsafe...streams* F. divides 'lave/Our'. Cf. Introd. p. xxvi. Most agree that something is prob. omitted here. Yet the general sense is not in doubt: How insecure (and humiliating) a time it is for us when we can only keep honour bright by flattering. He seems to fear exposure as well as assassination from Ban.: the two would go together.

38. *But...eterne* She speaks his thought and he then reveals his intention.

copy (v. G.)=lease or (more prob.) mould. K. cites Massinger, *Fatal Dowry*, iv, 1, 'die, and rob the world/Of Nature's copy that she works form by'— an obvious echo. Cf. also *Oth.* 5. 2. 11.

39–40. *There's comfort...jocund* A sudden revelation of the 'deep damnation' into which he has fallen.

41. *Hecate's* F. 'Heccats'. Cf. note 2. 1. 52.

42. *shard-borne* Cf. *Ant.* 3. 2. 20; *Cymb.* 3. 3. 20. Meaning disputed in all three instances. Most edd. interpret 'borne on its scaly wings', and this sense for 'shard' seems to fit *Ant.* and *Cymb.* best. But the only parallel in O.E.D. is Gower, *Conf.* iii, 68 (of a dragon) 'Whos scherdes [=scales] schynen as the Sunne', and O.E.D. is definite that 'shard-borne' = 'dung-bred' (quoting Dryden, *Hind and Panther*, l. 321, 'Such souls as shards produce, such beetle things'). Yet the context in *Ant.* 3. 2. 20 suggests that O.E.D. is wrong; and its quotations under 11, 4 show 'shard' often = 'shell'.

43. *Hath...peal* 'hath tolled night's slumbrous curfew' (Gr.).

45. *dearest chuck* At once intimate and 'jocund'. Another horrifying glimpse into his mind; cf. note, ll. 39–40.

47. *Scarf...pitiful day* Cf. the different mood of 1. 7. 21–5.

49. *bond* i.e. Ban.'s life, with quibble on usual sense. Cf. *Ric. III*, 4. 4. 77: 'Cancel his bond of life.' Cf. Apperson, 140, and *1 Hen. IV* 3. 2. 157, 'the end of life cancels all bands'.

50. *paled* (Staunton's conj.) F. 'pale' (cf. 'cabined, cribbed, confined', 3. 4. 24 and *Cymb*. 3. 1. 19) it develops another aspect of 'bond' in typical Sh. fashion and only involves a simple *e : d* misprint. 'Pale' is colourless.

51. *rooky wood* Disputed. Most interpret 'rookery'; others take as 'roky (=dim, misty) wood', among them Dav., which reads 'the thick shady grove'. After 'light thickens' the second is apt, after 'crow' the first seems tautological; cf. p. 89. But 'roky' is a northern or E. Anglian word, prob. unknown to Sh. Perhaps a misprint of 'reeky' (='steamy, full of rank moisture', O.E.D. 1a).

55. *Things...ill* The tyrant's motto. Cf. Seneca, *Agamemnon*, l. 115, 'per scelera semper sceleribus certum est iter'.

3. 3.

S.D. Camb. 'A park near the palace'. The clues for locality are: 'something from the palace' (3. 1. 131), the sound of horses (l. 8, below) and the fact that they go almost a mile about to the gates, which Ban. and Fle. reach, as 'all men do', on foot (ll. 11–14), clearly by a short cut up a steep hill.

The presence of the 3 Murd. has exercised critics, some maintaining him to be Macb. incognito. This is irreconcilable with Macb.'s consternation at the news of Fleance's escape (3. 4. 21 f.), and with 'Thou canst not say I did it' (ibid. 50). I suggest that Sh. adds him (perhaps orig. introducing him at the end of 3. 1) to show that Macb., tyrant-like, feels he must spy even upon his own chosen instruments.

4. *To...just* exactly as Macb. himself prescribed.

6–7. *Now spurs...inn* Suggests a public highway.

7. *and near* (F 2) F. 'end neere'.

8. *I hear horses* Cf. 4. 1. 139–40. Lawrence (*Pre-R. Stud.* 217–18) shows that the sound of galloping 'off' could be produced in the old theatres. And in *Woodstock* (3. 2. 129) a character rides on horseback on to the stage (see ed. A. P. Rossiter, 1946).

9. S.D. F. '*Banquo within*'.

Give...ho! To his retinue, who go off with the horses.

10. *within...expectation* on the list of expected guests. Cf. *Rom.* 1. 2. 68 f.

16. *Let it come down* i.e. a 'rain' of blows.

S.D. '1 Murd. dashes out the torch—acc. to instructions as he thinks—and Fleance escapes in the darkness' (Gr.).

3. 4.

S.D. Camb. 'Hall in the palace'.

1–2. *at first And last* once for all.

11. *Be large* etc. He catches sight of 1 Murd. at this point.

14. *thee...within* outside you than inside him. Cf. Abbott, *Sh. Gram.* § 207.

21. *perfect* v. G.

23. *broad and general* free and unrestrained. Cf. *Oth.* 5. 2. 220, 'liberal as the air'.

25. *saucy* v. G.

safe A callous euphemism; cf. 'provided for', 1. 5. 66.

32. *ourselves* each other; cf. *Ado*, 2. 1. 331.

33–5. *The feast...home* A feast during which the host is not constantly assuring his guests they are welcome is nothing but a tavern-meal; or if it's just food they want, they might as well eat at home.

37. *Meeting* social gathering; cf. l. 109.
remembrancer v. G.

S.D. F. reads 'Enter the Ghost', etc.—doubtless from beneath the stage; the empty stool being immediately in front of a trap. Adams (p. 213) places it in the inner-stage; but that would surely bring it uncomfortably near the royal table, though the allusion in *The Puritan* to 'the ghost i' th' white sheet...at the upper end o' th' table' (cf. Introd. p. xxix, n. 3) seems to put it near the back of the outer stage. Some take the apparition to be a hallucination. True, nobody but Macb. sees it, but we have Forman as witness that it was visible to the Globe audience, and Stoll (pp. 190–217) proves its objectivity. Others again transfer the entry to l. 43; but F.'s is more effective, since it allows the audience to see the ghastly spectre glaring down the table as Macb., all unconscious, vents his appalling hypocrisies.

40. *our...roofed* all the rank and distinction of Scotland under our roof.

46. *The table's full* At first Macb. merely observes that the stool is occupied; then, he takes the seated corpse as some horrible practical joke (l. 49); last, he *knows*, and forgetting everything else, addresses the Ghost direct [Gr.]. Cf. his gradual realisation of the dagger, 2. 1. 33 ff.

48. *Here...highness?* The F. prints this as two lines, dividing 'Lord./What', in order, I suggest, to mark the pause as Macb. recognises the figure seated upon his stool. Cf. p. 91.

50. *Thou...did it* 'Some strange idea is in his mind that the thought of the dead man will not haunt him, like the memory of Duncan, if the deed is done by other hands' (Bradley, pp. 360–1).

55. *upon a thought* in a moment.

57. *passion* attack, fit.

58. *Are you a man?* Certainly an aside; so I think is the rest of this colloquy, during which the guests say nothing and presumably obey L. Macb. by continuing the feast. But all rise for the toast just before Macb. sees the second apparition, and are no doubt intended to hear what he says ll. 93 ff.

62. *air-drawn* A contemptuous quibble: (*a*) painted on air, (*b*) drawn through the air, so as to lead 'you to Duncan'.

64. *Impostors to* i.e. which usurp the name and power of true fear.

65–6. *A woman's story...grandam* Cf. *Dæm.* (p. 40), 'they are like old wiues' trattles about the fire... meere illusions'.

69. *Prithee, see there!* As at *Ham.* 3. 4. 125 f., the Ghost makes some gesture before vanishing.

72–3. *our monuments...kites* the only safe way with corpses is to let the vultures eat them. Cf. Scot, *Witchcraft,* v, vi, 'Some write that after the death of Nabuchadnezzar his sonne Eilumorodath gave his bodie to the ravens to be devoured, least afterwards his father should arise from death'.

75–83. *Blood...murder is* Spoken broodingly to himself.

76. *purged* With a glance at 'purge'=blood-letting, v. G.

humane (F.) 'Human' and 'humane' were not distinguished at this period.

gentle Proleptic; cf. 1. 6. 3.

78. *time has* (White; Camb.) F. 'times has'.

81. *twenty...crowns* Cf. l. 27.

mortal deadly.

83–4. *My worthy...lack you* Finding taunts of no avail, 'she changes her tactics and...endeavours to recall him to his senses by assuming an ordinary tone of voice....The device proves successful' (Moulton, 166).

88. F. prints the Gh.'s entry here; Camb. at l. 92; Gr. after 'Would he were here!', following Darm. Cf. end of note l. 37 S.D. above.

91. *thirst* long for ('for' not required at this date).

92. *all to all* i.e. 'let everybody drink to everybody' (K.).   93 S.D. see pp. lxix, lxxvi above.

95. *speculation* v. G.

98. *Only...time* Spoken with 'the falling accent of hopelessness' (Gr.).

101. *th'Hyrcan tiger* Cf. *Ham*. 2. 2. 454 and G. 'Hyrcan'.

104. *dare...desert* Where none could part the fighters or help the wounded. Cf. *Ric. II*, 1. 1. 65 note.

105. *If trembling I inhabit then* if I then harbour a single tremor. Much discussed and emended; but 'inhabit' (=house) occurs again at *A.Y.L.* 3. 3. 9, 'O knowledge ill-inhabited! worse than Jove in a thatched house'. Cf. O.E.D. 4 for other examples.

106. *The baby of a girl* a baby girl. Cf. 'that scoundrel of a man' [Darm.]. 'A girl's doll', the usual gloss, has no relevance to timidity.

110. *most admired disorder* Prob. = amazing lack of self-control; v. G. 'disorder'.

112–13. *You...owe* 'You make me doubt my own courage' (Darm.); v. G. 'disposition', 'strange', 'owe'. 'He is...staggered by the fact that everyone except himself is unmoved' (Clar.).

116. *mine* i.e. my colour.

119–20. *Stand...at once* Thus she dispenses with the long business of ceremonial departure, including lining-up in order of precedence and individual leave-taking.

122–44. Perhaps the most terrible passage in *Macbeth*. Notice his disconnected thought; her brief replies 'in listless, submissive words, which seem to come with difficulty' (Bradley, p. 376) and include 'not a word of reproach' (Moulton, p. 166); and above all the reference to sleeplessness.

122. *blood; they say, blood* (Whalley) F. 'blood they say:/Blood'. The two punctuations are virtually equivalent, since in 17th c. print a colon often introduced a noun clause. Cf. Simpson, p. 78. For the proverb cf. *Mirror for Magistrates*, 1571, p. 112, 'Take hede ye princes by examples past,/Bloud will have bloud, eyther at fyrst or last'. Macb. returns to his brooding of ll. 75–83.

123. *Stones* i.e. under which the murderer has concealed the corpse.

trees Prob. alluding to the tree which reveals the murder of Polydorus (*Aeneid*, iii. 22–57).

1.24. *Augures* (F.) Perhaps a minim-error for 'auguries' (cf. *Ham.* 5. 2. 217). But 'augure' (=augury) is poss., being found in Florio's *Worlde of Wordes*, 1598, v. Camb. vii, 378 (Note VIII).

understood relations 'incidents which were perceived to have reference to the question' (Schmidt, who cites *Merch.* 4. 1. 248 [245], where 'hath full relation to' = has full bearing upon). This seems better than J.'s, usually accepted, 'connexion between events, as understood by diviners', or K.'s 'reports properly comprehended'.

125–6. *brought forth...blood* Cf. *Dæm.* p. 80: 'as if the blud wer crying to the heauen for reuenge of the murtherer, God hauing appoynted that secret supernaturall signe, for tryall of that secrete unnaturall crime'.

127. *Almost...which is which* A symbolical timing of the central moment of the play; borne out by the immediate reference to Macd. who is to usher in the dawn.

128–9. *Macduff denies...bidding?* Cf. 3. 6. 21–2.

129. *Did you...him, sir?* i.e. did you send him a definite invitation and receive a refusal?

130. *by the way* casually.

but I will send For the result of this summons,
v. 3. 6. 39 f.

131–2. *There's...fee'd* Cf. Hol. 'For Macb. had
in euerie noble mans house one slie fellow or other in
fee with him'.

133. *betimes* A sudden resolve to be acted on at
once. Macb. is beginning to behave like a man subject
to fever (cf. Introd. p. lxi). Spies are not enough; he
will make the witches, who know everything, reveal the
names of all his foes.

Weïrd F. 'weyard'.

136. *All causes...way* everything else (or 'every
consideration') must afford scope.

136–7. *I am...so far* Cf. *Ric. III*, 4. 2. 63–4;
M.N.D. 3. 2. 48.

140. *acted ere...scanned* 'done first and scrutinised
after' (Gr.). Contrast Hamlet's 'That would be
scanned' at 3. 3. 75, almost the same point of the play.

141. *You lack...sleep* Cf. 3. 2. 17–22, 2. 2. 35 and
4. 1. 85–6; with 5. 1. For 'season' v. G.

142–3. *My strange...use* my strange delusions are
the terrors of the beginner not yet hardened by
practice. N.B. he now assumes that the Ghost was
imaginary.

144. *We are...deed.* Dreadful words.

in deed (Theo.) F. 'indeed'.

3. 5.

This sc. is an interpolation by Middleton; v. Introd.
p. xxiv. S.D. 'A heath' (Camb.) < 'the Heath' (Rowe).
'Thunder' denotes the use of traps, and all four 'enter'
from beneath, the witches prob. through the main trap
in the centre of the outer stage and Hecate by one of the
smaller ones.

10–13. *all you...for you* No relevance to Macb.; but seems to echo jealous speeches by Hecate in 1. 2 of Middleton's *Witch*.

15. *the pit of Acheron* Edd. ridicule the placing of Acheron, properly one of the rivers of Hades, in Scotland. But, as 'pit' shows, Hell itself is clearly implied (without reference to any river), a meaning gen. given to Acheron in Eliz. lit.; and Hell may be reached as readily from Scotland as from any other country.

20. *I am for th'air* Cf. Hecate in *The Witch*, 3. 3. 35, 'I'm for aloft'.

24. *vap'rous drop profound* Prob. the *virus lunare* (Lucan, *Pharsalia*, vi. 669), 'a foam which the moon was supposed to shed on particular herbs, or other objects, when strongly solicited by enchantment' (Steev.). For 'profound' v. G.

27. *artificial sprites* The apparitions in 4. 1.

29. *confusion* v. G.

32. *security* v. G.

33. S.D. F. 'Musicke, and a Song' and (at l. 35) 'Sing within. Come away, come away, &c.' Cf. pp. 87–8. The song comes from 3. 3 of *The Witch* and is printed in full (i.e. some 35 ll.) both in the 1673 Q. of *Macbeth* and in Dav. (1674). Perhaps the orig. intention was to sing only the first two lines here, viz.:

> Come away! come away!
> Hecate, Hecate, come away!

It has not been observed that the manner of Hecate's exit as well as the song has been followed. In both plays a car with an attendant spirit bears her aloft, i.e. is lowered and then drawn up by a windlass through a trap in the 'heavens' above the stage. 'Sits in a foggy cloud' (l. 35) shows that, in *Macbeth* at least, the car is concealed in billowing folds of light material such as were commonly used to add mystery to these stage-flights. Lastly the music was needed to conceal the noise of the pulleys. Cf. Adams, ch. x (pp. 335–66). N.B. Dav. prints the S.D. 'Machine descends' at l. 35.

3. 6.

S.D. The sc. gives no clue to locality; Theo. read 'A Chamber', Camb. (after Cap.) 'Forres. The palace'.

3. *borne* v. G. 'bear'. Through Len.'s irony we catch echoes of how Macb. himself spoke of these events in public.

8. *Who cannot...thought* i.e. who can want the thought. 'There can be no doubt that Sh. occasionally wrote a sentence that does not mean what he intended, though at the time of writing he evidently thought that it did. Sometimes it means the exact opposite: e.g. *Macb.* 3. 6. 8–10', Greg, *Ed. Problem*, p. xi, n. 2.

monstrous A trisyllable.

12. *tear* hack at. The way Macb. went to work in his pretended 'fury' (cf. 2. 3. 106 f.).

22. *tyrant's* Not 'usurper's' (Clar.) but 'a blood-thirsty king's'. The first time the term is applied to Macb. Hol., speaking of his 'tyranlike wrongs', relates that 'at length he founde suche sweetenesse by putting his nobles thus to death that his earnest thyrst after bloud...might in no wise be satisfied'.

24. *son* (Theo.) F. 'Sonnes'.

25. *holds* withholds.

27. *pious Edward* Edward the Confessor.

30. *upon his aid* in his behalf.

31. *Siward* F. 'Seyward'; Hol. 'Sywarde'.

35. *Free from...knives* rid our feasts, etc. of bloody knives; v. G. 'free'.

36. *free honours* honours honestly earned, i.e. not acquired by servility or as a reward for crime.

38. *the king* (Hanmer) F. 'their King'.

40, *He did* Cf. 3. 4. 129–30.

absolute...I' point-blank refusal (from Macd.). Hol. connects this refusal with Macb.'s fortification of the castle of Dunsinane, in the building of which Macd. refused to assist personally.

43. *clogs me* Implies that he will find some difficulty in delivering it to his terrible master.

49. *I'll send...with him.* Cf. l. 30.

4. 1.

S.D. Camb. (after Cap.) 'A cavern. In the middle, a boiling cauldron'. F. 'Thunder. Enter the three Witches'. Acc. to 3. 5. 15 the locality is 'The pit of Acheron', a contemporary staging of which may be seen in Jonson's description, in *The Masque of Queenes*, of an 'ougly Hell; which, flaming beneath, smoaked unto the top of the Roof', and from which twelve 'witches, with a kind of hollow and infernal music, came forth...all differently attir'd; some with ratts on theyr heads; some, on theyr shoulders; others with oyntment-potts at theyr girdles; all with spindells, timbrells, rattles, or other veneficall instruments, making a confused noyse, with strange gestures' (Jonson, vii, 282–3). This, which provides hints for my S.D., was prob. itself suggested by *Macbeth*, as was certainly the case with the 'cauldron in the centre' staged in 5. 2 of Middleton's *Witch*, a palpable imitation of the present sc. Lawrence (*Pre-R. Stud.* p. 162 f.) and Adams (pp. 209–11) agree that the 'cauldron' was set up above the trap in the inner stage and that the 'apparitions' rose from it.

1. *brinded cat* i.e. Graymalkin (1. 1. 8).

2. *hedge-pig* Cf. *Temp.* 2. 2. 10–12. In 1. 1,

2 Witch's familiar is a toad. But Sh. now wishes to use 'toad' (l. 6) for another purpose.

3. *Harpier* The familiar of 3 Witch. Steev. conj. it to be a corruption of 'Harpy' and J. C. Maxwell (privately) that it is a misreading of 'Harpya' for 'Harpyia' (v. *Aen.* iii. 226). Cf. 'Harpyr' (*1 Tamb.* 2.7.50).

5. *In the...entrails throw* Jonson's Witches similarly bring 'media magica', which they bury in the ground (v. Jonson, vii, 289–96), winding up their charm by chanting 'Around, around' and by 'a magicall Daunce full of praeposterous change and gesticulation ...dauncing, back to back, hip to hip, theyr handes joyn'd, and making theyr circles backward to the left hand, with strange, phantastique motions of theyr heads and bodyes' (ibid. pp. 300–1). Cf. note, 'hand in hand', 1. 3. 32.

6–8. *Toad...venom* Cf. *Newes* (p. 16), 'She confessed that she tooke a blacke toade and did hang the same up by the heeles, three daies, and collected and gathered the venome as it dropped', to the end that she might bewitch K. James.

6. *cold* Either this is dissyllabic or l. 6 lacks a syllable. Steev. reads 'coldest'.

7. *one* (Cap.) F. 'one:' which ruins the sense.

10–11. *Double...bubble* i.e. the purpose of the 'charm' is to double the hardships and sorrows of the world (cf. l. 18). As they speak the words, they pause, I take it, and stir the ingredients in with their spindles or broomsticks.

14–16. *newt...blind-worm* Cf. *M.N.D.* 2. 2. 11. Both are now known to be harmless.

17. *wing*, F. 'wing:'.

23. *Witches' mummy* Cf. G. 'mummy' and *Dæm.* (p. 43). The Devil 'causeth them to joynt dead corpses, and to make powders thereof, mixing such other thinges there amongst, as he giues unto them'.

24. *ravined* O.E.D. queries 'glutted', which is Clar.'s gloss. Mal. writes, 'I believe our author, with his usual licence, used "ravin'd" for "ravenous", the passive participle for the adjective'. 'Glutted' (e.g. with human flesh) seems the more probable.

27. *yew* A graveyard tree, supposed poisonous.

28. *in...eclipse* Cf. 'digged i'th' dark' (l. 25). The uncanny darkness of an eclipse was peculiarly consonant with witchcraft. Cf. *Lycidas*, l. 101.

29. *Turk...Tartar* Esp. precious, because un-christened, like the 'Jew' (l. 26) and the 'birth-strangled babe' (l. 30).

34. *ingredience* (F.) Cf. note 1. 7. 11.

37. *Cool...blood* Proceeding as usual by con-traries, they select the blood of the most lustful of animals to cool their concoction.

38. S.D. F. 'Enter Hecat, and the other three Witches'. Camb. print 'to' for 'and', which they take as a misprint. But this makes Hecate a witch, which she is not. Lawrence (*Sh.'s Work.*, p. 38) suggests that the F. S.D. was written by Middleton, who intended Hecate to bring 'other three witches' for the song at l. 43 and the dance at l. 132, both of which would need more than three to be effective. N.B. Five or six witches take part in the corresponding sc. of *The Witch* (5. 2. 37). See pp. xxvii and 88.

39–43. *O, well done!...put in* Another interpola-tion by Middleton. 'Smooth operatic, iambic lines' (as in 3. 5) instead of the 'impressive staccato of the trochaic lines' elsewhere in Sh.'s witch-scenes (Gr. p. xi).

39. *O, well done!* Cf. *Masque of Queenes*, l. 111. 'Well done, my Hagges' (Jonson, vii, 287).

40. *gains* 'There are no gains: the Sisters... disappear without waiting for a reward' (K.).

42. *Like elves and fairies* Another incongruity.

43. S.D. *Black spirits* etc. Another song from *The Witch* (also printed by Dav.), headed 'A Charm-Song, about a Vessel' and beginning (5. 2. 60):

> Black spirits and white, red spirits and gray,
> Mingle, mingle, mingle, you that mingle may!

An exit for Hecate, not given by F., was surely intended here; otherwise she should address Macbeth and speak ll. 125–32.

46. *Open, locks* See Scot, bk. xii, ch. xiv, 'A charme to open locks'; and Spalding, p. 113.

50. *by that...profess* in the name of your art.

52–4. *Though you...up* Perhaps a reference to the storm raised by witchcraft on K. James's voyage to Denmark; cf. *Dæm.* p. 46; *Newes*, p. 17.

55. *bladed corn...lodged* Cf. Scot, *Discoverie*, 1, ch. 4, 'Some [write] that they can transferre corne in the blade from one place to another'; and *2 Hen. VI*, 3. 2. 176; *Tit. And.* 4. 4. 71; *Ric. II*, 3. 3. 162; *Hen. VIII*, 5. 5. 32.

lodged beaten down.

57. *slope* Not found as vb. (=bend) elsewhere in Sh. or indeed before Milton (*Lyc.* l. 31; *Par. Lost*, i, 223) who perhaps takes it from this passage. Cap. conj. 'stoop' (<sp. 'stope').

58–60. *the treasure...sicken* Cf. 1. 3. 58 (note); 3. 2. 16 (note); *Par. Lost*, ii, 910 ff.; *Lear*, 3. 2. 8, 'Crack nature's moulds, all germens spill at once'; and *Wint.* 4. 4. 475, 'Let Nature crush the sides o'th' Earth together, And mar the seeds within'. Curry (ch. 11) shows that Renaissance thought, deriving from Augustine (*De Trinitate*), conceived the potentialities and generative powers of nature as latent in the 'rationes seminales' or seeds, both material and spiritual, which God in the beginning infused into Chaos; and that these 'virtues of things' hidden 'in the close Prison of Grosse and Earthie bodies' could to some extent be acted upon by demons or witches employing them. Cf. the 'élan vital' of Bergson and the 'Life Force' of G. B. Shaw. *sicken* become surfeited.

59. *germens* (Globe, O.E.D.) F. 'Germaine,'.
all together (Pope) F. 'altogether'.

63. *Call...'em* Note the 'fierce intensity of purpose' (K.).

67. *high or low* i.e. in the ranks of Hell.

68. S.D. Upton's interpretation, now generally accepted (though not by K.), runs:

The armed head represents symbolically Macbeth's head cut off and brought to Malc. by Macd. [and on the stage the same 'head' would serve in both cases.—J.D.W.]. The bloody child is Macd. untimely ripped from his mother's womb. The child with a crown on his head, and a bough in his hand, is the royal Malc., who ordered his soldiers to hew them down a bough, and bear it before them to Dunsinane.

Acc. to A. E. Parsons ('The Trojan Legend in England', *M.L.R.* xxiv, 404–7) the 'child crowned is James himself, crowned in his cradle, bearing his genealogical tree'. Cf. also H. N. Paul as cited p. xx, n. 2 above [1950].

69. *He knows...thought* Macb. does not recognise himself, but the audience do, and the irony of the words prepares them for equivocation to follow.

72. S.D. 'descends'. This F. S.D. shows that the Apparitions come up through the trap-door.

76. *More potent...first* The words seem to dispose of K.'s idea that Apparitions 1 and 2 both represent Macd.; Macb. is less potent than Macd.

82. *what need...thee?* what fear need I have of thee?

83. *assurance double* (Pope) F. 'aſſurance: double'.

84. *of fate* i.e. from fate.

88. *round* Cf. 1.5.27. *top* Literally and figuratively.

90. *care* F. 'care:'.

93. *Dunsinane* (F2) F. 'Dunsmane'. The only instance of correct accentuation; Dúnsináne elsewhere in the play. Cf. note l. 97 and 5. 2. 12.

97. *Rebellious dead* (F.) Most edd. accept Theob.'s conj. 'Rebellions head', which accords with l. 91. But H. W. Donner (*Acta Acad. Aboensis Humaniora*, xviii; cf. *T.L.S.* 23 and 30/9/49) points out that Macb. refers in 3. 4 (N.B. 3. 4. 80–2), to the 'rising' of Banquo's ghost which 'rises' again at l. 122 below. Cf. also Roy Walker, *The Time is Free*, pp. 143–4. [1950.]

98. *Birnam* F. 'Byrnan'—and often later. A hill opposite Dunkeld on the Tay, visible from Dunsinane 12 miles off.

106. *noise* music, v. G. Adams (pp. 189–91) suggests that the cauldron sinks to give the audience a clear view of the kings, as each passes rapidly across the lighted doorway at the back of the inner-stage.

111. S.D. F. 'A ſhew of eight Kings, and Banquo laſt, with a glaſſe in his hand'. 'Shew'=dumb-show (cf. *Ham.* 3 2. 133 note). K. notes that Hoboyes (Hautboys) play in F. *Ham.* as here (S.D. l. 106). That Ban. should carry the glass is inconsistent with l. 119 (v. note). The eight kings are those of the Stewart dynasty: Robert II (son of Walter Stewart, supposed descendant of Ban.) who married the grand-daughter of Robert Bruce, Robert III and the 6 Jameses. Mary Q. of Scots omitted, because only kings spoken of.

113. *hair* J. proposed 'air' (cf. *Wint.* 5. 1. 128) and I suspect he may be right. Despite l. 123 (v. note) 'hair' seems oddly specific.

116. *this?*—(F.) *Start* i.e. from your sockets, that I may see no more; cf. *Ham.* 1. 5. 17.

117. *crack of doom* sound of the last trump. Cf. Introd. pp. xviii–xix; v. G. 'crack'.

119. *The eighth* (F. 'eight') This should be James I

of England. Did they dare to show his image on the stage? If not, that perhaps explains why F. gives to Banquo the 'glass' (i.e. the 'prospective glass' or magic .mirror; cf. Greene, *Friar Bacon*, scc. vi, xiii).

121. *two-fold balls...sceptres* Chambers (*Wm. Sh.* i, 473) writes:

[This] can have nothing to do, as suggested by some commentators, with the triple style of King of Great Britain, France, and Ireland, adopted by *Procl.* 1003 of 20 Oct. 1604. The earlier English style was triple, and there were no sceptres for France and Ireland. The 'two-fold balls' must be the 'mounds' borne on the English and Scottish crowns, and the 'treble sceptres' the two used for investment in the English coronation and the one used in the Scottish coronation.

122. *sight!...*F.'fight:' 'Pause syllabique' (Darm.). The sudden and unexpected apparition of the murdered Ban. quite unnerves Macb., and what follows is spoken aghast. The cry 'But no more *sights*!' at l. 155 harks back to this 'horrible' moment.

123. *blood-boltered* having his hair matted with blood, v. G. Macb.'s obsession with Ban.'s head and its 'twenty trenchéd gashes' (3.4.27, 82) is adduced by K. to explain 'hair' at l. 113; but why should the 'hair' of Robert II be made to suggest the matted hair of Ban.?

124. *What, is this so?* 'As Macb. is staring at the blood-boltered Ban., the apparitions vanish, and...he turns to the sisters, only to find that they too have vanished' (K.).

125-32. *Ay, sir...pay* An interpolation, as most agree, which ruins a fine theatrical effect. But K. over-reaches himself when he condemns the last two lines as 'absurdly out of tune', since (as Ver. notes) they are spoken in mockery and refer to Macb.'s rude 'welcome' at l. 48, while Hazlitt calls ll. 125-6 a 'bitter taunt'.

129. *I'll charm...sound* Bullen (Middleton, v. 446)

compares Hecate's words in *The Witch*, 5. 2. 85–6, 'Come my sweet sisters; let the air strike our tune'; followed by the S.D. 'They dance the Witches' Dance, and exeunt'.

130. *antic round* fantastic dance. Cf. the description of the Witches' dance in the *Masque of Queenes*, cited note l. 5.

135. S.D. Len. had evidently stood on guard without the cavern.

139–40. *I did hear...horse* Cf. note 3. 3. 8.

142. *Macduff is fled* 'As in 1. 3. 104 the predictions begin to fulfil themselves instantly and thus their trustworthiness is established in Macb.'s mind' (K.).

145–6. *The flighty purpose...with it* 'Our deeds never keep pace with our purposes unless we act at once' (Gr.).

149. *acts, be* F. 'Acts: be'.

153–5. *That trace...sights!* Omit the rhyming tag 'No boasting...cool', which merely repeats what has already been said, and we are left with a regular pentameter for the alexandrine, etc. Cf. p. xxiv.

155. *no more sights!* He need not fear. 'The Witches have done their work, and after this purposeless butchery his own imagination will trouble him no more' (Bradley, p. 363).

4. 2.

S.D. From Camb. Hol. relates that Macb. besieged the castle, which offered no resistance. 'But neverthelesse Makbeth most cruel caused the wife and children of Makduffe, with all other whom he found in that castell, to be slaine.' For Macd.'s desertion see Introd. p. xxxix.   2. *patience* 'self-control' (K.).

4. *Our...traitors* i.e. his flight laid him open to the charge of so being.   7. *titles* v. G.

9. *the natural touch* a parent's instinct

11. *Her...nest*. Absolute construction.

17. *fits o'th' season* what convulsions the time may bring forth. It is Macb. of course to whom the 'fits' belong.

19. *And...ourselves* without knowing it.

19–20. *when we...we fear* when our fears make us entertain all sorts of rumours; cf. *K. John*, 4. 2. 145.

22. *none* (Camb. conj.) F. 'moue'—a simple minim-error, v. MSH, i, 106 f. Cf. *Ant.* 1. 4. 44–7.

24–5. *Things...before* 'Another metaphor from the sea' (Darm.).

29. *It...disgrace* i.e. I should break down.

32. *As birds do* The boy remembers ll. 9–11 (and Sh. *Matth.* vi. 26).

35. *pitfall* v. G.

36. *Poor* No traps are set for '*poor* birds'.

44–50. *Was my father...hanged* The boy casts back to ll. 4–18. But see Introd. pp. xxix–xxxi.

45. *he was* i.e. to her, she imagines.

47. *One...lies* i.e. is false to, or equivocates in, his oath of allegiance (or his marriage-vow).

59. *how wilt...father?* With the repetition of the question at l. 38 we return to the orig. theme.

65. *in your...perfect* i.e. I well know who you are.

68–9. *ones./To...thus*, (Camb. after F. 2) F. 'ones/ to...thus.'

82. *shag-haired* (Steev.) F. 'ſhagge-ear'd'. 'Heare' is a common sp. of 'hair' in Sh. (cf. *V.A.* ll. 51, 147, 191; *K. John* (F.), 5. 2. 133, 'vnheard' for 'unhaired'), and *g* and *h* are similar letters in his hand; thus 'shagheard' might easily be misread 'shaggeard'. For 'shag-haired villain' cf. *2 Hen. VI*, 3. 1. 367 and Add. IV (c) to *Sir Th. More*, ll. 64–73 (Malone Soc. Reprint). See *O.E.D. ruffian* 2: 'one distinguished as a swaggering bully...by his dress or appearance (esp. by wearing the hair long).'

4. 3.

A sc. gen. contemned by critics; e.g. 'the only tedious one in the play' (E.K.C.); 'the dialogue is dull and forced' and 'the earlier part...is a perfunctory paraphrase from Hol.' (Gr.). Cf. also Bradley, pp. 57–8. Yet it is undoubtedly by Sh. (see notes, ll. 22, 64, 80, 219); while it falls into 3 parts: (i) the testing of Macd., (ii) the account of the King's Evil, (iii) the news of the death of Lady Macd. and children; and of these no. (iii) is not 'dull' and nos. (i) and (ii) were prob. 'sweet, sweet, sweet' flattery for a monarch's 'tooth', v. Introd. pp. xxxi–xxxiii.

S.D. Dyce and Camb. 'England. Before the King's palace'. For 'Edward the Confessor', v. 1. 146 (note) and 3. 6. 27.

3. *mortal* v. G. *sword*, F. 'Sword:'. *good* brave.

4. *Bestride* Cf. G, *downfall'n* (Warb.) F. 'downfall'.

6. *Strike...face* Cf. *2 Hen. IV*, 1. 3. 91–2, 'with what loud applause/Didst thou beat heaven'.

10. *friend, I* F. 'friend: I'.

13. *well:* F. 'well,'.

14. *young* And so not dangerous.

15. *deserve* (Theo.) F. 'diſcerne' (*n : u* error).

wisdom For the omission of ''tis' or ''twere' cf. l. 191 and 3. 2. 32.

19–20. *recoil...charge* give way to a royal command. A suppressed image from gunnery; cf. *2 Hen. VI*, 3. 2. 331.

19. *may* = is permitted to.

20. *I shall* Omitted by Pope as unnecessary to sense and metre.   22. *Angels...fell* v. Introd. p. lxvi.

24. *so* like grace.

hopes i.e. for Scotland; cf. l. 114.

25. *there where* i.e. by the action in which. Without

some understanding with Macb. how could he have
left wife and child?

26. *rawness* v. G.

29–30. *Let...safeties* i.e. I have no wish to cast
doubts upon your honour, only to protect myself.

33. *wrongs* ill-gotten crown, etc.

34. *affeered* (Hanmer) F. 'affear'd', v. G. Suggested
by 'check'.

44–132. *But for all this* etc. Sh. follows Hol.
closely (except at ll. 97–100, v. note) and Malc.'s device
seems crude to mod. minds. Yet doubtful if Sh.'s
audience saw anything but shrewd policy in it, since it
diverts Macd.'s attention from the testing (ll. 8–31),
which had deeply offended him, while it tests him still
further and proves him 'honest' up to the hilt. Further,
it has an important dramatic function: just as the
character of Laertes is exposed in *Hamlet*, 4. 5 and 4. 7,
as a foil to the hero, so here at the same moment of the
play an image of the true Prince is set forth as a foil to
the villain.

46. *sword*, F. 'Sword;'.

51. *grafted* made part of my being.

52. *opened* i.e. like buds.

58. *Luxurious, avaricious* 'These epithets surprise
us. Who would have expected avarice or lechery in
Macb.?' (Bradley, p. 363). But luxury (=lust), avarice
and deceit are the three vices Malc. proceeds to charge
himself with (acc. to Hol.) and he 'merely admits, for
the sake of argument, that Macb. has them' (K.).

63. *cistern* i.e. a 'tank of stagnant foul water'
(Darm.); cf. *Oth.* 4. 2. 61 and Hol. 'abhominable
fountaine of all vyces'.

64. *All continent...o'erbear* Cf. Sh.'s favourite
river image, v. Spurgeon, pp. 92–4.

65. *will* lust.

66–7. *Boundless...tyranny* absence of self-control is like tyranny in the 'little kingdom' of man's nature.

69. *But fear not yet* 'Macd. is testing Malc. in his turn' (K.) and so leads him on to further confession.

71. *Convey* v. G. Borrowed from Hol.

72. *cold, the* F. 'cold. The'.

77. *ill-composed affection* evil disposition.

80. *Desire...house* Cf. Son. 29. 7.

his that man's.

81–2. *And my...hunger more* Cf. Ham. 1. 2. 144–5.

82. *that* so that.

85. *sticks deeper* Cf. 3. 1. 49.

85–7. *grows...root...slain kings* Cf. Hol. 'Avarice is the roote of all mischief and for that crime the most part of our kings have bene slaine'.

86. *summer-seeming* i.e. a transitory heat, like summer, that 'fades before the frost of age' (Gr.).

89. *Your mere own* property entirely your own.

portable Suggested by 'importable' in the corresponding paragraph of Hol.

90. *weighed* counterbalanced.

91. *The king-becoming graces* etc. Cf. Hol. 'there is nothing that more becommeth a prince than constancie, veritie, truth and iustice'; and *Bas. Dor.* (p. 38), 'Iustice...Clemencie, Magnanimitie, Liberalitie, Constancie, Humilitie, and all other Princely vertues'.

94. *fortitude* constancy.

95. *relish* v. G. and cf. 'smacking' (l. 59).

96–7. *In the division of...ways* Metaphors from performing (i) music (v. G. 'division'), (ii) drama. Cf. *2 Hen. IV*, 4. 5. 125–6.

97–100. *Nay...unity on earth* Cf. Introd. pp. xxxi–xxxii, and K. James's speech of 1603 to Parliament (McIlwain, pp. 269 ff.) on the blessings of outward and inward peace conferred upon Britain in his person.

98. *the sweet milk* Cf. 1. 5. 16 (note).

99. *Uproar* Not found as vb. elsewhere.

107. *interdiction* A term in Scots law='a restraint imposed upon a person incapable of managing his own affairs', while by 'voluntary interdiction' a man, 'conscious of his facility' or weakness of character, might resign the conduct of his affairs to another (v. O.E.D. 3).

accused F. 'accuſt' Most edd. follow F 2 'accurſt'; but, as Gr. notes, '"accused" makes good sense'—better, I think, after 'interdiction', as just interpreted.

108. *blaspheme his breed* slander the royal house of Scotland.

108–11. *Thy royal father...lived* No hint of this in Hol. K. James and Q. Anne might take it to themselves, if they chose.

111. *Died...lived* Cf. *Temp.* 5. 1. 313 'Every third thought shall be my grave'.

113. *Hath* (F.) Rowe, etc. 'Have'. Cf. Franz, pp. 565 ff.

119. *modest wisdom* wise precaution.

120–1. *but God...and me!* 'A solemn oath that what he is about to say is true' (K.).

125–6. *yet unknown to woman* Draper compares James's insistence upon prenuptial chastity in *Bas. Dor.* (McIlwain, p. 34).

128–31. *At no time...upon myself* See Introd. p. xxxi. 133. *thy* (F 2) F. 'they'.

here-approach Cf. 'here-remain', l. 148.

135. *Already* (F.) Rowe and some edd. 'All ready'. *at a point* v. G. 'point'.

136–7. *the chance...quarrel!* May our chances of success (v. G. 'goodness') be as great as is the justice of our quarrel.

140–59. *Comes the king forth* etc. Cf. Introd. pp. xxxii–xxxiii. Exhibits the true prince (cf. note ll. 44–132) in another way.

142–3. *convinces...art* defeats the utmost efforts of science.

146. *the evil* 'The King's Evil' or scrofula was for centuries thought curable at the touch of any king descending from Edward the Confessor, who was said to have exercised the power first, though no record of it goes back beyond Henry II. Henry VII instituted a special service for the occasion (cf. l. 154) and began the presentation of gold coins (cf. l. 153). James I continued the practice, while professing scepticism of its efficacy, since 'the age of miracles is past'; v. K. *Witchcraft*, p. 316, and *Sh. Eng.* i, 427.

156. *virtue* healing power; cf. *Mark*, v. 30, and Hol. (Boswell-Stone, p. 40) 'He left that vertue... unto his successors the kings of this realme'.

157. *gift of prophecy.* The words are Hol.'s, yet also applicable to James, who (the bishops declared at the Hampton Court Conference) 'spoke by the power of inspiration' (Harington, i, 181–2).

159 f. *See who comes here* etc. The rest of the sc. is Sh.'s invention; cf. the reception by Brutus of Portia's death (*Caes.* 4. 3. 147–95).

160. *My countryman* He recognises him by his dress, which suggests that the Scots wore something distinctive on Sh.'s stage, perhaps a blue bonnet (cf. *1 Hen. IV*, 2. 4. 352).   168. *rend* (Rowe) F. 'rent'.

170. *modern ecstasy* commonplace excitement.

174. *too nice...true!* too pointed and yet too true!

175. *doth hiss* gets [the speaker] hissed for stale news.

183. *out* i.e. in the field. Cf. *2 Hen. IV*, 3. 2. 118.

185. *power a-foot* forces mobilising.

191–2. *none...out* Christendom has none to show.

194. *would* should.   195. *should* would.

196. *fee-grief* v. G.

206. *quarry* v. G. Cf. *Ham.* 5. 2. 362.

deer A quibble.

209–10. *Give sorrow...break* Malc. offers the
advice approved by the best contemporary psychology;
cf. note 2. 2. 33–4.   212. *must be* had to be.

216. *He has no children* Is 'he' Macb. or Malc.?
Bradley (pp. 489–92) argues at length for Malc.;
cf. *K. John*, 3. 4. 91, 'He talks to me that never had
a son'. Others, who prefer Macb., quote *3 Hen. VI*,
5. 5. 63–4, 'You have no children, butchers! If you
had,/The thought of them would have stirred up
remorse' (=compassion), or interpret the words, 'How
can I revenge? Macb. has no children to kill'. (Cf.
Stoll, p. 197 n. 20.) The reader must take his choice.
But note (i) Macd. is at first stunned, makes Ross repeat
the news twice over, and only at l. 220 seems to become
conscious of Malc.'s persistent efforts, doctor-like, to
break into the obsession, which if allowed to prevail
would lead to madness (cf. 2. 2. 33–4 note); (ii) yet the
word 'comforted' might well sting a man so stunned
into a momentary reaction, expressed in a bitter aside.
That L. Macb. had 'given suck' (1. 7. 54 and note) is
irrelevant to the problem, since she might have had as
many children as Q. Anne (the second) and yet be without one now, and there is no hint of a child to Macb.
anywhere in the play.

217. *hell-kite* Vergil's 'immanis voltur' (*Aen.* vi,
597).

219. *at one...swoop* Now proverbial. Two senses
present: (*a*) at one pounce of the 'hell-kite', (*b*) at one
sweep of the stakes, by which Macd. loses all the prizes
of life; cf. *Ham*. 4. 5. 142 (Q2), 'soopstake'.

220. *like a man* That touches him at last.

224–7. *Sinful...souls* i.e. they died as a punish-
ment for my sins, not theirs. An answer to 'Did
heaven...part?' with no reference to their being
'rawly left', as some suppose; Macd. '*must* be from
thence' (l. 211). See p. xxxix.

235. *too* i.e. let him escape damnation as well as my
sword. Cf. *Ham*. 1. 2. 182–3; 3. 3. 73–95.

tune (Rowe) F. 'time'.

236. *power* army.

238–9. *the Powers...instruments* The 'Powers'
were a separate order in the angelic hierarchy whose
special function was the repulse of Satan's forces when
Divine Wisdom judged they had proceeded far enough
(cf. Curry, pp. 70, 72–3, and note 2. 1. 7–9 above).

239–40. *Receive...day* The tag adds little. Cf.
Introd. p. xxiv and n. 2.

5. 1.

S.D. 'Dunsinane' (Cap.); 'A room...castle' (Mal.).
F. 'Doctor of Physicke' denotes the appropriate gown.

1. *two* F. 'too'.

4. *since...field* Cf. 4. 3. 184–5.

5. *night-gown* v. G.

7. *write...seal* Evidently a letter to Macbeth.
Does Sh. suggest that she replies to the letter written
by him when in the field before (1. 5. 1–13)?

9–13. *A great perturbation* etc. The professional
medical language of the time. *perturbation in nature*
constitutional disorder. *do...watching* exhibit all the
symptoms of wakefulness. *actual* v. G.

20. *close* concealed.

22–3. *light...continually* 'Darkness which she
invoked (1. 5. 49 f.) is now her terror' (Gr.). Cf. l. 35.

25. *are shut* (F.) Rowe and most edd. 'is shut'.
Cf. *Oth*. 4. 3. 95; *Son*. 112, 10–11, 'my adder's sense
...stoppéd are'.

29. *washing her hands* Cf. 2. 2. 67–8, 'A little water
clears us of this deed: How easy is it then!' Tragic
irony.

34. *One · two* The bell she struck at 2. 1. 61.

35. *Hell is murky!* A sudden glimpse.into the abyss. at her feet. Cf. ll. 22–3 (note) and 1. 5. 49 ff. 'Come thick night, And pall thee in the dunnest smoke of hell'.

36. *a soldier and afeard?* Cf. her taunts at 1. 7. 39–41, 49.

36–7. *What...accompt?* Cf. 1. 7. 77–9. Blank verse.

38–9. *Yet who...blood in him?* This takes us with her into Duncan's chamber and adds to what we know from 2. 2. 55–7, 64.

42–4. *No more...starting* By a natural transition the dream now shifts to the banquet after Ban.'s murder.

49. *smell of the blood* 'Macb.'s imagination is visual: it is the *colour* of the blood that appals him (2. 2. 61–3). ...The sense impression that poisons L. Macb.'s memory comes from smell' (Gr.). Verplanck compares the smell of blood that Cassandra scents before the murder of Agamemnon (Aeschylus, *Ag.* ll. 1306–11).

51. *Oh! oh! oh!* A separate line in F.

58. *practice* v. G.

61–3. *Wash...grave.* The two murders are now confused; cf. 2. 2. 66–71; 3. 4. 78–82.

65. *to bed* As they do at the end both of 2. 2 and 3. 4.

67. *What's done...undone* Cf. her 'what's done, is done' (3. 2. 12) and his 'If it were done, when 'tis done', etc. (1. 7. 1).

70 f. *Foul whisperings* etc. The return to blank verse 'lowers the tension towards that of the next scene' (Bradley, p. 400).

75. *annoyance* injury. His fears are justified at 5. 8. 69–71.

5. 2.

S.D. 'The...Dunsinane' (Cap. and Camb.). Here are some of the 'worthy fellows' (4. 3. 183) that had risen against Macb., Len. among them (cf. 3. 6).

2. *uncle* More convenient for verse than 'grandfather' as Hol. describes him. *Siward* F. 'Seyward'.

3. *dear causes* grievous wrongs; v. G. 'dear', 'cause'.

4. *to the...alarm* i.e. to the field of battle.

5. *the mortified man* i.e. a corpse; v. G. 'mortified'.

6. *well* v. G.

8. *file* v. G.

10. *unrough* v. G.

11. *protest* v. G.

12. *Great...fortifies* Cf. Hol. 'To the ende he might more sickerly oppresse his subiects with all tyranlike wrongs, hee buylded a strong Castell on the top of an hill cleped Dunsinnane'.

15. *distempered cause* 'The purpose of ll. 11–24 is to prepare us for the almost maniacal excitement...in the next sc.' (K.). 'Cause', then, =not 'party', but 'sickness' (cf. *All's Well*, 2. 1. 114), while 'rule' =self-control, which 'belt' symbolises; cf. *1 Hen. IV*, 3. 3. 21–2, 151 (note).

17. *murders...hands* Cf. Seneca, *Her. Fur.* l. 1329, v. note 2. 2. 59–63.

20–2. *now...thief* Cf. 1. 3. 144–6; 1. 7. 34–6; 2. 4. 38; and Spurgeon, pp. 325–7 for the image of ill-fitting clothes that runs through *Macbeth*.

23. *pestered...start* ragged nerves for being jumpy.

24–5. *When...there* 'when all the faculties of the mind are employed in self-condemnation' (J.). The only *direct* suggestion in the play that Macb. has a conscience.

27–9. *the med'cine...of us* i.e. they are ready to help the true doctor (cf. 5. 3. 50), Malc., purge the land of its fever (cf. *L.L.L.* 4. 3. 95–6; *Ric. II*, 1. 1. 153), even if it means bleeding themselves to the last drop of their blood; v. G. 'purge'.

29–30. *Or so...weeds* 'A singularly infelicitous figure' (K.). After ll. 28–9, 'Or so much as it needs' is bathetic. See p. xxiv. For the notion that blood promoted vegetable growth, cf. *Ric. II*, 5. 6. 46; *3 Hen. VI*, 2. 2. 169.

5. 3.

S.D. 'Dunsinane...castle' (Cap. and Camb.). 5. 1 shows us L. Macb.'s break-down; 5. 3 shows us Macb.'s.

5. *consequence* (Singer) F. 'Confequences'. Both style and metre support the change.

8. *English epicures* Cf. Hol. i. 357, 'fine fare or riotous surfet...which came into the realme of Scotland with the Englishmen'.

9–10. *the mind...fear* The rhyme lends finality and a touch of complacency which are immediately contradicted by what follows.

15. *lily-livered* v. G.

boy A term of contempt; cf. *Cor.* 5. 6. 101.

19. *sick at heart* 'His frenzy gives place, in an instant, to profound dejection' (K.). Note the unfinished sentence in l. 20.

20. *Seton* F. 'Seyton'. Cf. F. 'Seyward' (3. 6. 31, 5. 2. 2, etc.) and 'weyward' for 'weird' (1. 3. 32, etc.).

21. *cheer...disseat me now* 'Cheer' connects with the thought of 'I am sick at heart'. 'But it breaks into the vivid metaphor in "push" and "disseat"' (Gr.). Bp. Percy read 'chair' for 'cheer', and if we suppose a play on that word, in Sh.'s day not dissimilar in sound, all is clear.

disseat (Cap.) F. 'diſ-eate'; F2 'diſeaſe'. Cf. *Oth.*
5. 1. 128–9, 'This is the night/That either makes me
or fordoes me quite'.

22. *way of life* J. conj. 'may of life', which, Raleigh
(*Sh.* p. 223) declares, was to 'make him speak like Pope';
yet cf. *Ado,* 5. 1. 76; *Hen. V,* 1. 2. 120; *Ric. II,* 3. 4.
48–9; and Sidney, *Ast. & Stel.* 21, 'If now the May
of my years much decline'. But 'way'=course, and
Macb. prob. refers to the progress of the seasons;
cf. *Son.* 73, 'That time of life thou may'st in me behold/
When yellow leaves, or few, or none, do hang' etc.;
and Seneca, *Her. Fur.* ll. 1258–9, 'Cur animam in ista
luce detineam amplius/Morerque nihil est; cuncta iam
amisi bona'.

23. *the sere* i.e. 'the withered state' (of old age).
See Onions and T.L.S. 24/x/1935.

29. S.D. Hol. merely includes 'Seiten' in a list of
names (i. 351) with no reference to Macb. But French
(p. 296) notes that 'the Setons of Touch were (and are
still) hereditary armour-bearers to the kings of Scotland'
and that this is Seton's function here. Cf. p. xlii,
and G. Seton, *History of the Seton Family,* 1896, i, 337.

39. *Cure her* (F2) F. 'Cure'. Clar. conj. 'Make
cure'; and, as many note, Macb. is thinking more of
himself than of his wife.

40. *Canst...diseased* The parallel from Seneca,
quoted for l. 22, continues: 'nemo polluto queat
Animo mederi'.

43. *oblivious* causing oblivion.

44. *stuffed...stuff* J. conj. 'charged' for 'stuffed';
cf. 5. 1. 53. Mal., Dyce, E.K.C., K. etc. defend F.
here, on the plea that Sh. is fond of such repetitions,
and instance 1. 5. 63–4; 3. 2. 20; 5. 2. 19. But
whereas those add point or charm, neither is afforded
by the repetition before us, which is clearly due, as most
edd. have agreed, to misprint or mistranscription (cf.

note 5.4.11, and p.89). Many emendations proposed, e.g. for 'stuffed'—full, foul, fraught, stained, clogged, etc.; and for 'stuff'—grief, load, slough, freight, etc. After 'charged' (for 'stuffed') the best, I think, is 'pressed', i.e. oppressed; cf. *Oth*. 3.4.176.

46. *himself* Spoken pointedly; the Doct. realises that Macb. is talking about himself as well as his wife.

48. *staff* The commander's truncheon; cf. *Ham*. I.2.204 (note).

50. *Come, sir, dispatch* This fidgeting with the armour, impatiently demanded, yet not needed, put on and then put off again, was no doubt made much of in Sh.'s theatre. Cf. 'Ric. III's distraction (4.4.440–56) on learning of Richmond's landing' (Gr.).

50–6. *If thou...English hence?* Dramatic irony, since, as was observed at 5.2.27–9, the best doctor is Malc. and the real disease, not the English, but Macb. himself.

52. *pristine* (F2) F. 'priſtiue'.

55. *senna* (F4) F. 'Cyme', prob.<'cynne', a sp. of 'sene', the usual 16th and 17th c. form (<Fr. 'sené' or 'cené').

5.4.

S.D. 'Country near Birnam wood' (Camb.). The rebels have now joined forces with Malc. and Siward, 'near Birnam wood' (5.2.5). Edd. add Lennox and Ross, who have nothing to say.

2. *chambers will be safe* i.e. not like Dunc.'s chamber in Macb.'s castle.

6. *discovery* reconnaissance.

9–10. *endure...before't* allow us to besiege it.

10. *'Tis...hope* Because only so can he keep his forces under his eye.

11. *to be gone* (Johnson) F. 'to be giuen'. Malone strongly inclined to J.'s conj. which gives good sense,

while 'given', prob. a transcriber's anticipation of 'given' in the next line, makes no sense at all. Cf. G. 'advantage'. 12. *more or less* v. G.

13–14. *constrainéd...too* Cf. *2 Hen. IV*, 1. 1. 196. *things* creatures; cf. *Ham*. 4. 2. 27.

14–16. *Let...soldiership* i.e. let us be wise after the event and get to business now.

16–18. *The time...we owe* i.e. 'time will soon show how our account stands' (Gr.).

19–20. *Thoughts...arbitrate* The couplet merely repeats what Macd. and Siward himself have just said in ll. 14–18, and might be omitted with no loss to the play, while 'due decision' (l. 17) makes a good antecedent to 'which' (l. 21). Cf. Introd. p. xxiv.

5. 5.

S.D. 'Dunsinane. Within the castle' (Mal. and Camb.).

1–2. *Hang...come:* (Rowe) F. 'Hang...walls,/ The Cry is ſtill, they come:'. Keightley conj. 'Hang out our banners! On the...walls/The cry.../come'.

1. *the outward walls* Sh.'s Dunsinane is 'a large castle with various walls and fortifications, which must be taken one after another' (K.). Cf. 5. 2. 12.

2. *The cry...come* Cf. 'ten thousand' (5. 3. 13); and 'false thanes' (5. 3. 7, 50) have now joined the English (cf. 5. 2. 18).

5. *forced* reinforced.

9–15. *I have...start me* Cf. 1. 3. 135 and 3. 4. 143. 'Hard use' has now banished fears; but, as ll. 17–28 show, all 'human kindness' and interest in life have gone also; v. G. 'treatise', 'direness'.

17. *should...hereafter* would have died sometime. He 'does not even ask the manner or the cause' (K.).

18. *such a word* 'as Death' (E.K.C.).

23. *Out...brief candle!* Contrast *Prov.* xx. 27, 'The spirit of man is the candle of the Lord', and *Meas.* 1. 1. 32–5.

24. *shadow* Suggested by 'candle' and itself suggesting 'player' (cf. *M.N.D.* 5. 1. 210).

24–5. *a poor player...struts and frets* 'Shows Macb.'s contempt, not for the actor, but for human life. "Poor" expresses pity' (K.). For 'struts and frets' cf. *Troil.* 1. 3. 153–6; *Ham.* 3. 2. 32.

38. *false* (F 2) F. 'fhlfe'.

42. *pall in* (Johnson) i.e. fail in (cf. G.). F. 'pull in'. 'I pull in' is at once too deliberate, as if 'resolution' were a stop in an organ upon which Macb. is playing, and disturbs the rhythm.

43. *th' equivocation of the fiend* Cf. *2 Hen. VI*, 1. 4. 60–75 and Introd. p. xxx.

50. *wish...undone* Cf. Introd. p. lxiii; 3. 2. 16; 4. 1. 58–60.

estate = at once 'structure' and 'organisation'.

51. *Ring...bell* Cf. 2. 3. 74. The bell, which summons everyone in the castle for the final sally, may recall to the audience the clangour that followed the discovery of Duncan's murder.

5. 6.

S.D. 'Dunsinane. Before the castle.' (Camb.). Before the castle-bell has ceased, the sound of drums is heard, and Malc., Siward and Macd. appear, followed by their 'moving grove'.

4. *battle* v. G.

6. *order* plan.

10. S.D. F. 'Exeunt/Alarums continued'. This refers to the trumpets (cf. *2 Hen. VI*, 2. 3. 95), not the castle-bell, as some suppose; and they are sounded

intermittently until the death of Macb. at 5. 8. 34. Scenes 5. 6, 5. 7, and 5. 8 are continuous.

5. 7.

S.D. 'Another part of the field' (Camb. after Cap.). Rowe, Pope, etc. continue the scene.

1. *tied...stake* When baited, the bear 'was attached by a long chain to a stake in the middle of a ring' (*Sh. Eng.* ii, 429) and at each 'course' (v. G.) some four to six mastiffs were loosed upon it. The 'outward walls' of the castle form the ring around which Macb. ranges in fury. Escape is impossible, but a bear at bay is a terrible beast. Cf. *Lear*, 3. 7. 54; *Caes.* 4. 1. 48–9.

4. S.D. F. 'Enter Young Seyward'.

11. S.D. Hol. relates that 'one of Siwards sonnes chaunced to be slayne' in the battle; Sh. uses this to give Macb. one fight before he meets Macd., and represents the 'son' as a boy to increase our detestation of the 'butcher'.

13. S.D. F. 'Exit./Alarums. Enter Macduffe'. For 'alarums', which here='the noise' (l. 14) of fighting, cf. *Hen. V*, 4. 6. 35; *1 Hen. VI*, 5. 5. 85.

17. *wretched kerns*. It is fitting that the only troops now loyal to Macb. are the Irish mercenaries upon whom 'the merciless Macdonwald' had relied in 1. 2. 12–13.

23. S.D. The 'action gives no opportunity for the removal of the dead Siward', which suggests 'some manipulation' of the text, says Chambers (*Wm. Sh.* i, 472). But when old Siward enters he does not see his son, and we learn at 5. 8. 44 that the body has been 'brought off the field', prob. by servitors.

29. *strike beside us* i.e. deliberately miss us; cf. *3 Hen. VI*, 2. 1. 130–2.

S.D. F. 'Exeunt. Alarum/Enter Macbeth'. Pope first introduced a fresh sc. division here, which Camb. adopted and read 'Another part of the field' (after Dyce).

5. 8.

1. *the Roman fool* Suicide was the common end of defeated Roman leaders, e.g. Brutus, Cassius, and Antony in Sh.'s own plays. But supposing Macb. to be a reader of Plutarch, Antony surely would seem to him the 'fool' par excellence.

5–6. *my soul...already* 'The only real touch of remorse in Macb.' (E.K.C.).

9. *intrenchant* v. G.

14. *the angel* 'Demons, though cast out of heaven ...are still angels' (Curry, p. 71). Cf. *Son.* 144.

18. *my better...man* i.e. courage, which is to him the supreme virtue.

19–20. *these juggling fiends...sense* Cf. *The Færie Queene*, III, iv, 28:

> So tickle be the termes of mortall state,
> And full of subtile sophismes, which doe play
> With double sences, and with false debate,
> T' approue the vnknown purpose of eternal fate.

I owe this note to Dr Percy Simpson.

20. *palter...double sense* Cf. note 5. 5. 43.

25. *monsters* Cf. *Temp.* 2. 2. 29 ff. Human 'monsters' of various kinds were lucrative shows in London in Sh.'s time.

26. *Painted...pole* i.e. your picture set on a pole outside the booth.

27–9. *I will...curse* Cf. *Ant.* 4. 12. 33–7; 5. 2. 208–21.

33. *warlike* K. found this so banal that he condemned 'Before...shield' as spurious, noting that

the words could be omitted without impairing the metre. John Hilton suggested (privately) 'warlock shield'—a brilliant guess, I think, though implying that Sh. had some Scots.

34. S.D. F. 'Exeunt fighting. Alarums./Enter Fighting, and Macbeth slaine'. Pope omitted 'Enter ...slain', and began a fresh sc. at this point. He was right in the latter, in which mod. edd. have not followed him, and wrong in the former, in which they have. Clearly ll. 35–75 are spoken within the castle, which Malc., Siward, etc. entered at 5. 7. 29; and this being so there is no contradiction, as all have assumed, between 'Enter...flaine' here and the S.D. at l. 53. What I suppose happened in Sh.'s theatre was an exciting duel between two practised swordsmen (one of them Burbage), begun on the main stage and ending on the inner stage, before which the traverse would be drawn to conceal the dead body of Macb. At 'Exeunt fighting' they passed through the door into the tiring-house; 'Alarums' denoted the sound therefrom of the duel supposedly continued out of sight along the foot of the wall; and at 'Enter fighting' they reappeared on the inner stage, where the great contest was concluded. K. notes 'Here a new scene might well be marked'.

[5. 9.]

S.D. For 'retreat' and 'flourish' v. G.

35. *arrived* in the castle.

36. *go off* v. G.

39–49. *Your son...death* Based on Hol. (*Chron. of Ed. the Confessor*), though he does not refer to the son's youth.

41. *prowess* A monosyllable.

42. *the...station* 'the post from which he did not flinch' (Clar.).

47. *God's soldier...he!* Let God receive him as his crusader; cf. *K. John*, 2. 1. 566.

53. S.D. 'on a pole' (Mal. from Hol.) makes 'stands' (l. 54) explicable.

55. *the time is free* the world can breathe again.

56. *compassed...pearl* i.e. already encircled or crowned with the jewels of Scotland, her nobility.

60. *spend...expense* Idiomatic use; cf. *Numbers* xxii. 10, 'die the death of the righteous' [Clar.].

61–2. *reckon...with you* i.e. reward you well for your services.

63. *earls, the first* etc. 'He created many Earles, etc. ...These were the first Earles that have beene heard of amongest the Scottishe men' (Hol.).

69. *fiend-like queen* Cf. Introd. pp. xlvii–xlviii, lxvii–lxviii.

70–1. *by self and* by her own. Cf. 5. 1. 74–6.

73. *in measure...place* in due proportion, time and place.

GLOSSARY

Note. Where a pun or quibble is intended, the meanings are distinguished as (*a*) and (*b*).

ABSOLUTE, positive; 3. 6. 40

ACTUAL, 'exhibited in deeds' (O.E.D. 1); 5. 1. 12.

ADDITION, title; 1. 3. 106; 3. 1. 99

ADDRESS (refl.), prepare; 2. 2. 24

ADHERE, agree, suit, cohere; 1. 7. 52

ADMIRED, amazing, to be wondered at; 3. 4. 110

ADVANTAGE, favourable opportunity; 5. 4. 11

AFFECTION, disposition; 4. 3. 77

AFFEER, confirm (legally). Orig. a commercial term = fix the market price; 4. 3. 34

AGITATION, movement, activity; 'slumbry agitation' = sleep-walking; 5. 1. 11

ALARUM (vb.), call to action; 2. 1. 53

ALARUM BELL, tocsin, town or castle bell, rung in time of danger or as a call to action; (theat.) the large bell 'in the wooden tower above the tiring-house'; 2. 3. 74; 5. 5. 51

ALL-HAIL (vb.), greet with the cry 'all-hail!'; 1. 5. 6–7

ALL-THING, altogether, entirely; 3. 1. 13

AMAZE, utterly confuse (not 'astonish'); 2. 3. 108; 5. 1. 77

AMAZEDLY, 'like a man in a trance' (K.); 4. 1. 126

AMAZEMENT, stupefaction; 2. 4. 19

ANNOYANCE, harm; 5. 1. 75

ANTIC, fantastic; 4. 1. 130

ANTICIPATE, forestall; 4. 1. 144

APPLY TO, be specially directed towards; 3. 2. 30

APPROVE, prove; 1. 6. 4

ARGUMENT, subject of conversation; 2. 3. 120

AROINT, begone! (cf. *Lear*, 3. 4. 129). A word of unknown orig., only found in Sh. and his imitators; 1. 3. 6

ARTIFICIAL, produced by art (or magic); 3. 5. 27

ASSURANCE, solemn promise; 4. 1. 83

AUGER-HOLE, very small place; lit. hole made by a carpenter's auger (cf. *Cor.* 4. 6. 87); 2. 3. 122

AUGURE, divination; 3. 4. 124

AUTHORIZE, vouch for, warrant; 3. 4. 66

AVOUCH, vouch for, answer for; 3. 1. 119

BADGED, marked plainly for all to see. Retainers wore coloured 'badges' to show to whose service they belonged 2. 3. 101

BANE, destruction; 5. 3. 59

BAREFACED, open, undisguised; 3. 1. 118

BATTLE, division of an army; 5. 6. 4

BEAR, (i) exercise, carry out, perform; 1. 7. 17; 3. 6. 3, 17; (ii) 'bear in hand', abuse with false pretences or appearances; 3. 1. 80

BELDAM, old woman (term of contempt); 3. 5. 2

BELLMAN, watchman, who called the hours and formerly 'announced deaths and called on the faithful to pray for the departed' (O.E.D.); 2.2.3

BENEFIT, natural advantage or 'gift' (O.E.D. 3 b). Cf. *A.Y.L.* 4. 1. 32; 'Disable all the benefits of your country'; 5. 1. 10

BENISON, blessing; 2. 4. 40

BESTOW (reflex.), lodge; 3. 1. 29; 3. 6. 24

BESTRIDE, defend a fallen friend (cf. *1 Hen. IV*, 5. 1. 122, 'if thou see me down in the battle and bestride me'); 4. 3. 4

BILL, list; 3. 1. 99

BIRTHDOM, fatherland; 4. 3. 4

BLOOD-BOLTERED, having the hair clotted with blood (cf. O.E.D. *balter*, vb. 5. obs. exc. in dial. 'to form tangled knots or clots, to stick together by coagulation'); 4. 1. 123

BODEMENT, augury, presage (cf. *Troil.* 5. 3. 80); 4. 1. 96

BOND, (i) life (v. note); 3. 2. 49; (ii) legal agreement to fulfil a contract; 4. 1. 84

BOTCH, 'flaw or blemish resulting from unskilful workmanship' (O.E.D.); 3. 1. 133

BREAK, impart, disclose; 1.7.48

BREECHED, covered (as by breeches); 2. 3. 116

BRIEFLY, quickly; 2. 3. 133

BRINDED, early form of 'brindled'; 4. 1. 1

BROAD, free, unrestrained; 3. 4. 23; 3. 6. 21

BROIL, battle (cf. *1 Hen. IV*, 1. 1. 3); 1. 2. 6

BRUIT, proclaim, announce; 5. 7. 22

BUY, acquire, win; 1. 7. 32

CARD, 'The Shipman's Card' = the compass, lit. the circular card with the 32 points marked upon it; 1. 3. 17

CARELESS, uncared for, worthless, 1. 4. 11

CASE, clothe, surround; 3.4.23

CAST, (i) (*a*) throw to the ground, (*b*) vomit (cf. *Meas.* 3. 1. 92); 2. 3. 40; (ii) 'cast the water' = diagnose by examination of the urine; 5. 3. 50

CATCH, seize; 1. 5. 17

CAUSE, (i) business, affair; 3. 1. 33; (ii) consideration; 3. 4. 136; (iii) ground for accusation; 5. 2. 3; (iv) case, sickness; 5. 2. 15

CENSURE, judgement, opinion; 5. 4. 14

CHALLENGE, blame, accuse (cf. *Tit. And.* 1. 1. 340); 3. 4. 42

CHAMBERLAIN, one who waits on a king or lord in his bedchamber; 1. 7. 63

CHAMPION (vb.), oppose in a 'wager of battle' (cf. *Ric. II*, 1. 3. 5). In the sense of 'stand up, defend', the vb. not found before 19th c.; 3. 1. 71

CHARGE (sb.), (i) office, duty, commission; 2. 2. 6; (ii) command; 4. 3. 20 .

CHAUDRON, entrails; 4. 1. 33

CHECK, rebuke, call to account; 4. 3. 33

CHOPPY, chapped; 1. 3. 44

CHOPS, jaws; 1. 2. 22

CHOUGH, jackdaw; 3. 4. 125

CHUCK, chick. A term of endearment (cf. *Oth*. 3. 4. 49); 3. 2. 45

CLEAR (adj. and adv.), innocent, spotless; 1. 5. 70; 1. 7. 18; 2. 1. 28

CLEARNESS, freedom from suspicion of evil; 3. 1. 132

CLEPT (p.p.), called, named; 3. 1. 93

CLING, shrivel up (cf. O.E.D. 3c); 5. 5. 40

CLOSE (vb.), (i) enclose; 3. 1. 98; (ii) heal, join; 3. 2. 14

CLOSE (adj. and adv.), secret, hidden; 3. 5. 7; 5. 1. 20

CLOUDY, angry, sullen; 3. 6. 41

COIGN, corner; 1. 6. 7

COMBINED, in collusion; 1. 3. 111

COMBUSTION, civil uproar (cf. *Hen. VIII*, 5. 4. 51); 2. 3. 58

COMMAND UPON, lay commands upon; 3. 1. 16

COMMEND, offer; 1. 7. 11

COMMISSION (in), deputed to perform a certain action; 1. 4. 2

COMPASS, surround; 5. 8. 56

COMPOSITION, agreement, peace terms; 1. 2. 61

COMPT (in), under obligation to render an account at audit-time like the steward of an estate; 1. 6. 26

CONFOUND, ruin, destroy; 2. 2. 11; 4. 1. 54; 4. 3. 99

CONFUSED, disorderly; 2. 3. 58

CONFUSION, ruin, destruction; 2. 3. 66; 3. 5. 29

CONJURE, adjure; 4. 1. 50

CONSENT, (*a*) collusion, complicity (cf. *A.Y.L.* 2. 2. 3), (*b*) counsel, advice (cf. *Wint.* 5. 3. 136); 2. 1. 25

CONSEQUENCE, future event; 1. 7. 3; 5. 3. 5

CONSTANCY, firmness of mind, courage; 2. 2. 68

CONSTRAIN, force into service, conscript; 5. 4. 13

CONSTRUCTION, interpretation; 1. 4. 12

CONTINENT, (*a*) containing, restraining, (*b*) chaste; 4. 3. 64

CONTRIVER, schemer, plotter; 3. 5. 7

CONVERT (intrans.), change; 4. 3. 229

CONVEY, contrive in secret (cf. *Lear*, 1. 2. 109—'I will convey the business as I shall find means'); 4. 3. 71

CONVINCE, overpower, defeat completely (Lat. 'convinco'); 1. 7. 64; 4. 3. 142

COPY. Either (*a*) copyhold, tenure (cf. 3. 2. 49) or (*b*) image, pattern (v. note); 3. 2. 38

CORPORAL, (i) corporeal, having a body; 1. 3. 81; (ii) bodily; 1. 7. 80

COUNTENANCE (vb.). Meaning doubtful: either (i) face, or (ii) be in keeping with, or perhaps a quibble on both; 2. 3. 80

COURSE (sb.), the onset of the dogs in bear-baiting; 5. 7. 2

Coz, 'cousin', used of any close relationship; 4. 2. 14

CRACK, 'a sudden sharp and loud noise as of something breaking or bursting...formerly applied to the roar of a cannon, of a trumpet, and of thunder' (O.E.D.); 1. 2. 37; 4. 1. 117

CRAVE, require; 3. 1. 34

CRIB, confine as in a hovel (cf. 2 Hen. IV, 3. 1. 9); 3. 4. 24

CROSS, thwart; 3. 1. 80

DAINTY, punctilious, particular; 2. 3. 144

DAREFUL (adj. or adv.), bold, defiantly; 5. 5. 6

DEAR, (a) grievous, dire, (b) heart-felt, i.e. that touches closely; 5. 2. 3

DEGREE, rank; 3. 4. 1

DELICATE, mild, pleasant; 1. 6. 10

DELIVER, communicate; 1. 5. 10; 3. 3. 2

DEMAND, ask; 4. 1. 61

DEMI-WOLF, cross between wolf and dog; O.E.D. does not record elsewhere; 3.1.93

DENY, refuse; 3. 4. 128

DIGNITY, rank; 5. 1. 55

DIRENESS, horror; 5. 5. 14

DISCOVERY, reconnaissance; 5. 4. 6

DISJOINT, fall to pieces; 3. 2. 16

DISORDER. Either (i) agitation of mind (cf. K. John, 3. 4. 102) or (ii) commotion, confusion; 3. 4. 110

DISPATCH (sb.), management (with grim pun on vb. (ii) below); 1. 5. 67

DISPATCH (vb.), (i) make haste; 5. 3. 50; (ii) put to death; 3. 4. 15

DISPLACE, banish; 3. 4. 109

DISPOSITION, habit of mind, nature; 3. 4. 113

DISPUTE, resist, struggle against; 4. 3. 220

DISTANCE, discord, variance. The orig. sense; 3. 1. 115

DISTEMPERED, diseased, distracted; 5. 2. 15

DIVISION, variation, descant; 4. 3. 96

DOUBT, fear; 4. 2. 66

DRAB, strumpet; 4. 1. 31

DRENCHED, drowned; perhaps after 'swinish sleep' with play on 'drench' = draught or dose of medicine administered to an animal (cf. 1 Hen. IV, 2. 4. 104); 1. 7. 68

DUDGEON, haft, handle; 2. 1. 46

DUN, dark; 1. 5. 50

DUTY, respect, reverence; 3. 4. 92; 4. 1. 132

ECSTASY, (i) frenzy; 3. 2. 22; (ii) excitement; 4. 3. 170

EFFECT, (i) fulfilment, execution; 1. 5. 46; (ii) manifestation; 5. 1. 10

EMINENCE, honour, distinction; 3. 2. 31

ENCOUNTER, meet, respond to; 3. 4. 9

ENDURE, 'suffer without opposition' (Schmidt); 5. 4. 9

ENKINDLE UNTO, 'excite...to hope for' (A. C. Bradley); 1. 3. 121

ESTABLISH (the estate), settle (the succession); 1. 4. 37

ESTATE, (i) government, succession to the crown; 1. 4. 37; (ii) 'th'estate of the world' = the cosmic order, the universe; 5. 5. 50

EVEN-HANDED, impartial, un-
biased (cf. *Merch.* 2. 7. 25,
'weigh with even hand');
1. 7. 10

EXPECTATION, those expected.
Abstract for concrete; 3. 3.
10

EXPEDITION, haste; 2. 3. 110

FACT, evil deed, crime; 3. 6. 10

FACULTIES, powers, prero-
gatives; 1. 7. 17

FANTASTICAL, imaginary; 1. 3.
53, 139

FARROW, litter of pigs; 4. 1. 65

FATAL, ominous; 2. 1. 36; 2. 2.
3; 3. 5. 21

FAVOUR, (i) indulgence; 1. 3.
149; (ii) expression; 1. 5.
71

FEE-GRIEF, grief that is 'fee' or
private property; 4. 3. 196

FELL (sb.), skin with hair on it,
scalp; 5. 5. 11

FILE (sb.), list, catalogue; 3. 1.
94; 5. 2. 8

FILE (vb.), defile, corrupt; 3.
1. 64

FIRSTLING, first-fruit, or first-
born of a flock (cf. *Deut.* xv.
19); 4. 1. 147, 148

FIT, periodical paroxysm of
fever (cf. *Cor.* 3. 2. 33, 'the
violent fit o'th' time'); 3. 4.
21, 55; 4. 2. 17

FITFUL, subject to fits (q.v.) or
paroxysms; 3. 2. 23

FLAW, outburst, lit. gust of
wind (cf. *2 Hen. IV*, 4. 4.
35); 3. 4. 63

FLIGHTY, swift, fleeting; 4. 1.
145

FLING OUT, kick out and
plunge wildly; 2. 4. 16

FLOURISH, 'a fanfare of horns,
trumpets, etc. to announce

the approach of a person of
distinction' (O.E.D.); 1. 4.
1 S.D.; 5. 8. 35 S.D.

FLOUT, insult; 1. 2. 49

FOISON, abundance; 4. 3. 88

FORCE, reinforce; 5. 5. 5

FORGE, invent, trump up; 4. 3.
82

FORK, forked tongue; 4. 1. 16

FOUNTAIN, source; 2. 3. 97

FRANCHISED, free; 2. 1. 28

FREE (vb.), banish, get rid of
(cf. *Cymb.* 3. 6. 80; *Temp.*
Ep. 18); 3. 6. 35

FRENCH HOSE, 'usually of mid-
thigh length, shaped like
pumpkins, and stuffed with
hair, flocks, or bombast'
(Linthicum, *Costume in Eliz.
Drama,* p. 205). But the
Porter seems to allude to a
tighter kind; 2. 3. 13

FRET, chafe (cf. *3 Hen. VI*, 1. 4.
91); 5. 5. 25

FRUITLESS, having no issue;
3. 1. 60

FRY, spawn; 4. 2. 83

FUME, 'a noxious vapour, supposed formerly to rise to the
brain from the stomach';
chiefly as the result of in-
toxication (O.E.D.); 1. 7. 66

FUNCTION, the operation of
mind or body (cf. *Oth.* 2. 3.
354); 1. 3. 140

FURY, frenzy, madness; 2. 3. 106

GALLOWGLASS, heavy-armed
foot soldier from Ireland (cf.
2 Hen. VI, 4. 9. 26); 1. 2. 13

GENIUS, guardian spirit; 3. 1.
55

GENTLE, made gentle or calm;
1. 6. 3; 3. 4. 76

GENTLY, quietly, without a
struggle; 5. 7. 24

GERMEN, germ, seed (cf. *Lear*, 3. 2. 8); 4. 1. 59

GET, beget; 1. 3. 67

GIN, snare, trap; 4. 2. 35

GIVE OUT, proclaim; 4. 3. 192

GLASS, magic mirror (v. note); 4. 1. 119

GO, (i) pass, 3. 1. 91; (ii) 'go off', die (cf. *Ant.* 4. 13. 6); 5. 8. 36

GOLDEN, very favourable (cf. *A.Y.L.* 1. 1. 6, 'report speaks goldenly'); 1. 7. 33

GOOD MAN, brave man; 4. 3. 3

GOODNESS, success; 4. 3. 136

GOOSE, tailor's smoothing-iron (so called because the handle is like a goose's neck); 2. 3. 14

GOSPELLED, submissive to the gospel precepts; 3. 1. 87

GOUT, clot, thick drop; 2. 1. 46

GRACE (sb.), (i) honour, distinction; 1. 3. 55; (ii) holiness; 4. 3. 23, 24, 159

GRACE (vb.), honour; 3. 4. 41, 45

GRAFT, implant, incorporate; 4. 3. 51

GRAVE, weighty; 3. 1. 21

GRAYMALKIN, *or* Grimalkin (lit. little grey Mall or Mary), common name for a cat; 1. 1. 8

GRIPE, grasp; 3. 1. 61

GROW, (i) advance in dignity; 1. 4. 29; (ii) cling to (cf. *Hen. VIII*, 5. 5. 50, 'like a vine grow to him'); 1. 4. 32

GUISE, fashion, practice; 5. 1. 19

GULF, gullet; 4. 1. 23

HARBINGER, an officer of the royal household, who preceded the king on his journeys to procure lodgings; 1. 4. 45

HARM, evil, wickedness; 3. 5. 7; 4. 3. 55

HARNESS, armour; 5. 5. 52

HARP, guess (O.E.D. cites Cotgrave, 1611, 'to harpe at the matter'); 4. 1. 74

HARPIER, name of a demon (v. note); 4. 1. 3

HAVING (sb.), possession (cf. *Tw. Nt.* 3. 4. 343); 1. 3. 56

HEAT-OPPRESSÉD, fevered; 2. 1. 39

HEAVILY, sorrowfully; 4. 3. 182

HEAVY, drowsy (cf. *Temp.* 2. 1. 186, 191); 2. 1. 6

HECATE, goddess of the infernal region, queen of night, ghosts and magic, and guardian of witches (cf. *M.N.D.* 5. 1. 382 note); 2. 1. 52; 3. 5. 1 etc.

HERALD (vb.), usher; 1. 3. 102

HERMIT, beadsman; 1. 6. 20

HOLD, (i) keep, withhold; 3. 6. 25; (ii) entertain; 4. 2. 19

HOME (adv.), to the full; 1. 3. 120

HOMELY, humble; 4. 2. 67

HORRID, horrible; 1. 3. 135; 1. 7. 24

HOSE, breeches (v. *French hose*); 2. 3. 13

HOUSEKEEPER, watch-dog; 3. 1. 96

HOWLET, owl or owlet; 4. 1. 17

HURLYBURLY, uproar, tumult; 1. 1. 3

HUSBANDRY, thrift, economy; 2. 1. 4

HYRCAN, of Hyrcania, province of Persian empire on shores of Caspian, mentioned by Pliny (*Nat. Hist.* bk. viii, c. 18) as a breeding-place for tigers; 3. 4. 101

ʸIELD, reward (lit. yield); 1. 6. 13

ILLNESS, evil, wickedness. The orig. sense; as 'sickness' not found before the end of 17th c.; 1. 5. 19

IMAGE, idea (cf. *M.N.D.* 5. 1. 25); 1. 3. 135

IMPRESS, conscript; 4. 1. 95

INCARNADINE, lit. make the colour of flesh, 'turn blood-red' (K.); 2. 2. 62

INDUSTRIOUS, zealous, energetic; 5. 4. 16

INFORM (v. note); 2. 1. 48

INGREDIENCE, the composition of a drug or poison, a mixture (v. note); 1. 7. 11; 4. 1. 34

INHABIT (vb.), house, harbour (v. note); 3. 4. 105

INITIATE, 'belonging to a novice or unpractised person' (O.E.D.); 3. 4. 143

INSANE, producing insanity; 1. 3. 84

INTEMPERANCE, excess; 4. 3. 66

INTERDICTION, exclusion (v. note); 4. 3. 107

INTEREST, right or title to a share in; 1. 2. 66

INTERMISSION, delay, interval of time; 4. 3. 232

INTRENCHANT, invulnerable (cf. *trench*); 5. 8. 9

INVENTOR, contriver; 1. 7. 10

JEALOUSY, suspicion; 4. 3. 29

JUMP (vb.), risk, hazard; 1. 7. 7

JUTTY (sb.), 'projecting part of a wall or building' (O.E.D.); 1. 6. 6

KERN, light-armed foot soldier from Ireland (cf. *Ric. II*, 2. 1. 156); 1. 2. 13, 30; 5. 7. 17

LACE, 'diversify with streaks of

colour' (O.E.D. 6. Cf. *Rom.* 3. 5. 8); 2. 3. 112

LAP, wrap, encase; 1. 2. 55

LARGE, unrestrained; 3. 4. 11

LATCH, catch; 4. 3. 195

LATED, belated; 3. 3. 6

LAVISH, insolent, wild (cf. *2 Hen. IV*, 4. 4. 64); 1. 2. 58

LAY ON, strike hard; 5. 8. 33

LILY-LIVERED, cowardly. The liver was the seat of courage in the old physiology; 5. 3. 15

LIMBEC, alembic, distilling vessel (full of alcoholic fumes); 1. 7. 67

LIMITED, appointed (cf. *Meas.* 4. 2. 163); 2. 3. 51

LINE, strengthen, support; 1. 3. 112

LIST, the lists; 3. 1. 70

LODGE, beat (crops) down flat; 4. 1. 55

LOON, worthless fellow; 5. 3. 11

LUXURIOUS, lascivious; 4. 3. 58

MAGGOT-PIE, magpie. Both prefixes are shortened forms of Margaret, a pet-name for the bird when caged; 3. 4. 125

MANSIONRY (collective sb.), dwellings; 1. 6. 5

MARTLET, house martin; 1. 6. 4

MATE, confound, stupefy; 5. 1. 77

MAW, stomach; 3. 4. 73; 4. 1. 23

MEASURE, proportion; 5. 8. 73

MED'CINE, doctor; 5. 2. 27

MEMORIZE, make memorable; 1. 2. 41

MERE, absolute, utter; 2. 3. 94; 4. 3. 89, 152

METAPHYSICAL, supernatural;
1. 5. 28

METTLE, life-stuff, substance,
ardour, spirit; 1. 7. 73

MINION, darling, favourite, the
pick of; 1. 2. 19; 2. 4. 15

MINISTER, attendant spirit (cf.
Temp. 1. 2. 275; 3. 3. 87);
1. 5. 47

MINUTELY, every minute; 5. 2.
18

MISCHIEF, evil deed; 1. 5. 49

MISSIVE, messenger (cf. *Ant.*
2. 2. 74); 1. 5. 6

MODERN, commonplace, ordinary; 4. 3. 170

MODEST, moderate; 4. 3. 119

MORE AND LESS, high and low
(cf. *2 Hen. IV*, 1. 1. 209);
5. 4. 12

MORTAL, deadly, fatal; 1. 5.
40; 3. 4. 81; 4. 3. 3

MORTALITY, human life; 2. 3.
92

MORTIFIED, dead (cf. *Caes.* 2.
1. 324; *Lear*, 2. 3. 15); 5. 2.
5

MOTIVE, incentive, person or
object which prompts love,
devotion, etc.; 4. 3. 27

MOULD, (*a*) model, pattern
(tailor's), (*b*) bodily form
(O.E.D. 10b); 1. 3. 145

MOUSING, accustomed to prey
on mice; 2. 4. 13

MOVE, disturb, agitate; 3. 4.
48

MUMMY, a common drug, orig.
made from Egyptian mum-
mies, the spices of which
perhaps lent it some virtue,
but often of other dead
bodies. Sir Th. Browne
writes: 'The common opinion
of the virtues of mummy
bred great consumption there-

of, and princes and great men
contended for this strange
panacea, wherein Jews dealt
largely, manufacturing mum-
mies from dead carcases and
giving them the names of
kings' (Fragment on Mum-
mies: *Works*, ed. G. Keynes,
v. 461); 4. 1. 23

MUSE, wonder; 3. 4. 85

NAPKIN, handkerchief; 2. 3. 6

NATURAL, partaking of natural
or human affection; 4. 2. 9

NATURE, (i) human nature,
natural habit, feeling or instinct; 1. 2. 11; 1. 3. 137;
1. 5. 49; 2. 1. 8; 2. 4. 16, 27;
(ii) physical or mental con-
stitution; (and so) vital
force, life; 1. 7. 68; 2. 2. 7;
2. 3. 113; 3. 4. 28; 5. 1.
9

NAUGHT, worthless, wicked; 4.
3. 225

NAVE, navel. O.E.D. records
no other instance of this
meaning, though the words
are etym. akin; 1. 2. 22

NEAR, nearer (cf. *Ric. II*, 5..1.
88); 2. 3. 140

NERVE, sinew; 3. 4. 102

NICE, precise, exact; 4. 3. 174

NIGHTGOWN, dressing-gown; 2.
2. 70; 5. 1. 5

NIMBLY, briskly, breezily; 1. 6.
2

NOISE, music (cf. *Temp.* 3. 2.
133); 4. 1. 106

NONPAREIL, one who has no
equal; 3. 4. 19

NOTE (sb.), (i) notoriety; 3. 2.
44; (ii) list; 3. 3. 10

NOTION, intellect, mind. The
only meaning in Sh.; 3. 1.
82

OBLIVIOUS, causing oblivion; 5. 3. 43

ODDS (at), at strife; 3. 4. 127

OFFEND, irritate; 3. 4. 57

OFFERING, ceremony, ritual, prayer; 2. 1. 52

OFFICE, (i) duty, task assigned; 3. 3. 3; (ii) (plur.) servants' quarters; 2. 1. 14

OLD, plenty of, abundant (cf. *M.W.W.* 1. 4. 4); 2. 3. 2

ONCE, ever; 5. 5. 15

OUT, in the field, up in arms; 4. 3. 183

OVERCOME, come over, pass over; 3. 4. 111

OWE, own, possess; 1. 3. 76; 1. 4. 10; 3. 4. 113

PADDOCK, toad; 1. 1. 9

PAIN, trouble; 2. 3. 49

PALL, (i) shroud; 1. 5. 50; (ii) fail (cf. *Ham.* 5. 2. 9); 5. 5. 42

PALTER, shuffle, prevaricate, equivocate; 5. 8. 20

PART, depart, die; 5. 8. 52

PASS, review, go through point by point (Clar.); 3. 1. 79

PASSION, agitation, sorrowful emotion; 3. 4. 57; 4. 3. 114

PATCH, fool; 5. 3. 15

PEAK, waste away; 1. 3. 23

PENT-HOUSE, sloping roof over door or window to protect it from the weather (v. note); here, eyelid; 1. 3. 20

PERFECT, (i) reliable; 1. 5. 2; (ii) (*a*) completely satisfied (cf. *Tim.* 1. 2. 90), (*b*) whole and sound; 3. 1. 107; 3. 4. 21; (iii) fully acquainted; 4. 2. 65

PERTURBATION, disorder, anomaly; 5. 1. 9

PESTERED, harassed; 5. 2. 23

PHYSIC (vb.), 'treat with remedies, relieve, alleviate' (O.E.D.); 2. 3. 49

PITFALL, fowler's snare, 'in which a trapdoor...falls over a cavity or hollow' (O.E.D.); 4. 2. 35

PLANT, 'establish or set up (a person or thing) in some position or state' (O.E.D. 5c; cf. *L.L.L.* 1. 1. 164; *Ric. II*, 5. 1. 63; *All's Well*, 2. 3. 159); 1. 4. 28; 5. 8. 65

POINT, 'at a point', ready, fully equipped (cf. 'at point', *Lear*, 1. 4. 347; *Ham.* 1. 2. 200); 4. 3. 135

POORLY, meanly, unworthily (cf. *Ric. II*, 3. 3. 128); 2. 2. 72

PORTABLE, bearable; 4. 3. 89

POSSET, 'drink composed of hot milk curdled with ale, wine, etc. formerly used as a delicacy and as a remedy' (O.E.D.); 2. 2. 6

POST, fast-riding messenger; 1. 3. 98

POSTER, one who travels 'post', i.e. swiftly; 1. 3. 33

POWER, forces; 4. 3. 185; 236; 5. 2. 1; 5. 6. 7

PRACTICE, skill, art; 5. 1. 58

PREDOMINANCE, ascendancy. Astrol.; 2. 4. 8

PRESENT (adj.), instant; 1. 2. 66

PRETENCE, aim, intention; 2. 3. 131

PRETEND, aim at, intend; 2. 4. 24

PRIDE, highest pitch (cf. *1 Hen. IV*, 1. 1. 60); 2. 4. 12

PROBATION, proof (cf. *Meas.* 5. 1. 156); 3. 1. 79

PRODUCE FORTH, bring to light; 5. 8. 68

PROFESS, claim knowledge or skill in; 4. 1. 50

PROFOUND, deep-hanging, 'and therefore ready to fall' (Clar.); 3. 5. 24

PROOF, impenetrable armour; 1. 2. 55

PROPER, fine (contemptuous); 3. 4. 60

PROPORTION, adjustment, proportioning (O.E.D. 6); 1. 4. 19

PROSPECT, the range of vision; 1. 3. 74

PROSPEROUS, profitable; 3. 1. 21

PROTEST, proclaim; 3. 4. 105; 5. 2. 11

PROVOKE, stimulate; 2. 3. 26

PURGE (sb.), cleansing, purification (by blood-letting). Not in O.E.D., but v. 2 Hen. IV, 4. 1. 65, 'Purge the obstructions which begin to stop Our very veins of life', and Ric. II, 1. 1. 153; 5. 2. 28

PURGE (vb.), purify by purgative; 5. 3. 52

PURVEYOR, officer sent on in advance to provide food for the king and his retinue; 1. 6. 22

PUSH, attempt, crisis (cf. Ham. 5. 1. 289, 'put the matter to the present push'); 5. 3. 20

PYRAMID, spire; 4. 1. 57

QUARREL, cause; 1. 2. 14

QUARRY, heap of slaughtered deer at the end of a chase (cf. Ham. 5. 2. 362); 4. 3. 206

QUESTION, discuss; 2. 3. 128

RANCOUR, malicious enmity; 3. 1. 66

RAPT, lost in reverie; 1. 3. 57, 142; 1. 5. 5

RAVELLED, tangled, knotted; 2. 2. 37

RAVIN UP, swallow up greedily (cf. 'ravin down', Meas. 1. 2. 125); 2. 4. 28

RAVINED, glutted, (or) ravenous (v. note); 4. 1. 24

RAWNESS, unprotected condition (cf. O.E.D. 'raw' 6, excoriated, and Hen. V, 4. 1. 139–40, 'children rawly left'); 4. 3. 26

RAZE OUT, erase, blot out; 5. 3. 42

REBUKE, repress (cf. K. John 2. 1. 9); 3. 1. 55

RECEIPT, receptacle, container; 1. 7. 66

RECEIVE, believe, accept as true; 1. 7. 74, 77

RECOIL, give way suddenly (like a spring or a gun); 4. 3. 19; 5. 2. 23

RECOMMEND (refl.), make itself agreeable; 1. 6. 2

REFLECTION, shining; 1. 2. 25

RELATION, recital; 4. 3. 173

RELISH, trace, hint; 4. 3. 95

REMEMBRANCER, one engaged or appointed to remind another; 3. 4. 37

REMORSE, pity (cf. Temp. 5. 1. 76), relenting (cf. Merch. 4. 1. 20); 1. 5. 43

RENDER, surrender; 5. 7. 24

REPEAT, recite; 4. 3. 112

REPETITION, report, account; 2. 3. 84

RESOLVE (refl.), make up one's mind; 3. 1. 138

REST, remain; 1. 6. 20

RETREAT, a signal on the trumpet to recall a pursuing force (cf. *2 Hen. IV*, 4. 3. 70); 5. 8. 34 S.D.

RONYON. A term of abuse, lit. scabby, mangy (cf *M.W.W.* 4. 2. 180); 1. 3. 6

ROUND, (i) crown; 1. 5. 29; 4. 1. 88; (ii) round dance; 4. 1. 130

ROUSE, bestir oneself, rise up; 3. 2. 53; 5. 5. 12

RUB, roughness, unevenness. A term of bowls (cf. *Ham.* 3. 1. 65); 3. 1. 133

RUGGED, (i) 'wrinkled with care or displeasure; frowning' (O.E.D. 3b); 3. 2. 27; (ii) rough, shaggy; 3. 4. 100

RUIN, destruction, death; 2. 3. 114

RUMP-FED. Either, fed on rump, the best beef, or, fat-rumped (for 'fed' = fattened, v. O.E.D.); 1. 3. 6

SAG, sink 'through lack of strength or effort' (O.E.D. 2); 5. 3. 10

SAUCY, (i) importunate, pushing; 3. 4. 25; (ii) impertinent; 3. 5. 3

SCAN, examine, consider; 3. 4. 140

SCARF UP, blindfold; 3. 2. 47

SCHOOL (vb.), control, discipline; 4. 2. 15

SCORCH, slash, cut; 3. 2. 13

SCORE, reckoning, debt; 5. 8. 52

SCOUR, wash away purge; 5. 3. 56

SCRUPLE, doubt; 2. 3. 129

SEASON, that which keeps things fresh, preservative; 3. 4. 141

SEAT, situation; 1. 6. 1

SEATED, firmly fixed (cf. 'the seated hills', *Par. Lost*, vi, 644); 1. 3. 136

SECURITY, over-confidence; 3. 5. 32

SEEL, blind. Lit. sew (a falcon's) eyelids together; 3. 2. 46

SELF-ABUSE, hallucination (cf. *Ham.* 4. 7. 49); 3. 4. 142

SELF-COMPARISONS, qualities equal to his own (cf. *Ant.* 3. 13. 26); 1. 2. 56

SENNET, flourish on a trumpet; 3. 1. 10 S.D.

SENSE, apprehension; 5. 1. 25

SENSIBLE TO, perceptible by; 2. 1. 36

SERE (sb.), withered state; 5. 3. 23

SET, (i) stake; 3. 1. 112; (ii) 'set forth', display; 1. 4. 6; (iii) 'set down before', besiege (cf. *Cor.* 1. 2. 28); 5. 4. 10

SETTLED, determined, resolute; 1. 7. 79

SEV'NIGHT, week; 1. 3. 22

SEWER, 'attendant at a meal who superintended the arrangement of the table, the seating of the guests, and the tasting and serving of the dishes' (O.E.D.); 1. 7 S.D.

SHARD-BORNE, supported on 'shards' = scaly wing-cases (cf. note); 3. 2. 42

SHIFT (vb.) 'shift away', slip away unobserved; 2. 3. 145.

SHIFT (sb.) 'make a shift' = manage somehow or other; 2. 3. 40

SHOUGH, shag-haired kind of dog; 3. 1. 93

SIGHTLESS, invisible; 1. 5. 48; 1. 7. 23

SINGLE, feeble; 1. 3. 140 (with quibble on 'single' = individual); 1. 6. 16

SKIPPING, light-footed; 1. 2. 30

SKIRR, scour; 5. 3. 35

SLAB (adj.), viscous, glutinous; 4. 1. 32

SLEAVE, filaments of silk (v. note); 2. 2. 37

SLEEK (vb.), smoothe. Gen. applied to the hair; 3. 2. 27

SLIVER, tear off a twig (cf. *Lear*, 4. 2. 34); 4. 1. 28

SLOPE, bend (v. note); 4. 1. 57

SOLE, mere; 4. 3. 12

SOLELY, absolutely, entirely; 1. 5. 69

SOLEMN, official, ceremonial; 3. 1. 14

SOOTH, true; 5. 5. 40

SORE, dreadful; 2. 4. 3

SORRY, woeful, wretched; 2. 2. 20, 21; 3. 2. 9

SPECULATION, power of sight, 'intelligent or comprehending vision' (O.E.D.; cf. *Troil.* 3. 3. 109); 3. 4. 95

SPONGY, soaked to capacity (with drink); 1. 7. 71

SPRITE, spirit; 2. 3. 79; 4. 1. 127

SPY. Meaning doubtful (v. note); 3. 1. 129

STAFF, lance (lit. shaft); 5. 7. 18

STAMP, coin (cf. *M.W.W.* 3. 4. 16); 4. 3. 153

STANCHLESS, insatiable (cf. *Tit. And.* 3. 1. 14); 4. 3. 78

STAND, (i) 'stand upon', be particular about, insist upon; 3. 4. 119; (ii) 'stand to 't', (*a*) be resolute, (*b*) fall to work (cf. *Temp.* 3. 3. 49); 3. 3. 15

START (sb.), impulse. As we now say 'fits and starts' (cf.

Lear, 1. 1. 304, 'such unconstant starts'); 3. 4. 63

START (vb.), (i) jump from its place; 4. 1. 116; 5. 2. 23; (ii) startle, cause to start; 5. 5. 15

STATE, (i) 'state of man' = (*a*) all the mental and physical attributes of manhood, (*b*) the 'little kingdom' (*Caes.* 2. 1. 67–8; cf. *K. John*, 4. 2. 245–6); 1. 3. 140; (ii) chair of state (cf. *1 Hen. IV*, 2. 4. 372, 'this chair shall be my state'); 3. 4. 5

STATION, place, position; 3. 1. 101; 5. 8. 42

STAY, await; 4. 3. 142

STICK DEEP, go deep; 3. 1. 49; 4. 3. 85

STILL, always; 3. 1. 21

STRAIGHT, immediately; 3. 1. 139

STRANGE, (i) unaccustomed, unfamiliar; 1. 3. 145; (ii) astonished as at something new or strange; 3. 4. 112

STUDY, 'to be studied in' = to have got up a part perfectly; 1. 4. 9

SUBORN, procure one to do an evil action; 2. 4. 24

SUDDEN, impetuous, violent (cf. *A.Y.L.* 2. 7. 151); 4. 3. 59

SUGGESTION, prompting, temptation; 1. 3. 134

SUMMONS, call to surrender (to sleep); 2. 1. 6

SURCEASE, discontinuance, death; 1. 7. 4

SURMISE, speculation; 1. 3. 141

SURVEY, perceive, notice; 1. 2. 31

SWAY, direct my actions, control myself; 5. 3. 9

SWELL, overflow, burst forth (cf. 'swelling', full to bursting, *1 Hen. IV*, 3. 1. 199; *Tit. And.* 5. 3. 13); 1. 2. 28

SWELLING, increasing (in grandeur or greatness); 1. 3. 128

SWELTERED, 'exuded like sweat as if by heat' (O.E.D.); 4. 1. 8.

SWOOP, (*a*) pounce, (*b*) sweep of the stakes; 4. 3. 219

TAINT, be infected with; 5. 3. 3

TAKE OFF, kill, destroy; 3. 1. 104; 5. 8. 71

TAKING-OFF, murder; 1. 7. 20

TEEM, bring forth (cf. *Hen. V*, 5. 2. 51); 4. 3. 176

TEMPERANCE, moderation, self-control; 4. 3. 92

TEMPERATE, self-controlled; 2. 3. 108

THICK-COMING, coming rapidly (one after the other; cf. 1. 3. 97); 5. 3. 38

THOUGHT, 'upon a thought' = as quick as thought, in an instant; 3. 4. 55

TIME, world, society; 1. 5. 62, 63; 1. 7. 81; 4. 3. 72

TITLE, possession; 4. 2. 7

TOUCH, feeling (cf. *Temp.* 5. 1. 21); 4. 2. 9

TOWER, 'mount up, as a hawk, so as to be able to swoop down on the quarry' (O.E.D.); 2. 4. 12

TOY, trifle; 2. 3. 93

TRACE, follow; 4. 1. 153

TRADE, have dealings with; 3. 5. 4

TRAIN, false lure, lit. carrion dragged or distributed in a line to lure wild beasts into a trap; 4. 3. 118

TRAMMEL UP, enmesh. A trammel = a very effective net (for fish or fowl) in mesh of two sizes, by means of which the prey securely noosed itself in a bag; 1. 7. 3

TRANSPORT, carry away by violent emotion; 1. 5. 55

TRANSPOSE, change; 4. 3. 21

TREATISE, discourse, story; 5. 5. 12

TRENCH, cut; 3. 4. 27

TRIFLE, make trivial by comparison; 2. 4. 4

TUG, pull about roughly, maul; 3. 1. 111

UNBEND, slacken, relax (cf. 'bend up', 1. 7. 79); 2. 2. 45

UNDEEDED, without having achieved any deed; 5. 7. 20

UNFIX, loosen (cf. *2 Hen. IV*, 4. 1. 208); 1. 3. 135

UNMAKE, undo, ruin (O.E.D. 3); 1. 7. 54

UNMANNERLY, immodestly; 2. 3. 116

UNROUGH, unbearded, smooth-faced; 5. 2. 10

UNSEAM, rip up; 1. 2. 22

UNTITLED, having no claim (to the throne); 4. 3. 104

UPROAR (vb.), throw into confusion. Not found elsewhere; 4. 3. 99

USE (sb.), normal operation; 1. 3. 137

USE (vb.), keep company with; 3. 2. 10

UTTERANCE. 'A challenge or a combat "à l'outrance", to extremity, was a fixed term of the law of arms, when the combatants engaged "with an odium internecinum", an intention to destroy each other' (J.); 3. 1. 71

VALUED FILE, catalogue raisonné (Clar.), priced catalogue (Steevens); 3. 1. 94

VANTAGE, favourable opportunity or position; 1. 2. 31; 1. 3. 113; 1. 6. 7

VAULT, (a) cavern, cellar, (b) the earth (with sky as roof); 2. 3. 95

VIRTUE, healing power; 4. 3. 156

VISIT, afflict with disease; 4. 3. 150

VISITING (sb.), access of feeling; 1. 5. 44

VIZARD, mask; 3. 2. 34

VOLUME, space; 2. 4. 2

VOUCH, lit. warrant (a legal term); hence, back or recommend by words of welcome; 3. 4. 34

WAKE, arouse; 3. 6. 31

WANTON, capricious, unrestrained; 1. 4. 34

WARRANT (sb.), justification; 2. 3. 145

WARRANT (vb.), justify; 4. 3. 137

WASSAIL, carousal; 1. 7. 64

WASTEFUL, laying waste, devastating; 2. 3. 114

WATCH (vb.), sit up at night; 5. 1. 1

WATCHER (v. watch); 2. 2. 71

WATCHING (sb.), being awake; 5. 1. 10

WATER-RUG, rough-haired water dog; 3. 1. 93

WEAL, society, commonwealth; 3. 4. 76; 5. 2. 27

WEIRD, having to do with fate or destiny; 1. 3. 32 (v. note); 1. 5. 8; 2. 1. 20; 3. 1. 2; 3. 4. 133; 4. 1. 136

WELL, probably, very likely (cf. mod. 'it may well be that...'); 5. 2. 6

WHILE, till; 3. 1. 43

WIN, win over, gain one's confidence; 1. 3. 123, 125

WINK AT, shut one's eyes to; 1. 4. 52

WITHERED, 'gaunt, spectre-like' (Schmidt); 1. 3. 40; 2. 1. 52

WORM, serpent, snake; 3. 4. 29

WROUGHT, exercised, agitated; 1. 3: 149

YESTY, frothy, foaming; 4. 1. 53